SEED *to* SUPPER

Growing & Cooking Great Food
No Matter Where You Live

John Tullock

Health Communications, Inc.
Deerfield Beach, Florida

www.hcibooks.com

Library of Congress Cataloging-in-Publication Data
is available through the Library of Congress

© 2016 John Tullock

ISBN-13: 978-07573-1888-7 (Paperback)
ISBN-10: 07573-1888-6 (Paperback)
ISBN-13: 978-07573-1889-4 (ePub)
ISBN-10: 07573-1889-4 (ePub)

Publisher: Health Communications, Inc.
            3201 S.W. 15th Street
            Deerfield Beach, FL 33442–8190

Cover design by Larissa Hise Henoch
Interior design and formatting by Lawna Patterson Oldfield

CONTENTS

111   Chapter 3: **Gardening in Raised Beds**

Preserved Foods

Techniques

Baked Goods and Batters

Condiments

Food, Glorious Food

I grew up on a small farm that produced nearly everything we ate. My mother used to say that Grandma always began her shopping list with "sugar, coffee, oatmeal" because those were three staples we did not grow. Some folks in the neighborhood grew sorghum, though, and after they harvested the crop, squeezed the juice from it, and boiled down the juice to make syrup, Grandma could barter eggs for a quart or two. It has a special, grassy flavor all its own and is not quite as sweet as honey or agave nectar. You will find it listed in some of the recipes in this book. These days, sorghum is making a comeback as people seek out alternatives to refined sugar and corn syrup.

The best part of farm life was the abundance of garden-fresh vegetables that dominated every meal. Even breakfast might include fried potatoes, a tomato bread pudding, or fried green tomatoes. My dad remembered his mother frying squash blossoms dipped in batter and serving them with honey for breakfast. Other meals would include at least three vegetables, and twice that many on Sundays or when guests came by for dinner.

My family food traditions are rooted in the Southern Appalachians, but every region of the country has traditional

recipes featuring the farm-fresh ingredients typical of that locale. Home gardeners are seeking out the heirloom vegetables their ancestors grew and sharing recipes from their grandparents' time.

Not since the Greatest Generation marched off to war have Americans embraced home food gardening with such enthusiasm. Instead of aiding in the fight to protect democracy, this time we are working to save Earth's ecosystem, surely a goal with equivalent, if not greater, urgency. An increasing number of people are growing fresh, wholesome food. Home food production has taken off, even in urban areas where earnest apartment dwellers cultivate tomatoes and herbs under artificial lights, and in suburban sprawl-scapes, where lawns are giving way to lettuces and leeks.

According to the National Gardening Association, 2014 marked the first time food gardening surpassed flower gardening as a backyard hobby among Americans. Whether it's a few pots of herbs on a sunny windowsill or a traditional vegetable patch, the new American food garden represents a heartening response to the commodification of food and the industrialization of farming.

In *Seed to Supper*, I endeavor to provide a balanced, concise introduction to food gardening and to cooking with homegrown produce. The kitchen-tested recipes feature the most popular homegrown vegetables and fresh herbs, paired with meat and

dairy from the grocery store. You don't have to be an expert, either in the garden or the kitchen, to grow the ingredients or to create the recipes offered in this book.

Americans have rediscovered local products and are incorporating them into both traditional and contemporary recipes. In a few cases, I mention by name high-quality products from my region that anyone can buy online. I encourage readers to substitute similar ingredients when they come from producers close to your home. And if you simply use whatever brand you can find at the grocery, the recipe will still taste great.

We are each a part of a vast, living system that is the Earth's biosphere. Increasingly, we behave more like a virulent pathogen than the rational beings we consider ourselves to be. Whether for good or ill, we undeniably interact with and alter our environment every day. Our most intimate connection with the biosphere is via the food system. All of us, despite our differences, must eat. Some of us get way too much food, too many of us do not get enough, and the complex system of industrial food production and distribution scarcely serves anyone well, save the corporate moguls upon whose investments commercial farmers are forced to depend.

Industrial agriculture requires enormous inputs of petroleum and water. Increasingly, farmers are planting genetically modified varieties of staple crops in an effort to reduce labor costs, increase productivity, and secure enough profit to stay in business. Besides the unknown and potentially harmful environmental effects of the genetic modifications themselves, growing these crops almost always involves increased application of pesticides. For example, many genetically modified crops are "Roundup Ready," meaning they carry resistance to the herbicide glyphosate, marketed under the name Roundup by the Monsanto Corporation. Instead of traditional cultivation to control weeds in soybeans, farmers spray the crop with herbicide, which kills the weeds, leaving the soybeans to fight another day. For the most part, the environmental effects of these practices are unknown. According to the Institute for Responsible Technology, we learn the following:

> Currently commercialized GM crops in the U.S. include soy (94%), cotton (90%), canola (90%), sugar beets (95%), corn (88%), Hawaiian papaya (more than 50%), zucchini and yellow squash (over 24,000 acres). (Number in parentheses represents the estimated percent that is genetically modified.)*

The benefits of growing and cooking with homegrown produce are many. Unparalleled freshness, maximum nutrition, and outstanding flavor comprise the top three, but growing food saves energy, reduces our dependence upon fossil fuels, conserves water, promotes ecological diversity, and protects local landscapes from development. The exercise gardening affords is exactly the type recommended for our aging population, and a diet rich in fruits and vegetables—invariably a consequence of home food gardening—helps stem the rising tide of obesity. Any location in the

---

* Source: *http://www.responsibletechnology.org/buy-non-gmo/non-gmo-seed*, accessed January 9, 2015.

United States can produce a variety of vegetables, although local conditions will determine which vegetables do best in any given area. Where I live, the growing season is long, rainfall is reliable and abundant, and the list of potential crops is extensive. Because local conditions vary widely, I have focused upon the needs of the vegetables in the chapters on outdoor gardening. If you read my comments regarding what vegetables need and their dislikes, you can decide for yourself how easy or difficult a particular plant will be to grow in your individual circumstances.

For example, where summers are short, tropical vegetables such as okra and watermelons seldom succeed. On the other hand, in the Deep South, lettuce production is limited to the winter months and perhaps late fall and early spring. Otherwise, the temperature becomes too hot to support a crop. For these and other reasons, most people will find it difficult to produce all the vegetables they may want to eat. My advice is to focus on what will grow well and utilize your crops to the maximum, and then look to your local farmer's market, CSA, or organic food co-op for the rest. We should never avoid delicious, wholesome foods like bananas or cinnamon because we cannot grow them on the patio.

Instead of grouping recipes by season, and gardening advice by plant variety, I chose the novel approach of organizing growing and cooking information by the nature and size of the space available to the gardener. Thus, we begin with herbs and greens that can be successfully produced at a sunny window, then move on to larger containers on the patio or deck, then to raised beds in a corner of the yard, and finally to an integrated backyard landscape. Each increase in the gardener's growing room brings additional possibilities for the kitchen. Recipes accompany the growing advice for each crop discussed. The final chapter offers generalized advice for successful vegetable gardening, regardless of the amount of space devoted to the activity.

How to Read the Recipes

The recipes emphasize getting the best flavors out of ultra-fresh ingredients without the need for complex kitchen techniques. While some recipes require more preparation time than others, or include more ingredients, none is inaccessible to the average home cook. Neither are all recipes vegan or vegetarian. Pairings of seasonal produce with meat, chicken, and fish, as well as eggs and dairy products, creates a culinary palette offering greater interest and opportunity for exploration. Nevertheless, many recipes can be executed without resorting to animal products, so I offer suggestions for vegetarian substitutions.

To avoid repetition, I include here information that applies to all the recipes in the book. The recipes all begin with a list of the ingredients in the order in which they are used and the amount of each needed for the dish.

- Eggs are large in size.

- I always use plain, all-purpose flour. Sifting is unnecessary. If you need to blend in salt or baking powder, use a wire whisk to combine the dry ingredients.

- Measurements need not be precise, except for baked goods. Soups, stews, and other dishes will turn out just fine if you alter slightly the amounts of ingredients. You should have two types of measuring cups. For dry ingredients, these typically have a long handle and look like a miniature saucepan. For liquids, measuring cups are shaped like a small pitcher with graduations on the side. You can use these interchangeably, except when baking.

Food should look good as well as taste good. Having your own garden allows you to choose vegetable varieties based on their appearance. Green or orange tomatoes or purple carrots on the plate are sure to impress and please your family and friends. I find it a useful rule to try to have as much color on the plate as possible. This is a good way not only to make the meal pleasingly attractive but also to maximize the nutritional benefits from a varied selection of plant foods. I encourage you to be visually creative when serving the dishes listed in the following pages.

CHAPTER 1

At the Kitchen Window

Pots of herbs growing at the kitchen window have been around for a long time. Window-box gardens probably originated as a way to make fresh herbs and flowers easily accessible. The earliest ones were made of terra cotta and used by the Romans for growing plants used in cooking, for medicinal purposes, and in religious practices. Even as window boxes became more ornamental and less practical, planting schemes still called for the inclusion of herbs like basil and thyme. An exterior window box on a south-facing sill remains a great option for growing any of the plants mentioned in this chapter.

Seeing the Light

Outdoor growing in containers will receive more discussion in the next chapter, so we will begin by assuming you have only the indoor space near a window, or perhaps no window at all. In either case, you can use artificial lighting to produce an array of crops. Many options are available for lighting equipment, each with advantages and disadvantages.

Fluorescent Lighting

If the primary consideration is cost, fluorescent lighting offers the best option. A single compact fluorescent lamp, designed to replace a 150-watt incandescent bulb, will provide enough light for a twelve-inch diameter container of herbs and greens. For around ten dollars you can buy a clip-on reflector to hold the lamp.

If you aspire to a larger garden, fluorescent fixtures come in a variety of lengths. The most common and inexpensive size is forty-eight inches long, typically called a shop light, and holds two 40-watt lamps. The cost is quite reasonable. Two shop lights will illuminate a space of about eight square feet, enough for four standard nursery flats of plants.

Fluorescent fixtures made expressly for indoor horticulture are widely available. While more costly than the suggestions above, which can be found at any DIY store, these designs offer splash-proof housings, built-in timers, and other features. They also often feature T-5 lamps. These improved fluorescent lamps are half an inch in diameter, so more of them can be placed above a small space, increasing the light intensity and opening up greater possibilities for plant production.

High-Intensity Lighting

Another type of lighting equipment often sold for horticultural purposes employs metal halide lamps. These are sometimes also known as halogen quartz iodide, or HQI, lamps. Their light output is extremely bright but comes with several drawbacks.

First, the lamps get hot and are unsuitable for use in confined spaces or around young children. Spattering with water can result in an explosion, so the lamp must be well-protected. Second, they waste a lot of the electricity they consume, either releasing the energy as heat or as light wavelengths not particularly useful for plant growth. While commercial operations may use metal halide lamps, I do not recommend them for routine household use. The initial cost is also more than fluorescent lighting equipment.

LED Lighting

Light emitting diodes (LEDs) offer benefits of both fluorescent and high-intensity lighting systems. LED systems consume far less electricity per lumen of irradiance emitted. They are also compact. A 15-watt LED unit can produce as much illumination as a 200-watt high-intensity system. Moreover, LEDs can be precisely tuned to emit a particular wavelength. Thus, LED systems designed for horticulture emit most of their light in the wavelengths plants utilize.

The primary drawback to LED lighting is their high initial cost. However, if this cost is amortized over the useful life of the equipment, typically about ten years, and consideration is given to costs for replacement lamps for either fluorescent or high-intensity systems, LED lighting is the most economical choice.

Sunshine Only

If you opt to rely upon only the sunshine streaming through your windows, you can increase your success with vegetables and herbs with a few simple techniques. Choose the brightest window in the house. This is normally a south-facing exposure. If you have only east-west exposure, opt for the east side. Positioning a mirror on the room side of your windowsill garden will reflect more light onto the plants, as will placing aluminum foil underneath the pots to reflect light on the undersurfaces of the leaves.

Your Windowsill Garden

While the limitations of space and light availability will necessarily constrain the list of vegetables and herbs you can grow, that list nevertheless includes many useful and delicious options.

ARUGULA

Arugula is known also as the "peanut butter plant," because it tastes a bit like peanut butter. Rich in vitamins, arugula needs only a few weeks from seed to harvest. The cultivar Speedy is ready within a month. It adapts well to container growing.

Sow seeds one-fourth inch deep in a small pot and keep moist. Expect germination in about ten days. Plants will grow rapidly if the soil in the pot is kept moist, not wet, and the plants receive a weak fertilizer solution once a week.

Harvest baby arugula when the plants are about three inches tall. Let them get about twice that size for a more pronounced flavor. Use scissors to remove leaves half an inch above the soil line. Continue watering and feeding, and the plants will resprout. You can cut them two or three times before they become exhausted.

Rinse leaves if necessary, spin dry in a salad spinner, and store them in a plastic bag in the refrigerator, where they will keep for a week. Put a paper towel in the bag to absorb excess moisture.

In the Kitchen

Arugula is a delicious substitute for lettuce on a sandwich or in a salad, either alone or mixed with other greens. The recipes in this chapter will give you some ideas for capitalizing on its unique flavor.

Arugula Salad with Cranberries and Walnuts

If you grow arugula under lights out of season, this dish pairs it perfectly with ingredients available in winter.

YIELD: **2 SERVINGS**

2 cups loosely packed **baby arugula leaves**

1 cup assorted baby greens such as **lettuce** or corn salad

¼ cup **dried cranberries**

¼ cup **walnuts**, toasted (page 244) and coarsely chopped

2 tablespoons **walnut oil**

2 teaspoons **red wine vinegar**

1 tablespoon finely minced **shallot**

¼ teaspoon **salt**

Freshly ground **black pepper**

1. Wash the greens and spin them dry in a salad spinner or pat dry with paper towels. Place the greens in a bowl with the cranberries and walnuts and toss.

2. In a small bowl, combine the oil, vinegar, shallot, salt, and a few grinds of pepper. Whisk with a fork to emulsify.

3. Pour over the salad, toss well to coat, and divide the salad between two plates.

Potato Salad with Arugula Pesto

This nutrition-packed salad is as delicious as it is beautiful. I created this recipe to highlight the peanut butter taste of fresh arugula. The pesto is also delicious on pasta, on grilled pork, as a sandwich spread, or as a condiment for soup.

YIELD: **4 SERVINGS**

Potato Salad

2 cups **purple potatoes**, quartered *or* halved if large

1 small **yellow cauliflower**, separated into florets

1 cup **sugar snap peas**, trimmed as needed

1 small head **red leaf lettuce**, separated into leaves, rinsed, and spun dry

YIELD: **ABOUT 1 CUP**

Arugula Pesto

1 clove **garlic**, peeled

2 tablespoons **dry roasted unsalted peanuts**

¼ cup **unsalted butter**

¼ cup grated **Parmigiano-Reggiano cheese**

1 cup, packed, **arugula leaves**

¼ cup **extra virgin olive oil**

Potato Salad

1. Bring a large pot of water to a rolling boil. Add a tablespoon of salt and the potatoes. When the water returns to a boil, adjust the heat to maintain a steady boil and cook for 10 minutes. Test one of the potatoes for doneness. A wooden skewer should meet no resistance when the potato is pierced. You may need to cook the potatoes another 2 or 3 minutes, but do not allow them to become so done that they fall apart. As soon as they are done, drain them in a colander and rinse with cold water. Allow to drain while you continue with the preparation.

2. Bring another pot of water to a boil, add another tablespoon of salt, and drop in the cauliflower florets. Adjust the heat to a steady boil, and cook for 2 minutes. Add the peas and continue to cook 1 minute. Drain in a colander and rinse well under cold water. Allow to drain thoroughly.

3. Tear the lettuce into bite-size pieces and place in a large bowl.

4. Dry the prepared vegetables with kitchen towels and transfer them to the bowl with the lettuce. Add the pesto and toss to coat everything well. Serve immediately.

Arugula Pesto

1. With the motor running, drop the garlic through a food processor's feed tube to mince it. Drop in the peanuts and pulverize them. Turn off the food processor. Add the butter, cheese, and arugula. Process to a paste. Then pour the oil through the feed tube. The pesto should thicken and emulsify.

2. To store, transfer the pesto to a storage container and place a sheet of plastic film over the top, pressing down so the plastic is in contact with the surface of the pesto. This prevents darkening. Store the pesto in the refrigerator for up to one week. The pesto may also be frozen in small amounts, in which case it need not be protected with the plastic wrap. Just transfer the prepared pesto to small freezer containers, label, and freeze.

CORN SALAD

Also known as mâche and lamb's lettuce, this fast-growing plant ranks among the hardiest green crops, surviving even at 5 degrees. You can begin to harvest in as little as thirty days from the time seedlings emerge. Sow seeds thinly in small pots of growing mix, covering them with one-quarter inch of fine soil. Thin to one plant per pot once they have two sets of true leaves. You can transplant the extras to additional pots if you have room. Feed plants weekly and they will rapidly grow into rosettes large enough for a serving of salad. If you prefer, you can harvest individual leaves, beginning when the plants are three inches tall.

In the Kitchen

Corn salad's soft, nutty-tasting leaves are delicious by themselves or as a component of a mixed green salad, where they provide a counterpoint to more assertive greens, such as mustards. It can also substitute for spinach.

Cream of Corn Salad Soup

The rich, nutty flavor of corn salad shines in this simple cream soup. Serve it with a mixed vegetable salad accompanied by a crisp white wine for a light luncheon.

YIELD: **4 SERVINGS**

2 cups **corn salad leaves**

2 tablespoons **butter**

¼ cup finely minced **onions**

2 tablespoons **flour**

4 cups **milk**

¼ tsp **paprika**

Fresh **nutmeg**

Parmigiano-Reggiano cheese *or* hard-cooked egg yolks for garnish

1. Wash the corn salad leaves, then drop them into boiling water. When the water returns to a boil, cook for 1 minute. Drain. Rinse under cold water to stop the cooking and then drain thoroughly. Squeeze the corn salad by handfuls to express some additional liquid. Place the corn salad in a blender jar and reserve.

2. Melt the butter in a saucepan, and sauté the onions until they are softened. Stir in the flour until well combined. Add the milk slowly in a stream, stirring constantly. Continue to cook and stir until the soup thickens slightly. Pour into the blender jar with the corn salad and allow to cool about 15 minutes. Purée the soup, return it to the pan, and add the paprika, along with a few gratings of fresh nutmeg. Heat the soup until it is hot; do not allow it to boil. Taste for salt and adjust if necessary. Serve garnished with freshly grated Parmigiano-Reggiano cheese or minced hard-cooked egg yolk.

Mâche Salad with Blue Cheese, Blueberries, and Pecans

The nutty flavor of mâche pairs well with the sweetness of blueberries and pecans, while the rich tang of the blue cheese pulls everything together. If possible, make this dish with the small native pecans that are sometimes available.

YIELD: **2 SERVINGS**

2 cups **mâche leaves**, rinsed and spun dry

1 slice of **red sweet onion**, about ⅛ inch thick, separated into rings

½ cup **blueberries**

¼ cup **pecans**, toasted (page 244)

½ cup **crumbled blue cheese**

2 tablespoons **safflower** *or* sunflower oil

2 teaspoons **malt vinegar**

¼ teaspoon **salt**

Dash of **hot sauce**

Freshly ground **black pepper**

1. Chill two salad plates until very cold. Pile half the mâche leaves on each plate, top with some onion rings, a scattering of blueberries and pecans, and the blue cheese.

2. In a small bowl combine the oil, vinegar, salt, hot sauce, and a few grinds of black pepper. Whisk with a fork to emulsify.

3. Drizzle the dressing over the salad and serve at once.

CRESS

Sometimes called upland cress to distinguish it from watercress, cress has a spicy flavor, indicative of the mustard family to which it belongs. Another easy and fast-maturing green crop, cress is ready to harvest about six weeks after the seeds germinate. Easier to grow than watercress because it does not need so much moisture, cress can substitute in any recipe calling for its hydrophilic cousin.

Cress is a little pickier about its growing medium than other greens. Add perlite or sand to commercial potting mix to provide the quick drainage cress prefers, or use a mix intended for cacti. Weekly feeding with soluble fertilizer will keep cress growing quick and tender.

In the Kitchen

Use cress in a salad mix or in any recipe where its spicy bite is welcome. The following two recipes offer one traditional and one nontraditional way to use cress.

Cress Tea Sandwiches

One simply cannot serve a traditional high tea in the South without also serving these traditional sandwiches. This filling breaks with tradition, however, to lower the fat content dramatically by substituting white bean hummus for cream cheese.

YIELD: **16 SANDWICHES**

White Bean Hummus

1 cup dried **Great Northern beans**

1 **bay leaf**

2 cloves **garlic**

Sprig of **thyme**

½ teaspoon **salt**

Freshly ground **white pepper**

1 tablespoon **extra virgin olive oil**

Tea Sandwiches

8 thin slices of **homemade-style white bread**

Extra virgin olive oil

White bean hummus

½ cup chopped **cress**

2 tablespoons **mayonnaise** (optional)

2 tablespoons very finely minced **parsley** (optional)

White Bean Hummus:

1. Rinse the beans and remove any shriveled or yellowed ones. Add cold water to cover the beans by one inch. Soak the beans overnight in the refrigerator.

2. Drain the beans, rinse, drain again, then transfer them to a large saucepan or Dutch oven. Add enough cold water to cover them by one inch, the bay leaf, garlic, and thyme sprig. Bring to a boil. Adjust the heat and simmer until the beans are tender, about 1½ hours. Test by mashing a bean against the side of the pan with a spoon. When the beans are done, remove them from the heat. Pick out and discard the bay leaf and thyme sprig, and drain in a colander, reserving the liquid. Allow to cool for ten minutes.

3. Transfer the beans to the bowl of a food processor, along with the salt, several grinds of pepper, and the olive oil. Process to a smooth paste, adding a little of the reserved liquid to achieve the proper consistency for spreading. Taste and add more salt and pepper if needed.

Tea Sandwiches:

1. Brush one side of each bread slice with olive oil. This helps to keep the sandwiches from becoming soggy. Spread four of the bread slices on the oiled side with the hummus, leaving a border about one-quarter-inch wide all around the edge of the slices, and arrange them on a work surface. Top each slice with two tablespoons of chopped cress.

2. Spread the oiled side of the other four slices with hummus in a similar fashion, and place them hummus side down on the first four bread slices to make sandwiches.

3. Trim the crusts from the bread, using a kitchen knife. Then cut each sandwich diagonally into quarters to form a total of sixteen triangles.

OPTIONAL: While the sandwiches are delicious as is, you can fancy them up considerably with this simple trick. Carefully spread the long side of each sandwich with mayonnaise. Dip the mayonnaise edge into the minced parsley to decorate. Arrange the sandwiches on a platter. Cover with plastic wrap. They will keep for several hours.

Deviled Eggs with Cress

The bright flavor of cress adds an elegant note to this buffet staple. This recipe can easily be multiplied to produce as many appetizers as you like. Deviled eggs keep well and make an excellent picnic item. For easy peeling, choose less-than-fresh eggs for hard boiling. Place eggs in a large pan and cover them by one inch with cold water. If they stand up on their pointed ends, they will be easy to peel. Discard any egg that floats.

YIELD: **6 APPETIZERS**

3 **eggs**

⅛ teaspoon **onion powder**

¼ teaspoon **cider vinegar**

Pinch of **salt**

2 tablespoons **mayonnaise**

½ teaspoon **Creole mustard**

Dash of **hot sauce**

2 tablespoons chopped **cress**

1. Place the eggs in a large saucepan and cover with cold water. Set the saucepan over medium heat and bring slowly to a boil. Allow to boil 1 minute.

2. Remove the saucepan from the heat, cover, and let stand for 15 minutes. Drain the eggs and refill the saucepan with cold tap water. Allow the eggs to cool for 10 minutes, drain again, and refill the pan with cold water. After another 5 minutes of cooling, the eggs will be ready to peel, or you can store them in the refrigerator for a few days before continuing.

3. Carefully slice each peeled egg in half lengthwise, tip out the yolk into a bowl, and place the white halves on a serving plate. (A deviled egg plate is ideal.)

4. Add the remaining ingredients, except the cress, to the bowl with the yolks and mash with a fork to produce a uniform spread. Fold in the cress with the fork. Spoon the filling into the cavity of each of the white halves, distributing it equally. Refrigerate the eggs until ready to serve.

NOTE: Herbs or another full-flavored green, such as arugula, may be substituted for the cress.

LETTUCE

Of all the greens crops, lettuce comes in the greatest variety. The ubiquitous iceberg lettuce, crisphead, found on fast food hamburgers is among the more difficult types for a home gardener. Loose-head types form rosettes of individual leaves, but never a tightly compacted head. Butterhead lettuces have soft, rounded leaves and form neat heads. Romaine lettuces produce an upright, cylindrical head, while loose leaf varieties produce only clusters of leaves with little evidence of head formation. Windowsill growers should focus on loose leaf and Romaine types, both of which do well indoors. Heading lettuces typically do better if grown in a larger container outside. All these varieties come in forms that may be light green, dark green, brown, red, or variegated and with varying degrees of crinkling of the leaves. Grow multiple varieties for the prettiest salad combinations.

Lettuce seeds require light to germinate. Scatter the seeds thinly on the surface of the growing medium in a small pot, water well, and place the pot under lights immediately. At normal room temperatures, plants will sometimes emerge in as little as twenty four hours. Most of the seeds will have germinated within three or four days. Within two weeks, they should have true leaves. At this point, thin them by pulling with tweezers, removing all but one or a few plants, depending upon the size of the container. You can use the extra plants as microgreens or transplant them to additional pots if you have room. Feed weekly with a soluble fertilizer solution, and harvest as described for arugula. Most lettuces can be harvested three times before they start looking sickly.

In the Kitchen

Seldom eaten cooked, lettuce can nevertheless be used in dishes other than tossed salads. Here are some ideas for what to do with your lettuce harvest. You may substitute agave nectar for the sorghum or use a syrup made of two teaspoons brown sugar and a little water.

Southern Style Thai Lettuce Cups

Here us a southern take on a popular Thai dish. Substitute flavored tofu or seitan for the ham for a vegetarian version.

YIELD: **2 SERVINGS**

1 head **Bibb lettuce**

5 **cherry tomatoes**

2 tablespoons coarsely chopped, cooked **country ham**, preferably Benton's

2 tablespoons minced **green onions**

2 tablespoons chopped, fresh **mint leaves**

2 tablespoons chopped, fresh **Italian parsley leaves** (or cilantro)

1 tablespoon **lime juice**

2 teaspoons **sorghum syrup**

1 teaspoon **soy sauce** (or Thai fish sauce)

⅛ teaspoon **cayenne pepper**

1. Wash the lettuce and separate into leaves. Spin dry and reserve.

2. Wash and quarter the tomatoes and place them in a bowl with the remaining ingredients, stirring to combine. Cover and reserve in the refrigerator.

3. Arrange individual, cup-shaped lettuce leaves on serving plates. Spoon some of the tomato salad into each cup. Diners roll up the individual leaves around the salad and eat. Most people like sips of beer or whiskey between bites.

Lettuce Soup

We seldom think of lettuce as a cooked green, but this soup proves we should from time to time. One pound of fresh spinach leaves, or 1 cup of frozen then thawed spinach, can be substituted for the lettuce. The lettuce imparts a lovely blue-green color to the soup, while the spinach yields a forest green tint. If your garden produces an abundance of lettuce in late spring and you tire of salads, blanch the lettuce as directed in this recipe and then freeze in 1 cup portions. You can then make this soup whenever you crave a taste of springtime.

YIELD: **4 SERVINGS**

1 pound **lettuce leaves**

2 tablespoons **butter**

¼ cup finely minced **onions**

2 tablespoons **flour**

4 cups **milk**

¼ teaspoon **paprika**

Fresh **nutmeg**

Parmigiano-Reggiano cheese

Hard-cooked **egg yolk**

1. Wash the lettuce leaves. Drop them into boiling water. When the water returns to a boil, cook for one minute.

2. Drain then rinse under cold water to stop cooking. Drain thoroughly. You may want to squeeze the lettuce to express additional liquid. Place the lettuce in a blender jar and reserve.

3. Melt the butter in a saucepan, and sauté the onions until they are translucent. Stir in the flour until well combined. Add the milk while stirring constantly. Continue to cook and stir until the soup thickens slightly.

4. Pour the soup into the blender jar with the lettuce and allow to cool, about 15 minutes. Purée. If using an immersion blender, the cooling time is not necessary. Add the paprika and a few gratings of fresh nutmeg.

5. Reheat the soup to serving temperature; do not allow the soup to boil. Taste and adjust seasoning if necessary. Serve garnished with freshly grated Parmigiano-Reggiano cheese and/or minced hard-cooked egg yolk.

Spring Lettuces with Green Dressing

The dressing features ingredients you may also have growing along with lettuce.

YIELD: **4 SERVINGS**

4 to 6 cups **mixed spring lettuce leaves** *or* other leaves *or* a combination

Green Dressing

12 leaves **mizuna** *or* other mild mustard greens

2 large stalks of fresh **cilantro**

2 large sprigs of fresh **parsley**

1 large **clove garlic**, peeled

1 tablespoon **extra virgin olive oil**, more if needed

1 teaspoon **red wine vinegar**

½ teaspoon **salt**

Freshly ground **black pepper**

1. Have ready a bowl of ice water. Bring a pot of water to a boil. Holding the mizuna, cilantro, and parsley by the stems like a bouquet of flowers, immerse the leaves into the boiling water for 30 seconds.

2. Remove and then plunge into the ice water. Drain well. Cut off the unblanched portion of the stems and discard. Squeeze the greens dry and transfer to a blender jar. Add the remaining ingredients and blend until you have a uniform dressing, adding a little more oil if necessary to achieve the desired consistency. Serve immediately over mixed greens.

RADISH

Another member of the vast and useful mustard family, radishes lend themselves to indoor cultivation because they grow rapidly and do not require deep soil in order to produce usable roots. (By comparison, carrots are not so accommodating.) The size and shape of the root varies from round marbles to elongated, carrot-like forms. The round marbles are best for container culture. Some good cultivars include Sparkler, Cherry Belle, Red Head, and Pearl. All of these will be ready for harvest in a month after seedlings emerge. Even faster, Celesta produces roots within twenty-five days.

Sow radish seeds thinly on the surface of a pot of growing mix. Cover the seeds with about one-quarter inch of mix and water thoroughly. It is important that the seeds not dry out, so check regularly and water when they are starting to get dry. As soon as the seedlings emerge, thin them so they are about one inch apart each way. The final number of seedlings will depend upon the size of the pot they are in. Feed them at this point with a soluble fertilizer solution, and watch them grow. They should not require additional feeding. For the best root development, place your radish pots in the brightest available spot. They like plenty of light.

In the Kitchen

Most dishes calling for radishes do not involve cooking them, but they can be quite delicious when tenderized by brief exposure to heat. Try the soup described in the following recipe and see if you don't agree. The radish sandwiches are a classic combination, and the cornbread salad is a nontraditional salad in which radishes play a supporting role.

Japanese-Style Garden Vegetable Soup

Use tofu instead of chicken, if you prefer.

YIELD: **4 SERVINGS**

2 teaspoons **canola** *or* sunflower oil

½ teaspoon **sesame oil**

½ cup diced **radish**

¼ cup chopped **scallions**, white and green parts

¼ cup diced **celery**

¼ cup julienned **zucchini**

¼ cup julienned **shiitake mushrooms**

¼ cup julienned **snow peas**

4 cups **dashi** *(page 228)*

¼ cup diced **cooked chicken breast**

2 tablespoons **oyster sauce**

Salt

Freshly ground **black pepper**

Plain steamed **rice**, to serve

1 tablespoon chopped **cilantro** *or* parsley

1. In a heavy saucepan, heat the oils over medium heat and add the radish, scallions, and celery. Sauté for 2 to 3 minutes, or until the scallions are softened. Add the zucchini, mushrooms, and snow peas, and continue to sauté for 1 to 2 minutes, or until the snow peas are bright green. Add the dashi, bring to a boil, then reduce the heat and simmer gently, partially covered, for 20 minutes. Add the chicken and oyster sauce and stir to combine. Taste and add salt and pepper as needed.

2. Serve the soup over rice, garnished with the fresh herb.

Open-Faced Radish Sandwiches

This is a classic way to enjoy freshly harvested radishes.

YIELD: **2 SERVINGS**

6 to 8 freshly harvested **radishes** with leaves intact

2 slices **homemade-style wheat bread**

2 tablespoons **unsalted butter**, softened

¼ to ½ teaspoon coarse **sea salt**

Freshly ground **black pepper**

1. Carefully wash and trim the radishes, leaving them as intact as possible. Slice each radish lengthwise into thin slices, keeping the leaves attached. Lightly toast the bread. Spread each slice of bread with half the butter. Sprinkle with salt and pepper. Arrange the radish slices attractively on the bread slices. Serve immediately.

Cornbread Salad

From my friend Brock Street comes this recipe for cornbread salad. Use your favorite cornbread recipe or mine (page 248).

YIELD: **8+ SERVINGS**

1 8x8 pan of **cornbread**, or ½ of a 12-inch skillet of day-old cornbread, crumbled

12 **radishes**, trimmed and chopped

1 large **cucumber**, seeded and chopped

4 hard-cooked **eggs**, chopped

1 cup **mayonnaise**

¼ cup prepared **yellow mustard**, such as French's

2 cups **ranch dressing**, any brand or recipe

1. Place the first four ingredients in a large bowl and mix well. Combine the dressing ingredients in a separate bowl, mix well, and pour over the cornbread mixture. Stir gently to combine, and place the bowl in the refrigerator for at least 1 hour before serving. It is better the next day and can be made up to 3 days ahead. This will feed a crowd as part of a buffet.

SCALLION

Scallions, also known as green onions or spring onions, don't mind a bit of crowding and thus do very well in a pot, as long as they receive adequate moisture and fertilizer. All onions are heavy feeders and do best in rich, well-drained, sandy soil.

For indoor production, sow the seeds in small pots, covering them with one-quarter inch of growing medium. Keep the pots well watered, feed them weekly, and begin harvesting the onion tops when they are six inches tall. This will take only a couple of weeks after the seedlings emerge. If you want larger roots, thin the onions instead of merely harvesting the tops. The ones left in the pot will grow larger in diameter. You do not need to thin them all at once. Doing so over a couple of weeks' time will help prolong your harvest, because you can use the smaller ones in the kitchen.

In the Kitchen

Scallions go great in salads or as a garnish for almost any savory dish. They can be used anywhere you want to add a hint of onion flavor. The tops can be substituted in any recipe calling for chives.

Foo Yung Eggs with Scallions

Scallions star in this tasty take on egg foo yung. Vary the other ingredients to suit your taste and with what you have on hand.

YIELD: **2 SERVINGS**

3 **eggs**

¼ cup **chicken** *or* vegetable stock

1 cup shredded cooked **chicken breast**

6 **scallions**, white and green parts, trimmed

3 fresh **shiitake mushrooms**, stemmed and cut into thin strips

¼ cup shredded canned **bamboo shoots**

½ teaspoon **brown sugar**

Freshly ground **white pepper**

1 tablespoon **soy sauce**

3 drops **sesame oil**

1¼ cups (*about*) **vegetable oil**

Soy sauce

Hot sauce

1. In a large bowl, combine the eggs and stock. Beat very gently to combine; you should see some yolk and white remaining unmixed. Set aside while you prepare the vegetables.

2. In a large skillet or wok, heat one tablespoon of the oil until it ripples. Add the vegetables and stir fry over high heat for 1 minute. Transfer the contents of the skillet to the bowl with the eggs, stirring gently to combine. Add the sugar, pepper, soy sauce, and sesame oil, stirring again just to combine.

3. Wipe out the skillet and add the remaining oil to a depth of one-half inch. The amount will vary, depending upon the size and shape of the cooking utensil. Heat the oil until a drop of the egg mixture sizzles and turns brown. The temperature will be 325°F on a deep-fry thermometer. Using a ladle, scoop some of the egg mixture and carefully deposit it into the center of the oil. Fry until one side is golden brown, then turn with a spatula and fry the other side. Transfer the finished cakes to a plate lined with paper towels and keep warm in a low oven until all the cakes have been fried. Serve the cakes on warmed plates, and pass soy sauce and hot sauce.

NOTE: For a vegetarian version, substitute fresh bean sprouts for the chicken.

Kilt Lettuce

This dish has welcomed spring to Southern tables for two centuries or more. Kilt is the Appalachian pronunciation of "killed," referring to the way the lettuce is cooked by the hot dressing. The heirloom lettuce Black Seeded Simpson is the traditional variety used in this dish.

YIELD: **2 SERVINGS**

8 cups fresh leaf **lettuce**

8 **scallions**, each about ⅜ inch in diameter, trimmed

2 slices thick cut **bacon**, such as Benton's

2 tablespoons **cider vinegar**

1 tablespoon **water**

Freshly ground **black pepper**

1. Rinse the lettuce, spin it dry, and transfer it to a large metal bowl. Slice the scallions on the diagonal into one-inch pieces, using both the white and green parts. Add the scallions to the bowl with the lettuce and toss to combine.

2. In a heavy cast iron skillet, fry the bacon slowly until it is crisp and brown, turning occasionally. Transfer the bacon to paper towels to drain, reserving the drippings in the skillet. You should have about two tablespoons of drippings. If necessary, add a little oil or pour off some drippings to achieve the correct amount.

3. Combine the vinegar and water in a small bowl. Reheat the bacon drippings until a light haze appears above the pan. Add the vinegar, stir quickly to deglaze the pan, and immediately pour the hot dressing over the lettuce and onions. Stir quickly with a wooden spoon to wilt all the lettuce.

4. Seasoned the salad with a few turns of black pepper and top with the crumbled bacon. Serve at once.

CHERVIL

A relative of parsley, chervil has a similar grassy taste but with a distinctive light note of licorice that pairs beautifully with fish or delicate vegetables like peas and asparagus. The finely divided foliage is also attractive on the plate. Like other members of the carrot family, chervil is slow to germinate and the seedlings are weak. Once established, however, the plants grow rapidly and make a charming display. Pots of chervil grown indoors during winter can be moved outside in early spring, where they will continue to grow until the weather warms. Do this if you want to save seeds, as the plants will bloom when the air temperature gets high enough.

Seedlings will have trouble emerging if the growing medium is too coarse, so crumble it well with your fingers before filling the pot. Sow the large, needle-like seeds as described in this chapter for other greens, covering them with one-quarter inch of fine soil. It will take about two weeks or even longer for the seedlings to emerge, and they will grow slowly at first. Once true leaves appear, growth speeds up and the plants are sturdier. You can begin harvesting leaves when the plants are six inches tall and continue harvesting over a period of about two months. Because chervil prefers some shade, it is an ideal plant for a spot where the light is insufficient for more demanding crops.

In the Kitchen

Chervil's pretty foliage and delicate flavor shine in these two recipes. Use the potato chip windows to garnish mashed potatoes, or make a bunch and serve them like chips. The nontraditional take on shrimp scampi would make a great luncheon dish for a springtime gathering.

Chervil in Potato Chip "Windows"

This is a great little trick for garnishing the main dish for a dinner with company. Or just do it to get your kids to enjoy the flavor of fresh herbs. It seems like a lot of work, but once you get the hang of it, you can make these quickly. Store the chips in an airtight container at room temperature. They will keep for three days.

YIELD: **1 DOZEN PIECES**

1 large baking **potato**

1 tablespoon **butter**, melted

Small sprigs of **chervil**

Pinch of kosher **salt**

1. Preheat the oven to 425°F. Place a sheet of parchment paper on a baking sheet. Peel the potato, cut it in half lengthwise, and drop it into a bowl of cold water sufficient to cover it. This will keep the potato from darkening as you continue with the recipe.

2. Separate the chervil into individual leaves or groups of two or three leaves, as you prefer. Brush the parchment paper with some of the melted butter, coating it lightly all over. Remove a potato half from the water and pat dry with a kitchen towel. With a vegetable peeler or a mandoline slicer, remove paper-thin slices from the rounded side of the potato. Return the first few narrow slices to the water, and continue cutting until you have slices at least 1¼ inches wide.

3. Place a slice on the parchment then position a chervil leaf in its center. Top with another slice, pressing down so the chervil is visible through the top slice. The starch on the surface of the slices will help them adhere to each other. Continue until you have made as many "windows" as you like. With a sharp knife or pastry blade, trim the ends of the windows as neatly as you wish. Brush the tops of the windows with butter.

4. Place in the oven and bake until the edges are crisp and golden brown, 10 to 12 minutes. Remove from the oven and sprinkle with salt while they are still hot. Let them cool on the baking sheet then transfer to a suitable container until you are ready to use them. They can sit at room temperature for an hour or two before serving.

NOTE: Chop the smaller slices and trimmings of the potato and add them to soup.

Shrimp "Scampi" with Chervil

Chervil's hint of anise flavor goes great with shrimp. Try this dish as an alternative to the traditional version.

YIELD: **2 SERVINGS**

16 jumbo **shrimp**

1 tablespoon **olive oil**

1 tablespoon minced **onion**

2 tablespoons **shrimp stock** *(below)*

2 teaspoons freshly squeezed **lemon juice**

1 tablespoon minced **chervil**

1 teaspoon grated **lemon zest**

Shrimp Stock

Shells from 16 large **shrimp**

¼ medium **white onion**, in one piece

1 **bay leaf**

1. Peel and devein the shrimp, reserving the shells for the stock. Spread the shrimp on a tray lined with paper towels. Pat the shrimp thoroughly dry with paper towels.

2. Heat the oil in a heavy cast iron skillet until it ripples. Add the shrimp, spreading them out in a single layer with a metal spoon. Cook exactly 1 minute, then add the minced onion. Cook 2 minutes longer, then turn the shrimp with tongs. Cook an additional 3 to 4 minutes until the shrimp are just done through. With tongs remove the shrimp to a plate and keep warm.

3. Add the shrimp stock and lemon juice to the pan and deglaze, scraping up any browned bits with a spoon. Cook the sauce until it is slightly reduced. Add the chervil and lemon zest to the sauce, stir to combine, and pour over the shrimp. Serve at once.

Shrimp Stock:

1. Place the ingredients in a saucepan and cover with water. Bring to a boil, reduce the heat, and simmer until reduced to one-half cup. Strain the stock, discarding the solids.

CHIVES

The only member of the onion family found naturally in both the eastern and western hemispheres, chives are perennial, returning year after year from small, onion-like bulbs. Chives are easy to grow from seed, and because of shade tolerance they are a great candidate for indoor cultivation.

If you want to keep chives going for the longest possible season, fill a six- to eight-inch pot with growing mix and sow the seeds thinly on the surface. Water thoroughly and place in a warm, bright location. When the seedlings are an inch tall, feed them with soluble fertilizer. Repeat this feeding about every two weeks. You can begin harvesting the leaves when the plants are six inches tall, or leave them to mature. Chives will eventually reach a foot in height and may bloom if they receive enough sunshine. The blooms, pink-purple pompoms held at the tops of long stems, are edible and look beautiful garnishing a salad.

In the Kitchen

You can use chives in any recipe that will benefit from a light hint of onion. Snipped chives can garnish anything from salad to salmon. These two recipes are similar in that chives play the role of structural element as well as being a source of flavor.

Chive and Rice Flour Pancakes

These gluten-free savory pancakes are wonderful for wrapping fillings.
They can also be stacked with goodies in between and topped with a sauce.

YIELD: **8 PANCAKES**

1 cup **rice flour**

2 teaspoons **baking powder**

½ teaspoon **salt**

¼ teaspoon ground **white pepper**

1 **egg**, well beaten

1 cup **milk**, more if needed

¼ cup **chives**, snipped into 1-inch pieces

2 teaspoons plus 2 tablespoons **safflower oil**, divided

1. In a mixing bowl combine the flour, baking powder, salt, and pepper.

2. In a separate bowl, whisk together the remaining ingredients except for two tablespoons of oil, then whisk the liquids into the dry ingredients. Stir well to combine. Add a little more milk if the batter seems too stiff.

3. Place the batter in the refrigerator to rest for at least an hour.

4. Preheat the oven to 180°F. Heat the remaining two tablespoons of oil in a large skillet over medium heat.

5. Remove the batter from the refrigerator and stir to evenly distribute the chives. Ladle one-quarter cup of batter into the hot oil. Cook until bubbles appear on top and the edges begin to brown. Turn and brown on the other side. Work in batches so the pan will not become too crowded to easily turn the pancakes.

6. As each pancake is done, transfer it to a rack over a plate lined with paper towels. Keep the pancakes warm in the oven until you are ready to serve them.

Steamed Vegetable Bundles (tied with chives)

This is an easy way to dress up steamed vegetables for company. The trick is having the carrots done at the same time as the much softer asparagus and zucchini. Hence, precook the carrots before making the bundles. The simple seasoning lets the vegetables and subtle flavor of the chives shine through.

YIELD: **4 SERVINGS**

12 stalks **asparagus**

1 **zucchini**

2 large **carrots**

8 **chive leaves**, each about 9 inches long

2 tablespoons **fruity extra virgin olive oil**

Half a **lemon**

Coarse **sea salt**

Freshly ground **black pepper**

1. Snap off the bottom of the asparagus stalks. They should break naturally if you hold the stalk in one hand and bend back the bottom end with the other hand. Save the ends for the stock pot. Drop the stalks into a glass with an inch of water in the bottom, points up, like a bouquet of flowers. A pinch of sugar added to the water will enhance the flavor of the asparagus. Set aside while you prepare the rest of the dish.

2. Trim the ends of the zucchini and cut it lengthwise into slices ¼ inch thick. Stack the slices and cut them into strips that are ¼ by ¼ inch. Save the innermost slices, consisting of all or mostly seeds, for the stock pot and set aside the remaining slices.

3. Trim the carrots and cut them into strips, as you did with the zucchini. Bring a large pot of water to a rolling boil. Drop in the carrots, allow them to cook for 3 minutes, and then drain them in a colander. Run cold tap water over the carrots to stop their cooking. Set aside.

4. Bring another pot of water to a boil. Drop in the chives, count to three, and then drain the chives in a colander and run them under cold water.

5. Using some of each of the vegetables, assemble bundles and tie them together with the chives, using a chive near each end of each bundle. Set the bundles in a steamer basket. Place the basket over simmering water and steam the vegetables for 6 minutes. Remove with tongs to warmed plates. Drizzle the vegetable bundles with olive oil, sprinkle with salt and pepper, and squeeze a few drops of lemon juice over them. Serve at once.

NOTE: Long, thin, fresh green beans can be substituted for the carrots, and require precooking for 3 minutes, as well. Yellow squash can substitute for the zucchini.

CILANTRO

Cilantro makes an appearance in cuisines across the planet, earning it the reputation as the most-used of all herbs. This may be, at least in part, because it is extremely easy to grow. It does not mind crowding and grows almost as well in partial shade as it does in full sun. Therefore, it is an ideal candidate for growing in pots indoors. In addition to its other good qualities, cilantro develops a full, robust flavor when it is barely an inch tall. This means quick rewards for the novice grower eager to use the crop in the kitchen.

Sow the BB-size seeds of cilantro in pots of growing mix and keep well watered. Seeds take a long time to germinate—up to three weeks—so be patient. As soon as seedlings emerge, start feeding them with a weak solution of soluble fertilizer. Feed every week to keep them growing, especially if you harvest from time to time. Cut individual leaves with scissors to use as microgreens. More leaves will sprout from the crown. When the plants are six inches tall, you can pull entire plants from the pot. Use them, roots and all, in Thai style curries and many other dishes. When left to go to seed, a process that is unlikely to occur unless you move them outside during the summer, the resulting seeds are the spice we know as coriander.

In the Kitchen

Countless recipes include cilantro. The following shrimp recipe was inspired by a visit to Puerto Rico's rural southeastern coast.

Key Lime and Cilantro Shrimp Salad

Serve the salad over a bed of greens or sprouts.

YIELD: **2 SERVINGS**

Juice of 3 **key limes**

½ cup loosely packed **cilantro leaves**, finely minced

¼ cup **extra virgin olive oil**

¼ teaspoon **salt**

¼ teaspoon freshly ground **black pepper**

Dash of **hot sauce**

2 teaspoons **salt**

12 large **shrimp**, shelled and deveined

1. In a mixing bowl, combine the lime juice, cilantro, olive oil, salt, pepper, and hot sauce. Whisk to emulsify.

2. Bring a pot of water to a rolling boil. Drop in 2 teaspoons of salt and then the shrimp. Reduce heat to a simmer and cook just until the shrimp are pink, about 5 minutes.

3. Drain the shrimp thoroughly, transfer them to a bowl, and toss with the dressing. Serve at room temperature.

PARSLEY

In Italy they have the saying "I see you as often as parsley," referring to a person one encounters on a regular basis. Parsley is indeed universal in cooking, finding its way into innumerable dishes as a flavoring agent or garnish. Its fresh-tasting leaves are high in vitamin C and should be regularly included in salads.

Parsley is notoriously slow to germinate, but you can speed it up with the following approach. Place a half teaspoon of parsley seeds in a small bowl. Cover with lukewarm water and allow to sit overnight. Pour the water and seeds through a strainer, rinse under the tap, and then return the seeds to the bowl with more lukewarm water. Do this for four days in a row. On the fifth day, strain the seeds again and plant them in prepared pots as for chervil. They should emerge within a week. When true leaves appear, begin feeding with a soluble fertilizer solution. Continue feeding every two weeks. Parsley is a biennial, meaning it grows for one season and then blooms the second year. Therefore, it is relatively easy to keep plants going in containers for months. If this is your goal, transplant some of your seedlings to eight-inch pots to better accommodate the expansive root system.

In the Kitchen

Parsley brings nutrition-packed flavor to a wide variety of dishes. The parsley cream can be drizzled into a cream soup for dramatic effect. Winter tabouli is a great side dish with parsley as a main ingredient.

Parsley Cream

This flavorful cream makes a splendid garnish for any cream soup of a contrasting color. It is especially good with vichysoisse (page 64). Use vegetable or chicken stock, depending upon your preferences and the stock used in the soup being garnished.

YIELD: **ABOUT ½ CUP**

5 tablespoons **parsley leaves**

¼ cup chilled **stock**

¼ cup **heavy cream**

1. Bring a large pot of water to boil. Drop in the parsley leaves. Blanch the parsley for five seconds. Drain the leaves in a sieve and refresh them under cold running water. Drain well again. Purée in a blender with the chilled stock and cream.

Winter Tabouli

Making tabouli with homegrown parsley and home-canned tomatoes brings new life to this salad when fresh produce is scarce.

YIELD: **4 SERVINGS**

2 cups **home-canned tomatoes** with their juices

1 cup loosely packed fresh **parsley leaves**

½ cup **bulgur wheat**

2 **scallions**, white and green parts, chopped

1 tablespoon **extra virgin olive oil**

2 teaspoons freshly squeezed **lemon juice**

1 teaspoon dried **mint leaves**

¼ teaspoon **salt**

¼ teaspoon freshly ground **black pepper**

1. In a large bowl, stir all the ingredients together to combine. Refrigerate at least 1 hour. The wheat will absorb the flavorful juices. If you find the result too watery, drain the tabouli in a fine sieve prior to serving.

CHAPTER 2

Containerized Farming

With even a limited amount of outdoor space, growing food in large containers can be highly rewarding. New innovations in container design and the development of compact vegetable varieties have combined to make this type of gardening fun and almost foolproof.

If you have a sunny balcony, porch, or patio, you can grow an amazing amount of food in containers. The possibilities are limited only by the local climate, how much space you have, and the effort you are willing to make.

Choosing Containers

Vegetables are a lot like pedigreed dogs. They are not as rough and tumble as many other plants and require a bit of coddling. They will not, for example, tolerate too much crowding of the roots. Therefore, when looking for containers for a food garden, think larger rather than smaller. Some herbs and greens will grow in a six-inch pot, but you will get better production with less effort if you use at least twelve-inch diameter containers or larger for everything. The main reason for using larger containers, apart from avoiding crowding, results from the high water requirement of most vegetables. Smaller containers dry out more rapidly than larger ones, and in the summer this can mean you will have to water small containers more than once a day.

One way to avoid watering issues is to use self-watering containers. You can find numerous brands in garden centers and online, but the basic design is the same. A reservoir

holds several days' supply of water. Sitting above the reservoir is the container with growing mix. The design of the unit, typically involving a fabric mat under the grow container, allows water to wick up from the reservoir to the growing medium, where it is drawn toward the surface by capillary action, keeping the growing medium evenly moist but not soggy. This is an ideal situation for vegetable plants and frees the gardener from much of the task of watering. It is necessary to replenish the reservoir only from time to time.

If you don't mind watering, almost anything that will hold the growing medium and resist water damage can be used to grow crops. Plastic pots and planters are probably the most popular, but I have seen beautiful gardens growing in galvanized tubs, plastic five-gallon buckets, re-purposed shipping pallets, and various other odds and ends. As a rule, you want something at least six inches deep in order to provide root space, but beyond that, let your imagination wander. Flea market finds and household trash like empty food containers and milk bottles are all possibilities. Wooden boxes and crates add a rustic touch and look great with plants growing in them. Be sure to coat the inside of wood containers with a waterproof varnish or wood preservative to prevent rot, unless the containers are made of a naturally rot-resistant wood, such as cedar.

Growing Media

Plants growing in containers will do much better if they are grown in a soil-less medium instead of garden soil. The latter may not have the proper drainage characteristics needed for containers, as well as being a potential source for weed seeds, insects, and plant diseases. You will have fewer problems with your container garden if you use a commercially prepared sterile potting mix. Numerous brands are available, some containing only certified organic ingredients. Over the years, I have found little difference among them.

Feeding Container Crops

You have two basic options for feeding container crops. You can add a timed-release fertilizer to the growing medium when you fill the pot, or feed plants periodically with a soluble fertilizer solution. In my experience, either method works fine, but using timed-release fertilizer is less work. Plus, you don't have to keep track of when you last fed the plants and thereby avoid over-fertilization. Both types of fertilizers are available as organic or non-organic. Use whichever one suits you. In my experience, the plant growth will be the same.

To Sow or Not to Sow

Container crops can be grown from seed or transplants. Where possible, I suggest beginning gardeners use transplants purchased from a garden center. Some vegetables do not transplant well, but many of the most popular ones do, and you will have greater success with transplants. Once you gain some experience with growing vegetables, you may want to consider growing your own transplants (more about transplants in Chapter 6). Vegetables that are typically grown only from seed include most greens, carrots, beets, turnips, leeks, onions, beans, corn, and okra. Most others can be grown from transplants.

Many herbs should be grown from purchased plants, as the seedlings of thyme, rosemary, oregano, mints, and others do not come "true," that is, seedlings will vary in their flavor and intensity. Your best bet is to plant herbs that have been propagated from known cultivars. That way you get the cooking qualities you expect from any particular variety. This is not true for all herbs. Parsley, chervil, cilantro, dill, and basil are all good choices to grow from seed.

Your Container Garden

Growing in containers opens up several new possibilities for food crops. All of the vegetables and herbs mentioned in the previous chapter can be grown outdoors in larger containers. Any of them would be good candidates for a window box. Larger containers means a bigger harvest, too. While some of the vegetables listed later in this chapter could potentially be grown indoors, some, like tomatoes, present a challenge to the gardener to provide enough light. Hence, their inclusion in this chapter rather than the previous one.

ASIAN MUSTARDS

This category includes several related plants that have been developed through centuries of selection and breeding in Asia. They have found their way into American cuisine and are no longer limited to specialty markets and Asian grocery stores. They include mizuna, tatsoi, and bok choy, among others. All are quick to mature and are grown in the same way. These vegetables can be combined in a single container, because they all require the same conditions and typically mature within a few days of one another.

Fill a container with growing mix and sow the seeds, covering them with one-quarter inch of the mix. Water well and expect germination within seven to ten days. When seedlings have a pair of true leaves, feed them with a soluble fertilizer solution. If they seem too crowded, thin them to stand an inch apart each way. Most varieties will mature within a month. It is not necessary to feed them again unless the rate of growth slows noticeably. These plants do not grow well when daytime temperatures reach 80 degrees. In many parts of the United States, they can be produced in spring and again in autumn. In the Sunbelt, they can be grown as winter crops.

In the Kitchen

Asian mustards can be eaten either raw or cooked. Bok choy, with its substantial stalks, lends itself to cooking, while leafy mizuna and tatsoi can be added to salads. You can also add these leafy greens to soups.

Baby Bok Choy in Vegetable Herb Broth

Wow your dinner companion with this elegant but simple soup created from vegetables produced right in your kitchen.

YIELD: **2 SERVINGS**

4 **baby bok choy,**
trimmed

1 cup **vegetable stock**

2 tablespoons minced,
fresh, cool season **herbs**,
such as chervil, cilantro,
oregano, parsley, thyme,
or a combination

Salt

Freshly ground
black pepper

1. Bring the stock to a simmer in a large saucepan. Add the bok choy and 1 tablespoon of the herbs. Sprinkle with salt and a little pepper. Set the pan over medium heat and bring the stock to a simmer. Cover the pan, reduce the heat to low, and steam until a fork can be easily inserted into the base of the bok choy, about 10 minutes. Taste and adjust the seasoning. Serve the bok choy in bowls, ladling the broth over it. Garnish with the remaining herbs.

NOTE: *Use any of the vegetable stocks found in Chapter 5, "The Pantry." Each one will lend a different flavor profile to the finished dish.*

Stir Fry of Asian Mustards with Ground Pork

The tang of mustard greens melds perfectly with the richness of pork. Turnip greens and western mustard greens also benefit from this treatment.

YIELD: **2 SERVINGS**

2 cups loosely packed mixed **Asian mustards**, such as mizuna, tatsoi, and bok choy

2 teaspoons **vegetable oil**

Pinch of **salt**

8 ounces ground **pork**

1 piece **ginger**, about the size of a quarter, shredded

1 **clove garlic**, minced

1 tablespoon **soy sauce**

1 teaspoon **hot sauce**, or to taste

Rice vinegar to serve

1. Tear the leaves into bite-size pieces. Break or cut the bok choy stems into ½-inch pieces. Set aside in a bowl.

2. In a large skillet or wok placed over medium-high heat, heat the oil until it ripples. Add the salt. Add the pork and stir fry until it is no longer pink. Add the ginger and garlic and continue to cook for 30 seconds. Add the greens, toss to combine, cover the pan, and steam 1 minute. Remove the lid, add the soy sauce and hot sauce, and stir fry 1 minute longer. Serve at once, passing rice vinegar at the table so diners may season the dish to their preference.

DANDELION

Dandelions have become ubiquitous weeds in the New World, ironically because they were brought here as a food crop by European colonists. Wild dandelions can be gathered and eaten, but the taste is often bitter. Not so with the cultivated varieties, which make much larger leaves than wild ones typically do. To reduce the spread of dandelions outward from your garden, discard the pots at the end of the season. The perennial rootstock will sprout again the second year but will also bloom and go to seed. Grow them as an annual if you wish to avoid this. Besides being tasty, dandelion greens are an excellent source of vitamins and minerals.

Sow dandelion seeds on the surface of a pot filled with growing medium, barely covering them. When they germinate, feed every two weeks with a soluble fertilizer solution. When the leaves are large enough, begin harvesting. With regular watering and feeding, the plants should resprout and can be harvested two or three times before they become exhausted.

In the Kitchen

If they are small and tender, dandelion leaves can be added to salad mixes, but they are most often cooked. The simple braise highlights the special taste of dandelions, while the gumbo, traditionally eaten during the Christian Holy Week, blends dandelion with other greens.

Braised Dandelion Greens

Plain and simple cooking brings out the unique flavor of cultivated dandelion greens.

1 bunch **dandelion greens**

1 strip thick-cut **smoked bacon**, such as Benton's

6 **green onions**, white and green parts, chopped

½ cup **chicken stock**

¼ teaspoon **salt**

Freshly ground **black pepper**

1. Wash the greens and trim off the tough lower ends of the stems. Discard any yellowed leaves. Chop the dandelion greens into 3-inch pieces.

2. In a large, heavy skillet, preferably cast iron, cook the bacon over medium heat until it is crisp and brown. Transfer the bacon to a plate lined with paper towels to drain.

3. Reheat the fat in the skillet and add the dandelion greens and green onions. Cook, stirring until the greens have wilted and the white onions are becoming translucent. Pour in the chicken stock, reduce the heat to low, and simmer, stirring occasionally, until the liquid is reduced to two tablespoons. Add the salt and a few grinds of black pepper. Serve hot.

Gumbo Z'herbes

As with many traditional Southern dishes, gumbo z'herbes can be found in roughly as many versions as there are cooks. It is traditionally made on Holy Thursday or Good Friday in Louisiana. One constant seems to be the use of nine different greens, with symbolic reference to the Passion of Jesus. Shrimp or fish is substituted for the meats on Good Friday by observant Catholics, or animal protein may be omitted entirely.

YIELD: **8 SERVINGS**

8 ounces andouille **sausage**

8 ounces **ham**

2 tablespoons **bacon drippings** *or* vegetable oil

1 cup chopped **onions**

18 cups, in all, of **nine different greens,** such as dandelion, mustards, cabbage, Swiss chard, spinach, lettuce, scallions, beet tops, carrot tops, collards, turnip greens, or corn salad, washed and chopped or torn into bite-size pieces

2 cups **beef broth**

1 **bay leaf**

2 teaspoons fresh **thyme leaves**

1 teaspoon **Worcestershire sauce**

1 teaspoon **hot sauce**

Salt

Freshly ground **black pepper**

1. Split the andouille sausage lengthwise into quarters, then chop into ½-inch pieces. Cut the ham into ½-inch cubes.

2. Heat the oil in a large soup pot over medium heat. Add the meats and sauté until lightly browned on all sides. Remove with a slotted spoon to a heatproof bowl. Add the onions to the fat in the pot and cook, stirring occasionally, until they are translucent. Add the greens to the pot and cook, stirring until they have begun to wilt. Add the broth, bay leaf, and thyme, and bring the soup to a gentle boil. Reduce the heat and cook, covered, for 30 minutes. Add the meats, Worcestershire, and hot sauces to the pot, stirring to combine. Taste and adjust the seasoning, if needed, with salt and freshly ground black pepper. Serve the gumbo with steamed rice, passing additional hot sauce.

EGGPLANT

A member of the tomato clan, eggplant thrives on warm weather and ample rainfall. It is an ideal container subject, with miniature varieties bred just for the purpose, and it contributes bold, scalloped foliage and beautiful flowers, often blue or violet, to the container garden.

Unless you are extremely fond of eggplant, one or two containers should be sufficient for your needs. Wait until the weather is warm and settled before you plant. Purchase started plants at your local garden center. For one of the smaller varieties, fill a pot at least twelve inches in diameter with your preferred growing medium. For standard-size eggplants, use a larger pot, up to about five gallons. Set a plant in the center of the pot, and feed it with a soluble fertilizer solution. Plants should be fed about every two weeks until blooms appear. Make sure they receive an inch of water per week.

Eggplant can be a magnet for flea beetles. Where these pests occur, it is best to grow eggplant under cover until the first fruits appear. This is easy to do in a container. Just place some thin bamboo stakes around the circumference of the container and drape it with a row cover or other sheer fabric. Secure the fabric around the top of the pot with a piece of twine or wire.

Eggplant is ready to harvest when the skin is shiny. Dull-colored fruits are too mature to use. Fruits keep for about three days with refrigeration and should be eaten soon after picking for best quality.

Korean Eggplant

Common as a side dish in Korean restaurants, this eggplant is delicious with non-Asian food.

YIELD: **4 SERVINGS**

3 medium **Japanese eggplants**

2½ tablespoons **soy sauce**

2 **green onions**, chopped

3 cloves **garlic**, minced

1½ teaspoons **sesame seeds**, toasted

1½ teaspoons **sesame oil**

1 teaspoon **hot pepper flakes**, or as much as you prefer

1. Set a steamer over a pan of water and bring the water to a simmer.

2. Cut the eggplants into two or three pieces. Then cut each piece in half lengthwise. Place the eggplant in the steamer and steam for 15 minutes.

3. Remove the cooked eggplant to a bowl and set it aside until cool enough to handle. Tear each piece of eggplant lengthwise with your fingers. Place the eggplant in a storage container. Mix the rest of ingredients with the eggplant. Keep at room temperature for an hour or two before serving, or cover and refrigerate for up to 3 days. Bring to room temperature before serving.

Smoky Grilled Caponata

The key to this recipe is to remove as much moisture as possible from the eggplant before grilling. This permits it to absorb the dressing and also helps avoid a too-soft texture. The fresher the eggplant, the better your results will be.

YIELD: **6 TO 8 SERVINGS AS PART OF A BUFFET**

1 large or 2 small **eggplants**, a total of about 1½ pounds

Kosher salt

1 medium **onion**, peeled and thinly sliced

3 stalks **celery** with leaves, cut into ½-inch pieces

2 tablespoons **olive oil**

2 cups peeled, chopped **tomatoes** (or substitute canned diced tomatoes)

½ cup **wine vinegar**

1 tablespoon **sugar**

Olive oil for brushing the eggplant

½ cup pitted **olives**, preferably a green type

Freshly ground **black pepper**

¼ teaspoon **liquid smoke** flavoring

3 tablespoons chopped fresh **parsley leaves**

1. Trim the eggplant and cut it into lengthwise slices ¾-inch thick. Place the slices, in layers if necessary, in a colander set over a bowl to catch the liquid, and sprinkle them with kosher salt. If layering, salt each layer on both sides before adding more. Cover the eggplant with a plate and place a weight, such as a can of beans, on top. Allow the eggplant to stand at room temperature for 1 hour. Rinse the eggplant, discarding the bitter juices in the bowl. Place the slices on paper towels and blot thoroughly.
Set the eggplant aside while you complete the dish.

2. Heat the olive oil in a large skillet and cook the onion, stirring frequently, until it is translucent, about 10 minutes. Add the celery and cook for 10 minutes, stirring frequently. Add the tomatoes, cook 5 minutes, and add the vinegar and sugar. Cook an additional 10 minutes or so, until the tomatoes have broken down to form a sauce. This will take longer with fresh tomatoes and less time with canned tomatoes. Remove the mixture from the heat and let stand while you finish the eggplant.

3. Heat a grill pan until it is smoking hot. Brush the eggplant slices with oil and then grill them, a few at a time, until they are lightly browned and marked on both sides, turning them once or twice. Take care not to overcook them or they will be mushy. Transfer the slices to a cutting board until cool enough to handle and then cut them into cubes. Add the eggplant to the tomato mixture, along with the olives, a generous amount of pepper, smoke flavoring, and parsley. Stir to combine. Taste and add a little more sugar if you think it isn't sweet enough. You want a nice balance of sweet and sour flavors.

4. Cover the caponata and let it sit at room temperature for 24 hours. Refrigerate thereafter for longer storage, up to a week. Serve at room temperature.

If you prefer, grill the eggplant slices on an outdoor grill, using hickory chips for smoke. Place a handful of hickory chips on a square of heavy-duty aluminum foil. Bring up the corners to form a "purse" with a small opening at the top for smoke to escape. Place this over a low burner until smoke begins to drift from the purse, then start grilling the eggplant slices. Cover the grill and reduce the heat to low in order to capture the smoke flavor. You can also grill over hardwood charcoal (not briquettes) and omit the hickory chips. In either case, it is better to undercook rather than overcook the eggplant.

SPINACH

Nutritious spinach is another cool-season green crop that responds well to container cultivation. While you can simply scatter seeds over the surface of a large container, you will get better results if you start seeds separately and then transplant the baby spinach plants to their permanent quarters. Use a nursery tray with eighteen cells, fill with growing medium, and plant two or three seeds in each cell. Spinach is notorious for spotty germination. Not all the seeds will sprout, hence the recommendation to plant multiples. When at least one seed in each cell has sprouted, remove any smaller seedlings with tweezers, leaving only one plant per cell. Feed them at this time with soluble fertilizer solution. When the plants have two pairs of true leaves, transplant to individual six-inch pots, or to a larger container, spacing them six inches apart each way. Feed at transplant time and again every two weeks. Make sure the pots never dry out. This method can produce leaves the size of ping pong paddles. When the weather warms up, spinach will go to seed. You can replant in fall for a second crop. One of the main advantages of spinach over other greens is that it freezes well, and this is the preferred way to preserve it. Drop the leaves into boiling water, set a timer for three minutes, and drain the spinach when the time is up. Rinse well under cold water. Using your hand, squeeze out as much moisture as you can, then transfer the spinach to a suitable container and place in the freezer.

Cream of Spinach Soup

Few recipes bring out the flavor of spinach like this cream soup, and the rich forest green color looks great on the table. For a holiday version, garnish the soup with finely diced roasted red peppers in addition to the egg or cheese.

YIELD: **4 SERVINGS**

1 pound **spinach leaves**

2 tablespoons **butter**

¼ cup finely minced **onions**

2 tablespoons **flour**

4 cups **milk**

¼ tsp **paprika**

Fresh **nutmeg**

Parmigiano-Reggiano cheese or hard-cooked egg yolks for garnish

1. Wash the spinach leaves and then drop them into boiling water. When the water returns to a boil, cook for 1 minute. Drain. Rinse under cold water to stop the cooking and then drain thoroughly. Squeeze the spinach by handfuls to express some additional liquid. Place the spinach in a blender jar and reserve.

2. Melt the butter in a saucepan and sauté the onions until they are softened. Stir in the flour until well combined. Add the milk slowly in a stream, stirring constantly. Continue to cook and stir until the soup thickens slightly.

3. Pour into the blender jar with the spinach and allow to cool for about 15 minutes. Purée the soup, return it to the pan, and add the paprika, along with a few gratings of fresh nutmeg.

4. Heat the soup until it is hot; do not allow it to boil. Taste for salt and adjust if necessary. Serve garnished with freshly grated Parmigiano-Reggiano cheese or minced hard-cooked egg yolk.

Spinach Salad with Dates

Spinach has a luxurious flavor that pairs well with rich ingredients, like the dates featured in this recipe. Substitute any dried fruit you like.

YIELD: **2 SERVINGS**

2 tablespoons
extra virgin olive oil

1 tablespoon
white wine vinegar

1 tablespoon diced
red sweet pepper

1 teaspoon **Creole mustard**

1½ cups loosely packed
fresh **spinach leaves**

½ cup chopped **dates**

1 **mandarin orange**,
peeled and separated into
segments

2 **radishes**, thinly sliced

2 tablespoons chopped
fresh herbs of your choice

Salt

Freshly ground
black pepper

1. Combine the oil, vinegar, red pepper, and mustard in a small bowl. Reserve.

2. Arrange the other ingredients attractively onto two plates, scattering the herbs on top and seasoning with salt and pepper. Whisk the dressing ingredients and drizzle over the salads just before serving.

CARROTS

Carrots were not always orange. It is sometimes reported that the orange varieties were developed to honor the Dutch royal house of Orange; however, this view has not been documented. In recent years, carrots in other colors—notably purple, red, yellow, white, and bi-colored (purple and orange)—have enjoyed renewed popularity with gardeners and cooks. Different colors of carrots taste only slightly different from each other, and they are interchangeable in recipes.

Carrot seeds are reluctant to germinate, and the seedlings are weak. It is important to thin them as soon as true leaves appear or your crop will suffer. As a rule of thumb, you need a growing medium that is twice as deep as the carrot roots you expect to produce. Therefore, if you are growing in containers, it is best to stick with varieties that produce "baby" carrots about as long as your forefinger. Some other cultivars, such as Atlas, make rounded roots like a radish. These will produce carrots with as little as four inches of soil depth.

Fill your container with growing medium, water it well, and scatter the seeds thinly on top. Barely cover with a small amount of growing medium. Have patience and do not let the growing medium dry out. It may take three weeks for the seedlings to emerge. When the feathery true leaves appear, thin the plants to stand about an inch apart each way. Feed lightly with a soluble fertilizer solution and then cease feeding. Carrots do not need a lot of fertilizer, but they need constant moisture. Keep them watered. Harvest when the roots reach the size you expect. Most take about two to three months to yield a crop. Carrots keep well under moist refrigeration, or they can be canned or frozen.

Cream of Carrot Soup with Cumin and Thyme

YIELD: **2 SERVINGS**

1 cup chopped **onions**

2 tablespoons **unsalted butter**

1 sprig fresh **thyme**

2 cups chopped **carrots**

1½ cups **chicken stock**

½ teaspoon ground **cumin**

½ cup **heavy cream**

Salt

Freshly ground **black pepper**

2 teaspoons fresh **thyme leaves**

1. Place the onions and butter in a large saucepan and set over medium heat. When the butter melts, stir, cover, and reduce the heat. Cook for 5 minutes. Add the thyme sprig and carrots, cover, and cook gently until the onions are translucent, about 5 minutes more. Add the chicken stock and cumin, and then cover and cook for 20 minutes. Remove the thyme sprig. Transfer the soup to a blender jar and allow to cool for 15 minutes. If you use an immersion blender, it is not necessary for the soup to cool. Purée the soup then combine with the cream. Taste and add salt and pepper as needed.

2. The soup can be served at once, garnished with the thyme leaves, or cooled thoroughly and stored, covered, in the refrigerator for up to three days.

3. You can serve the soup chilled or reheat it gently over low heat. Do not allow the soup to boil after the cream has been added.

Roasted Carrots and Winter Vegetables

Roasting brings out the sweetness in carrots and other winter bounty. Sorghum and balsamic vinegar play well against the earthy-sweet flavor of the vegetables.

YIELD: **2 SERVINGS**

1 tablespoon **vegetable oil**

4 medium **carrots**, trimmed and cut crosswise in half

1 small **winter squash**, peeled, seeded and cut into bite-size chunks

1 small **rutabaga**, peeled and sliced lengthwise into eighths

¼ teaspoon **salt**

A few grinds of **white pepper**

Pinch of ground **mace**

1 tablespoon **sorghum syrup**

1 teaspoon **balsamic vinegar**

1. Preheat the oven to 325°F. Place the vegetable oil in a baking pan large enough to hold the vegetables in one layer. Add the vegetables, sprinkle with salt, pepper, and mace, and shake the pan to coat everything well with the oil and seasonings.

2. Set the pan on the middle rack and roast, turning the vegetables once with tongs, until the vegetables are softened and browned, about 45 minutes. While the vegetables are cooking, mix the syrup and the vinegar in a small bowl.

3. When the vegetables are done, remove them from the heat and immediately drizzle with the sorghum and vinegar mixture, tossing them to coat well. Serve at once.

NOTE: *If you cannot find sorghum, substitute agave nectar, reducing the amount to 2½ teaspoons.*

PEAS

Peas are a cool weather crop. Most of them require a trellis for support, so they are a bit more trouble to grow than other vegetables. The flavor of freshly picked peas prompts many gardeners to grow them every year despite the effort. For container cultivation of peas, first decide how you will support the vines and then choose a container that works with whatever arrangement you decide on. Peas climb via tendrils that like to curl around something about a quarter inch in diameter or less. Twiggy branches have traditionally been used, but more recently gardeners have discovered nylon trellis netting. If you grow them on a sunny balcony or deck, consider running strings from the container to the top of the railing. The peas will grow up the strings. Dwarf cultivars need no trellis and will produce peas in an eight-inch pot.

Fill a container at least eight inches deep with growing medium. Plant three peas to a spot, separating the planting spots by three inches each way, until you have filled the container. Place it where the pea shoots can reach your trellis, and water thoroughly. Peas are legumes, able to fix nitrogen from the atmosphere with the help of beneficial bacteria growing on the roots. Container gardeners should purchase a powdered inoculant to supply the bacteria. Often, packets of inoculant are found on the same rack with pea or bean seeds. If not, ask your local garden center. Extra, unused inoculant will keep in the freezer at least until the following season. The seeds will germinate in two weeks or less, and you should have pods ready to pick within ninety days.

Peas come in three varieties, all grown the same way. Shelling, or English, peas have tough pods that are inedible without significant effort in the kitchen. Snow peas have broad, flattened, edible pods that are eaten while the peas inside are immature. Snap peas have edible pods, and can be eaten at all stages of development until the seeds begin to mature and the pods turn yellow. For home gardeners, snow or snap peas make the most sense, as they will yield about twice as much weight of edible vegetables as the same size planting of shelling peas.

Creamy Chilled Vegetarian Snow Pea Soup

This is a fine recipe for using an abundant harvest of snow or snap peas.

1 quart **snow** *or* snap peas; loosely packed, trimmed, and washed

1 tablespoon **olive oil**

¼ cup chopped **onions**

¾ cup chopped **celery**

2 tablespoons chopped **scallions**

¾ cup **vegetable stock**

¾ cup **water**

¾ cup diced, peeled **potatoes**

1 wedge of **lime**

¾ teaspoon **sugar**

¾ teaspoon **sherry vinegar**

Salt

Freshly ground **white pepper**

Fresh **herbs** in season, finely chopped

1. Bring a pot of water to a rapid boil over high heat and add the peas. When the water returns to a boil, reduce the heat and parboil for 4 minutes. Drain the peas in a colander and rinse well under cold running water to stop the cooking and set the color. Drain and set aside.

2. Heat the oil over medium heat in a large saucepan. Add the onions, celery, and scallions, and sauté until the onions are translucent. Add the stock, water, potatoes, and lime wedge. Cover and simmer for 30 minutes. Remove the saucepan from the heat. Add the snow peas. Cool the pan, uncovered, at room temperature. Remove the lime wedge. Chill the soup overnight. Transfer the soup to a blender, purée, and pass it through a fine sieve to remove fibrous matter. Add the sugar and sherry, stirring to combine well. Taste and adjust the seasoning with salt and pepper.

3. Serve cold with a garnish of fresh chopped herbs.

End-of-Season Fresh Pea Soup

Here is a quick soup that uses ingredients you are likely to have or find in the market. I created this soup to utilize snap and snow peas from the garden that had been damaged by an early frost. You can use any peas you have on hand.

YIELD: **4 SERVINGS**

1 cup **snow** *or* **snap peas**

1 tablespoon **canola oil**

½ cup chopped **onions**

½ cup chopped **celery**

2 cups **chicken** *or* vegetable stock

1 tablespoon minced fresh **tarragon leaves**

Salt

Freshly ground **black pepper**

1. Trim the tips of the pea pods. If any of the peas have become large enough to shell, do so, placing the shelled peas in a separate small bowl and reserving the shells with the remaining trimmed peas. Bring water to a rolling boil in a saucepan. Add a big pinch of salt and the shelled peas. Cook for 1 minute, then drain through a sieve and rinse well under cold water to stop the cooking and set the color. Reserve the peas in a small bowl. Refill the pan with more water, bring it to a boil, and then add salt and the reserved pea pods and shells. Boil 3 minutes, then drain in a colander, rinse well under cold water, drain, and reserve in a bowl. The peas and pods may be prepared up to this point up to 24 hours in advance. Cover and refrigerate if not using immediately.

2. In a heavy-bottomed pot over medium heat, warm the oil. Add the onions and cook gently, covered, until they begin to soften. Add the celery, cover, and continue to cook until the onions are translucent. Add the stock and the tarragon, a pinch of salt, and a few grinds of black pepper. Bring to a boil, reduce the heat, and simmer for 10 minutes. Remove from heat and allow to cool slightly.

3. Place the reserved pea pods and shells in the jar of a blender. Add the soup mixture and liquefy. If you use an immersion blender, it is not necessary to cool the soup before blending. Pour the soup through a fine sieve to remove fibrous matter, allowing it to drain well. Press gently on the solids to extract all the liquid before discarding them. Add the reserved shelled peas to the strained soup. Reheat to serving temperature, adjust the seasoning, and serve. (You may also cool the soup to room temperature and store covered in the refrigerator for up to two days.)

4. Garnish with a few shreds of butterhead lettuce, some tarragon leaves, or other fresh minced herbs.

POTATOES

Among the first crops brought back to Europe by explorers, potatoes already had a long history of cultivation when the Europeans first arrived. Modern potatoes are the result of centuries of selection and hybridization among several wild potato species. Growing your own potatoes allows you to try varieties you will seldom see in the grocery store.

Despite wide variation in color, texture, and taste, potatoes can be easily understood as belonging to one of three groups, based either upon their time to maturity or upon their starch level, which has implications in the kitchen. Potatoes are classified as early, midseason, or late, with a range of maturity from 80 to over 120 days. In the kitchen, we think of baking potatoes with high starch content, boiling potatoes with low starch content and more moisture, and all-purpose potatoes with an intermediate level of starch. Baking potatoes are also good for mashed potatoes and French fries. Boiling potatoes lend themselves to potato salads, roasting, and grilling. All-purpose potatoes can fill any of these roles, though not always perfectly.

Potatoes grow well in large containers, and I do mean large. One of the best backyard methods is to grow them in a fifty-gallon heavy-duty trash-can liner. Roll the top of the liner down as you might a sock, and poke a few drainage holes in the bottom. Add a foot-deep layer of compost and growing medium, place two or three seed potatoes on top, and water well. When the potato foliage is six inches tall, add more growing medium to cover all but the uppermost inch of the leaves. Unroll the top of the bag to accommodate the growing mix. Repeat this procedure when another six inches of foliage has developed, then allow the potatoes to grow without further covering. Keep them well-watered during the growing season. When blooms appear, you can steal a few new potatoes by probing at the base of the stems with your fingers. Take care to cover any exposed roots or tubers with additional growing mix. When the foliage dies, remove it, wait two weeks, and then dump out the bag to harvest the potatoes. Handle them gently. Damaged skin invites mold and rot. Place the potatoes in a cool, dry place in the shade for a few days, then gently brush off any compost clinging to them, and store them in a basket in a cool, dark place.

Vichysoisse

I adapted this recipe for the classic chilled potato soup from Paul Bocuse's *Regional French Cooking*. This elegant but easily made delight makes the perfect brunch opener, or it can be a first course for a special dinner.
Best if done the day before, it improves in flavor as it rests in the refrigerator.
The traditional potato for this soup is the old stand-by, the Russet.
However, try making the soup with Red Pontiac or White Rose potato varieties. For a pretty, lemon-colored soup, use Yukon Gold or other yellow-fleshed potatoes. If you're feeling in an experimental mood, All Blue potatoes make an especially creamy vichysoisse with a bluish gray color.

YIELD: **4 SERVINGS**

2 tablespoons **unsalted butter**

2 large **leeks**, white part only, washed thoroughly and chopped

1½ cups diced peeled **potatoes**

3 cups **water**

1 sprig of **thyme**

1 sprig of **parsley**

½ cup **heavy cream**

Pinch of ground **mace**

Salt

Freshly ground **white pepper**

1. Melt the butter over medium heat in a large saucepan. When the foam subsides, add the leeks, turn the heat down to low, cover, and allow the leeks to "sweat" until they are tender, about 5 to 7 minutes. Add the potatoes, water, thyme, and parsley. Increase the heat and bring the soup to a boil. Adjust the heat to maintain a simmer and cook, partially covered, until the potatoes are very tender, about 30 minutes. Drain the soup in a colander placed over a heatproof bowl, reserving the liquid. Purée the vegetables in a blender or food processor with a little of the reserved cooking liquid. Return the soup to the pan, and then add ½ cup of the reserved liquid and the heavy cream. Place the pan over medium heat and stir with a wire whisk. Bring to a boil, whisking constantly, then remove from heat immediately and allow to cool to room temperature. Whisk in the mace. Chill the soup at least 4 hours and preferably overnight in the refrigerator. Taste the soup and season it with salt and white pepper. Serve in chilled bowls, garnished with parsley cream (page 40) or snipped chives.

NOTE: A bit of peeled, seeded, and finely chopped tomato or roasted sweet red pepper added as an additional garnish gives vichysoisse a red, white, and green look that is perfect for Christmas dinner parties.

Southern Style Potato Salad

It is important to select the right kind of potatoes for potato salad. Use a waxy, boiling potato such as Red Pontiac or Yukon Gold, not a baking potato.

YIELD: **8 SERVINGS**

3 pounds **potatoes**

¼ cup **Creole mustard**

1½ teaspoons **apple cider vinegar**

1½ teaspoons **sugar**

4 **eggs**, hard-boiled and peeled

6 **scallions**, white and green parts, chopped

2 stalks of **celery**, finely diced

½ cup chopped **sweet pickles**

2 or 3 **radishes**, trimmed and thinly sliced

Salt

Freshly ground **black pepper**

½ cup **mayonnaise**, approximately

Minced fresh **parsley** or dill for garnish

1. Wash potatoes well, but do not peel. This avoids too much water being absorbed as they cook. Bring a large pot of water to a boil. Add the potatoes and cook until the point of a knife meets little resistance when you pierce the potato. Start checking at about 15 minutes, although the exact time will depend upon the size of the potatoes, amount of water, and so forth. As soon as they are done, drain the potatoes, rinse briefly under cold water, and allow them to cool. When they are cool enough to handle but still warm, peel, trim out any dark spots, and chop them into bite-size pieces. Place the chopped potatoes in a large bowl.

2. While the potatoes are cooking, combine the mustard, vinegar, and sugar in a small bowl, stirring until the sugar is dissolved. When the potatoes are chopped and in the bowl, pour the mustard mixture over them and stir well to coat. Leave to cool to room temperature while you complete the preparation.

3. Chop the eggs and add to the potatoes. Add the scallions, celery, pickles, and radish slices, and stir to combine. Add salt and pepper to taste. Add the mayonnaise, a little at a time, until the salad holds together and is as moist as you prefer. Chill the potato salad overnight to allow the flavors to blend. Garnish with parsley or dill before serving.

Golden Potato Soup

A different take on potato soup that offers a hint of sweetness from the caramelized onions and carrots.

YIELD: **4 SERVINGS**

¾ cup **onion**

1½ tablespoons **butter**

¾ cup **celery**

2½ cups **chicken** *or* vegetable stock

½ cup *water*

¾ cup chopped **carrots**

2 cups chopped **yellow-fleshed potatoes**

1 sprig **thyme** *or* a pinch of dried thyme

½ cup **whole milk**

Salt

Freshly ground **pepper**

A grating or two of fresh **nutmeg**

1. Place a large, heavy-bottomed pot over medium heat and add the onions and butter. Adjust the heat so the onions cook very slowly. Cook them, stirring occasionally, until they are golden brown and fragrant. Take care to keep the heat low to avoid burning the onions. Add the other ingredients, bring to a simmer, and cook the soup for 30 minutes. Add the milk. Keep the soup hot, but do not allow it to boil after the milk has been added. Season to taste with salt, pepper, and nutmeg.

Korean-Style Potatoes

This dish is served as part of the banchan, or side dishes, that accompany a Korean meal. It is delicious with Western-style food, also.

YIELD: **4 SERVINGS**

1 to 2 tablespoons **olive oil**

2 to 3 **potatoes**, peeled and diced

2 **garlic cloves**, minced

1 small **onion**, cut in bite-sized pieces

2½ tablespoons **soy sauce**

1 tablespoon **corn syrup**

1 tablespoon **sugar**

½ cup **water**

1 tablespoon **sesame oil**

Sesame seeds to garnish

1. Rinse the potatoes to remove starch and then drain well. Place a heavy skillet over medium heat and add the olive oil. Add the potatoes and garlic and cook until the potatoes look a little translucent, then add the onion. Stir fry until the onions are translucent. Add the remaining ingredients, stir well, and reduce the heat. Simmer over medium heat until the potatoes are tender when tested with a fork. Add a little water if needed, but the liquid should be almost completely evaporated when the potatoes are finished. Cooking time is approximately 10 minutes. Remove the skillet from the heat and add one tablespoon of sesame oil and a sprinkle of sesame seeds.

2. You can substitute honey, agave nectar, sorghum, or maple syrup for the corn syrup. Each sweetener will add a slightly different flavor to the finished dish.

Deep Dish Vegetable Pie with Potato Crust

The idea for this heavenly pie is not mine. It comes from *The Moosewood Cookbook* by Molly Katzen. I have altered the recipe to include a wider variety of vegetables and to reduce the fat content, but the marvelous crust is unchanged from the original. Use a baking potato, such as Russet Burbank, to make the crust. The extra starch helps hold the crust together.

YIELD: **ONE 9-INCH PIE**

Oil for the pie pan

2 cups (packed) shredded **raw potatoes**

¼ cup finely minced **onion**

½ teaspoon **salt**

1 large **egg white**, lightly beaten

1 tablespoon **canola oil**

2 medium cloves **garlic**, minced

½ teaspoon **salt**

¼ teaspoon freshly ground **black pepper**

3 cups **assorted fresh vegetables**, diced, such as onions, broccoli, cauliflower, carrots, celery, peas, summer squash, winter squash, and green beans in any combination you like

½ cup **vegetable stock**, homemade or canned

1 tablespoon chopped fresh **parsley leaves**

1 teaspoon chopped fresh **basil** leaves

½ teaspoon chopped fresh **oregano** *or* a pinch of dried oregano

4 **eggs**

¼ cup **milk**

¼ cup grated **gouda, Swiss, Gruyere,** *or* other good melting cheese

(Continued on page 69)

1. Preheat the oven to 400°F. Oil a 9-inch pie pan. Combine the potatoes, onion, salt, and egg white in a bowl, stirring to combine well. Transfer the mixture to the pie pan. Place a sheet of plastic wrap over the potato mixture and pat it out into a uniform layer. Build a rim around the sides of the pan. Bake the crust for 30 minutes, then brush it with oil and bake 10 more minutes. Remove the crust from the oven.

2. Reduce the oven temperature to 375°F.

3. Set a large skillet over medium-high heat. Add the canola oil. When the oil ripples, add the garlic, salt, pepper, and vegetables. Stir fry until the vegetables begin to soften. Add the vegetable stock, cover the pan, and steam for 2 minutes. Remove the cover, increase the heat, and boil until almost no liquid remains. Stir in the parsley, basil, and oregano. Turn the filling into the prepared crust. In a bowl, beat the eggs with the milk, pour over the vegetables, and sprinkle the cheese on top. Bake until the eggs are firmly set and the top is lightly browned, about 45 minutes. Allow the pie to cool about 10 minutes before slicing. If you wish, garnish slices of the pie with additional chopped fresh herbs.

SNAP BEANS

Snap beans, or green beans, are among the easiest and most reliable crops for backyard growing and do very well in containers. They like a loose, well-aerated growing medium. I suggest combining three parts of commercial growing mix with one part sand or perlite. You should also incorporate a legume inoculant into the soil at planting time (page 60) to provide the beneficial bacteria that permit beans to make their own nitrogen fertilizer. Hundreds of bean varieties exist, but they are all grown in much the same way.

Beans exhibit two growth habits. Bush beans form compact mounds about eighteen inches in diameter. They usually bear one or two large flushes of beans and then peter out. Pole beans produce long vines that need a sturdy support to climb. They bear over a long season and need not be replanted. Besides the support, pole beans need a much larger container than bush beans do. While the latter can be grown in a twelve-inch pot with great success, pole beans need about five gallons of growing medium to accommodate their large root systems.

Plant beans when the weather is warm and settled. Seeds may rot in cold, damp growing medium. For bush beans, plant individual seeds every two inches around the perimeter of a twelve-inch or larger pot. After true leaves appear, thin out any sickly plants. Keep them well watered. When plants are about six inches tall, apply a tablespoonful of balanced organic fertilizer to the surface of the growing medium once. Additional feeding should not be required, especially if you have used the recommended root inoculant.

The procedure for starting and growing pole beans is identical to bush beans, although you must use a larger container and provide support for the vines. String, wire, thin bamboo poles, or anything similar that will permit the vines to climb to about six feet can be used. Just remember the saying "thin as a beanpole" and you can get as creative as you like with the support structure. Pick pole beans regularly to keep them producing.

Either bush or pole beans can be used for any green bean recipe. At the end of the season, the pods can be left to dry on the plants. They can then be harvested, shelled, and used as for any dried bean. Note, however, that the amount of dried beans you can get is likely to be small.

Three Bean Salad

A great summer dish that appears on salad bars and at gatherings throughout the South, three bean salad tastes better if allowed to sit overnight in the refrigerator before serving.

YIELD: **8 SERVINGS**

Dressing

½ cup **sugar**

½ cup **cider vinegar**

¼ cup **water**

1 teaspoon **salt**

Salad

1½ cups **Italian green beans**, trimmed and broken

1½ cups **yellow wax beans**, trimmed and broken

1 can **dark red kidney beans**, rinsed and drained well

¼ cup chopped **red onion**

2 tablespoons chopped **bell pepper**, any color

Dressing:

1. Combine the ingredients in a small bowl, stirring until the sugar and salt have dissolved.

Salad:

1. In a large pot of boiling salted water, separately blanch the fresh beans until they are barely tender, about 6 minutes per batch. Drain in a colander and refresh the beans under cold running water. Cool completely. Add the other ingredients and ⅔ cup of the prepared dressing. Stir well and chill at least 3 hours or overnight before serving.

Green Beans and "Shellies" with Country Ham

Toward the end of the season, pole bean plants will have both maturing and immature beans on them. Shelling out the mature beans and combining them with the immature ones creates a dish with rich bean flavor. To create a vegetarian version, substitute chopped, oil-packed sun-dried tomatoes for the ham.

YIELD: **4 SERVINGS**

1 tablespoon
bacon drippings
or vegetable oil

1 large center slice
(*about 3 ounces*)
of **country ham**,
preferably Benton's

1 medium **onion**,
chopped

½ teaspoon **yellow
mustard seeds**

¾ pound fresh **green beans**

¼ pound fresh **shelled
beans**, such as October
or cranberry beans

1½ cups **water**

Salt to taste

Freshly ground **black
pepper** to taste

1. In a large, heavy saucepan, heat the bacon drippings or oil and add the ham slice. Cook, turning once or twice, until the ham is bright red-brown and most of the fat has been rendered, 5 to 7 minutes. Transfer the ham to a plate, reserving the drippings in the saucepan. When the ham is cool enough to handle, separate and discard all traces of fat from the lean meat and chop the ham coarsely. The fat and lean should separate easily if the ham is properly cooked. If using sun-dried tomatoes, simply chop them and add with the beans.

2. Reheat the fat in the saucepan and add the onions. Cook, stirring occasionally, until they are translucent. Add the mustard seeds and cook, stirring until one or two seeds pop. Add the green beans, shelled beans, and water, and bring to a boil. Reduce the heat, cover, and simmer until the beans are tender. Stir in the reserved country ham. Taste, adjust the seasoning as needed, and serve.

Green Beans with Roasted Peppers

Tossing stir-fried green beans with roasted peppers and garlic creates a perfect side for an Italian meal.

YIELD: **4 SERVINGS**

1 pound fresh **green beans**

1 large **red** or yellow sweet pepper, roasted, seeded, and peeled *(page 243)*

2 tablespoons **olive oil**

3 cloves of **garlic**, minced

Salt

Freshly ground **black pepper**

1. Bring a large pot of salted water to a rolling boil. Drop in the beans and cook for 3 minutes. Drain the beans in a colander and place them under cold running water to stop the cooking and set the color. Slice the roasted pepper into narrow strips about 2 inches long.

2. Heat the oil in a large frying pan or wok until it ripples. Add the garlic and cook until it is a pale golden color, about 30 seconds. Add the beans and toss fry them until they are well coated with the garlicky oil and have begun to brown in a spot or two, about 2 minutes. Add the peppers, season with salt and pepper, and serve at once.

CUCUMBER

The cucumber is probably the most widely grown member of the squash family. The many cultivars can be divided into two groups. Pickling cucumbers, slightly curved and often with prickly spines, are smaller than slicing cucumbers, which grow straight and usually lack spines. While pickling cucumbers can be used raw, the slicing types do not always make crisp, tasty pickles. Plant breeders have created several compact cucumber varieties that are suitable for container growing yet produce an abundant harvest. Look for Little Leaf, Picklebush, Salad Bush, or Spacemaster.

Plant cucumbers when the weather is warm, with daytime temperatures above 65°F. Sow five seeds per twelve- or sixteen-inch container. Add a tablespoon of balanced organic fertilizer to the planting hole. When the seedlings have a pair of true leaves, pinch off all but the three strongest plants. Provide a trellis of string, wire, or thin branches for the tendrils to grasp. The seedlings need abundant water until they start to climb. After that, they will tolerate some drying. Using a balanced organic fertilizer, feed the plants a week after thinning them and again when blooms appear. Female blooms can be distinguished by the tiny cucumber below the petals. They will appear several days after male blooms form. In the meantime, male blooms can be harvested and used to garnish soup or salad. As blooming begins, start irrigating to maintain ample soil moisture if rainfall is insufficient. Proper watering will prevent misshapen fruits.

Cucumber fruits have the best quality when they are small and tender, typically at about three to six inches long, depending upon the variety. Pick them every day to keep the plants producing well. The most reliable method for home preservation is pickling.

White Gazpacho

A heavenly soup for a hot summer night when cucumbers are in season and garlic has been harvested, this version of gazpacho puts the emphasis on the cucumbers. Freshly harvested garlic will be relatively mild in flavor. If your garlic is pungent, use the smaller amount recommended.

YIELD: **2 TO 3 SERVINGS**

2 **cucumbers**, washed, peeled, and seeded

2 to 5 **garlic cloves**, peeled, ideally recently harvested and mildly flavored

½ cup **sour cream**

½ cup **chicken** or **vegetable** stock

¼ teaspoon ground **white pepper**

½ teaspoon kosher salt

¼ cup **tomatoes**, seeded, finely chopped

¼ cup finely chopped **scallion tops**

1. In a food processor, mince the cucumber and garlic. Add the sour cream, stock, white pepper, and salt. Process to combine. Thin with a little more stock if needed. Transfer to a covered container and chill at least two hours. Top each serving with a spoonful of tomatoes and a sprinkling of scallion tops.

Cucumber, Onion, and Tomato Salad

This chunky salad is a frequent player at the summertime dinner table in the South. It plays well all over the country, especially when made with garden-fresh ingredients.

YIELD: **2 SERVINGS**

1 **cucumber**

1 small **red onion**

1 **tomato**, preferably an heirloom variety

1 tablespoon **apple cider vinegar**

1 tablespoon **water**

½ teaspoon **salt**

A few turns of freshly ground **black pepper**

1 teaspoon **safflower** *or* sunflower oil

1. Trim the cucumber and slice it in half lengthwise. Using a teaspoon, scrape out and discard the seeds. Slice the cucumber halves crosswise into C-shaped pieces. Place the cucumber in a large bowl.

2. Trim and peel the onion and slice it into circles. Separate the circles into rings and add them to the bowl with the cucumbers.

3. Core the tomato and cut it into wedges or bite-size chunks, depending upon its size. Add the tomato and its juices to the bowl with the other vegetables.

4. In a small bowl, combine the remaining ingredients, stirring with a fork until the salt is dissolved. Pour the dressing over the salad and toss to coat.

5. Allow the salad to sit for an hour or so at room temperature before serving. It can also be refrigerated, covered, overnight. Bring to room temperature before serving.

Benedictine Spread

This versatile spread is named not for a monastic order but for Mrs. Benedict, a famed caterer of Louisville, Kentucky, who invented the recipe in the early twentieth century. Consequently, it is an essential component of a Derby Day buffet or tailgate party. Besides being good on sandwiches, the recipe can be used as a dip for almost anything dippable.

YIELD: **ABOUT 10 SERVINGS**

3 large **cucumbers**, peeled, seeded, and cut into chunks

2 tablespoons finely minced **white onion**

8 ounces **cream cheese**, softened

Heavy cream

Dash or more of **hot pepper sauce**

1. Place the cucumbers in a food processor and mince finely. Transfer the cucumbers to a clean dishcloth, gather up the corners to form a pouch, and twist, squeezing as much water from the cucumbers as possible. Transfer the cucumber to a bowl. Add the onion and cream cheese and mix well. If needed, add a little heavy cream to thin the mixture to the desired texture. Season with hot pepper sauce. Cover and refrigerate the spread overnight to allow the flavors to meld.

PEPPERS

Peppers rank among the best choices for container vegetable production. Each pepper plant bears an abundance of fruits that can usually be enjoyed over a long season, from the immature green stage until fully ripe. Even the largest plants can be accommodated in a hefty container, and the vast majority will grow superbly in a five-gallon pot, with smaller cultivars available for even an eight- or twelve-inch container. This holds true for both hot and sweet pepper types. Check catalog listings or other references to determine the mature size of cultivars in which you are interested. Among sweet bell peppers, Ace and Gourmet are compact forms, while Cayennetta is a compact-growing hot cayenne type. There are dozens more. You cannot go wrong if you place the plant in a five-gallon container.

Place a sturdy stake in the growing container when you plant it, as even the smaller plants may need support when they are laden with fruits. Tie the stem to the stake using strips of cloth or special soft ties available at many garden centers.

I recommend always purchasing pepper plants from your favorite garden center. The young plants are fussy, and problems during their early growth stages will reduce the yield later on. Peppers should be fed with a balanced soluble fertilizer solution at transplant time and every two weeks thereafter until the first blooms appear. They need plenty of phosphorus and calcium and will, therefore, benefit from the incorporation of bone meal into the growing medium. Add two tablespoons for a five-gallon container. Throughout the season keep the plants well watered but not soggy. It is wise to wait until the weather is warm and settled before transplanting peppers. Crops that grow during summer heat and then bear fruits in cooler fall weather are likely to be the most productive.

Grilled Fish with Three Pepper Sauces

This recipe is based on an idea from a restaurant menu I read years ago.
It takes an extremely simple recipe and turns it into something suitable for
a dinner party.

YIELD: **4 SERVINGS**

2 large green
**Anaheim chili
peppers**

2 large **red bell
peppers**

2 large **yellow bell
peppers**

2 tablespoons
safflower or
sunflower oil

1 large **shallot,**
finely chopped

3 cups **vegetable**
or **chicken stock**

½ teaspoon
kosher salt

Freshly ground
black pepper

4 6-ounce fillets of
any firm-fleshed
fish

Oil for brushing
the fish

Lemon wedges

1. Follow the instructions for roasting the peppers (page 243).
   After they are prepared, keep each type of pepper separate in
   small bowls. The peppers can be prepared up to this point a day
   in advance. Keep them refrigerated in covered bowls, and bring
   to room temperature before continuing with the recipe.

2. Heat the oil in a large saucepan over medium heat. Add the shallot and cook, stirring occasionally, until it is soft and translucent
   but not browned. Add the stock, salt, and pepper and bring to a
   boil. Remove the pan from the heat and set aside to cool slightly.

3. One by one, transfer the bowls of prepared peppers to a
   food processor. Purée, then add some of the seasoned broth
   to achieve a sauce consistency. The exact amount will vary,
   depending upon the peppers. Start with a tablespoon and add
   more as appropriate. As you complete each batch of purée,
   scrape it into a small saucepan, cover, and reserve. Repeat this
   procedure with each of the peppers until you have created all
   three sauces. Keep the sauces warm in a low oven while you
   prepare the fish. Warm the serving plates in the oven as well.

4. Brush the fish fillets with oil and sprinkle them with a little salt
   and pepper if you like. Place the fish in a grill basket and cook
   on a preheated charcoal or gas grill until done, about 2 to 3
   minutes per side.

5. When the fish is done, spoon a pool of each of the sauces into
   the center of a serving plate, forming a triangle. With a spatula,
   carefully transfer a piece of fish to the center of each plate.
   Garnish with lemon wedges and serve immediately.

White Chili

My friend Erik first introduced me to this concept over a decade ago. From his recipe, I developed my version using fresh produce.

YIELD: **4 TO 6 SERVINGS**

4 bone-in, skin-on **chicken thighs**, about 2 pounds

6 cups **water**

1 cup dried **Great Northern beans**, rinsed and soaked overnight in water to cover

2 medium **onions**, chopped

4 green **Anaheim chili peppers**, roasted, skinned, seeded, and chopped

¼ teaspoon ground **cloves**

¼ teaspoon ground **cayenne pepper**, more if you wish

2 teaspoons ground **cumin**

1 tablespoon minced fresh **oregano**

2 cloves **garlic**

Shredded **Monterey jack cheese**

2 green **onions**, chopped

Tortilla chips

1. In a large pot, combine the chicken thighs and water and bring to a boil. Skim off any scum that rises to the top. Adjust the heat so that the water maintains a gentle simmer, partially cover the pot, and cook for 30 minutes or until the chicken is tender. Remove the chicken pieces with a slotted spoon and set them aside to cool. Strain the broth through a fine sieve and reserve it.

2. Meanwhile, drain the beans and rinse them well. In another large pot, place the beans and enough water to cover them by 1 inch. Bring the water to a boil slowly, adjust the heat, and cook the beans at a slow simmer, partially covered, until they are tender, about 1 hour. Remove the beans from the heat and set aside. When they are cool, drain them, reserving the bean broth for another use. Reserve the beans in a bowl.

3. When the chicken is cool enough to handle, remove the skin and bones and discard them. Shred the meat into bite-size chunks. Reserve the meat in a small bowl.

4. Set a heavy-bottomed pot over medium heat and add ½ cup of the strained chicken broth. Sauté the onions in the broth until they are translucent. Add the remainder of the broth, spices, garlic, beans, chicken, and green chilies. Stir to combine well. Bring to a boil then adjust the heat and simmer until heated through, about 10 minutes. Serve the chili hot, topped with shredded cheese and some of the green onions. Pass a basket of tortilla chips.

TOMATO, DETERMINATE

Unquestionably the most popular vegetable among home growers, tomatoes come in two growth forms. Of these, the determinate form is most suited to container cultivation. We will discuss indeterminate tomatoes in the next chapter. Determinate tomatoes typically remain small, under six feet in height at maturity. Traditionally, they bear fruit in one or two flushes, and are therefore good candidates when you want an abundant harvest for preserving. More recently developed cultivars remain compact, even miniature, and yet bear over an extended period. These latter types are ideal when you want a regular supply of fresh tomatoes for salads or sandwiches.

Traditional determinate tomatoes, such as Marglobe, will grow best in a five-gallon or larger container. The smaller ones, such as diminutive Tiny Tim, are at home in an eight- to twelve-inch pot. Tumblin' Tom is a cultivar intended to cascade out of a hanging basket, producing lots of small, sweet fruits. Regardless of the varieties you select, they are grown the same way. Give tomatoes organically rich, well-drained, slightly acidic soil. They will do great in commercial growing mix enhanced with bone meal. Like peppers, tomatoes need phosphorus and calcium. Calcium deficiency is the main culprit in the condition known as blossom end rot, which can ruin a ripening crop. Tomatoes also need even moisture. Allowing the medium to dry out and then flooding the container with water may cause ripening fruits to crack. For this reason, tomatoes perform especially well in large self-watering containers.

Cornbread Panzanella

Panzanella is traditionally made with leftover wheat bread. Cornbread and tomatoes are made for each other, however, and this take on the summer salad will win you praise.

YIELD: **2 SERVINGS**

2 cups day-old homemade **cornbread**

1 medium **yellow tomato**

1 medium **red tomato**

½ medium **cucumber**

¼ cup chopped **red onion**

8 leaves fresh **basil**

2 tablespoons **extra virgin olive oil**

2 teaspoons **red wine vinegar**

¼ teaspoon **salt**

A few grinds of **black pepper**

Parmigiano-Reggiano cheese (optional)

1. Preheat the oven to 350°F. Cut the cornbread into 1-inch cubes and place them in a single layer on a baking sheet. Place in the oven while you prepare the vegetables. The cornbread is done when the edges of the cubes begin to turn brown. Check the pan every few minutes. When the cubes are done, remove them from the oven and set aside.

2. Trim the tomatoes and cut them into chunks. Place in a bowl. Peel the cucumber, if desired. Split in half lengthwise and use a spoon to remove the seeds. Chop into ½-inch chunks and add to the bowl. Tear the basil leaves into small pieces and add them to the bowl with the red onion. Combine the remaining ingredients except the cheese in a small bowl, mix well, and pour over the vegetables. Stir gently to combine. Refrigerate the mixture until ready to serve. A few minutes before serving, toss the toasted cornbread cubes with the vegetable mixture. Garnish with freshly grated Parmigiano-Reggiano, if desired.

NOTE: *You can also add fresh mozzarella to the salad if you wish. To prepare ahead, cool the cornbread to room temperature and store in an airtight container. Add the dressing to the salad and then cover and refrigerate.*

Old-Fashioned Tomato Bread Pudding

My grandmother made this from day-old biscuits and called it scalloped tomatoes. It is delicious by any name. The bread should be quite dry. If it seems too moist when you tear it, dry the pieces in a warm oven for ten minutes.

YIELD: **4 TO 6 SERVINGS**

2 cups peeled and diced **tomatoes**

2 tablespoons **unsalted butter**

2 tablespoons **brown sugar**

½ teaspoon **salt**

⅛ teaspoon freshly ground **black pepper**

Pinch of ground **cloves** *or* allspice

2½ cups 1-inch pieces of stale **yeast bread** *or* biscuits

1. Butter a loaf pan or deep casserole dish. Preheat the oven to 350°F. Combine the tomatoes, butter, brown sugar, salt, pepper, and spice in a small saucepan and heat to a simmer. Place a layer of bread in the bottom of the casserole. Add one-third of the tomato mixture. Continue to alternate a layer of bread with a layer of tomatoes, ending with bread. Place the pan in the oven and heat until bubbly and beginning to brown on top, about 30 minutes.

NOTE: *If you wish, top the dish with shredded cheese before baking. Substitute 2 cups of home canned tomatoes for the fresh tomatoes to make the dish out of season.*

Gazpacho

I discovered gazpacho in an Atlanta restaurant while in college and have been making it ever since. It is only worth making if you have excellent tomatoes. Don't let the long list of ingredients deter you. This dish requires only prepping and chopping the vegetables and herbs, along with measuring the other ingredients. No cooking is required. Choose average-sized vegetables for this dish. The exact proportions are not important.

YIELD: **6 TO 8 SERVINGS**

2 medium **tomatoes**, chopped

1 large **cucumber**, peeled, seeded, and chopped

1 **bell pepper**, seeded and chopped

1 medium **red onion**, chopped

3 tablespoons **breadcrumbs**, fresh or dry

1 clove **garlic**, minced

Juice of 1 **lemon**

3 tablespoons **extra virgin olive oil**

¼ cup minced fresh **parsley**

2 tablespoons torn pieces of fresh **basil**

2 tablespoons snipped fresh **chives**

1 teaspoon **salt**

½ teaspoon sweet **paprika**

3 cups water, **tomato juice**, **chicken stock**, *or* **vegetable stock**

Cubes of unpeeled, seeded **cucumber**

Minced **red** *or* yellow bell peppers

Chopped **scallions**

Fresh **basil** sprigs

1. You can use a food processor to chop the vegetables, but the texture will not be as good as if they are chopped by hand. When all the chopping is done, combine the vegetables, breadcrumbs, garlic, lemon juice, olive oil, herbs, salt, and paprika in a large bowl. Cover the mixture and place it in the refrigerator to chill. Separately chill the 3 cups of liquid. These components can be held in the refrigerator overnight, if desired.

2. When ready to serve, combine the vegetable mix with the chilled liquid. Stir well and serve garnished with cubed cucumber, minced peppers, chopped scallions, and a basil sprig.

3. The prepared vegetable mixture can also be frozen in convenient amounts. Thaw and then add an equal portion of water, juice, or stock and serve as suggested.

BASIL

Basil abhors cold weather. Below 38°F, basil leaves develop black spots and begin to drop. Grow basil outdoors when the weather has warmed up and nights remain above 60°F. Besides the typical green-leafed types with spicy, clove-like fragrance, cultivars that have lemon, lime, or anise notes are widely available. Compact, small-leaved forms, often known as Greek basil, are suitable even for the tiniest container gardens. Even the bigger ones will grow just fine in a twelve-inch or larger container. Basil combines well with other herbs and vegetables. Try growing it with tomatoes or peppers in a large, self-watering container.

Basil is easy to start from seed if you have a warm, sunny spot indoors or out. Sow seeds in small pots about a month before you wish to transplant them. Transplant when they have two pairs of true leaves. Basil grows well in commercial growing mix with a small amount of balanced organic fertilizer added. High fertility is not as important as abundant water. Do not allow the growing medium to dry out, or plants will drop leaves. Pinch off flowers as they appear. Beginning about two months after transplanting, the leaves can be harvested, and you can continue to harvest periodically for the remainder of the growing season. Regular harvesting keeps the plants bushy and productive. Harvest by cutting off the topmost six to eight inches of a stem. Immerse cut stems in a vase of water as for cut flowers. Do not refrigerate. If left at room temperature for two weeks or so, they will root. Transplant them into twelve-inch pots when the roots are about two inches long, and keep well watered until the plants resume growth. This is a good way to extend the growing season into cooler weather, although the plants need bright light to grow well indoors. You can even start basil cuttings from the grocery store in this manner.

Pesto

This classic Mediterranean condiment has many uses, and I have never tasted a commercially prepared one that compares to homemade. Vary the proportions of the herbs to suit what you have on hand or to emphasize whatever flavor you desire. Tossing potato gnocchi or cooked pasta with pesto creates a classic dish, but the sauce also can be used as a spread for sandwiches, a flavoring agent for cream cheese to create a dip, or to enhance a dish of steamed vegetables.

YIELD: **ABOUT 1 CUP**

1 clove **garlic**, peeled

¼ cup **unsalted butter**

¼ cup grated **Parmigiano-Reggiano cheese**

¼ cup tightly packed fresh **parsley** leaves

1 tablespoon shredded fresh **basil** leaves

1 tablespoon minced fresh **marjoram** leaves *or* ½ teaspoon dried marjoram

¼ cup **English walnuts**

¼ cup **extra virgin olive oil**

1. Using a food processor, drop the garlic through the feed tube to mince it finely. Stop the motor, add the remaining ingredients except the oil, and process to a thick paste by pulsing the machine. Add the oil by tablespoons, pulsing between additions just to incorporate it. Do not completely liquify the sauce; it should retain some texture.

2. Transfer the pesto into a storage container and place a sheet of plastic wrap over it, pressing the plastic against the surface of the pesto to exclude air. This will prevent darkening. Keep the sauce refrigerated and use within a week.

Peaches in Basil Syrup

One of the best ways to capture the flavor of basil is to infuse a simple syrup. The result makes a superb poaching liquid for summer fruits available when basil is at its peak.

YIELD: **2 SERVINGS**

1 cup loosely packed fresh **basil** leaves, plucked from the stems

1 cup **sugar**

1 cup **water**

Pinch of **salt**

2 fresh **peaches**

1. Rinse the basil leaves and spin dry in a salad spinner or pat dry with paper towels. Reserve. Place the sugar and water in a small saucepan. Set the pan over medium-high heat and bring to a boil, stirring until the sugar dissolves. Reduce the heat and simmer one minute. Remove the syrup from the heat and stir in the salt and the basil leaves. Cover and allow to cool to room temperature. Strain the syrup through a fine sieve, discarding the solids. The covered syrup will keep in the refrigerator for a week. Bring to room temperature before continuing.

2. Peel the peaches and remove the pits. In a large saucepan capable of holding the peaches in one layer, place the peaches and cover them with the syrup. You need only enough of the syrup to barely cover the peaches. Store any remaining syrup in the refrigerator. Set the saucepan over medium heat and bring to a boil. Cover, remove from the heat, and allow to cool to room temperature. Chill until cold or serve at room temperature.

NOTE: Mint, lemon verbena, or other herbs can be substituted for the basil.

EDIBLE FLOWERS

Many people are surprised to learn that numerous common flowers can be eaten. They are best used as a garnish for salads but can also star in cooked dishes such as the soup recipe below. Be certain of your identification when choosing flowers for the kitchen. Start them from seed. The ones listed are old standbys that anyone can grow. Use a twelve-inch container or larger for a mixed planting, or grow plants in individual six-inch containers.

Violas and pansies are rewarding candidates for the cool season. Pair them with dianthus and calendula for an edible and eye-catching container display. Fill the pot with commercial growing mix, adding two tablespoons of blood meal or four tablespoons of cottonseed meal per twelve-inch container. Sprinkle a few seeds of each variety on the surface of the mix and water well. When the seeds have germinated, thin them so only two or three individuals of each type remain in the container.

Daylilies offer a reliable way to have edible flowers in summertime from an easy-to-grow perennial plant. Choose one of the many compact forms of daylilies and grow it in a sixteen-inch container of commercial potting mix. Fertilize in spring as the foliage emerges and again when buds appear. The unopened flower buds of daylilies are reminiscent of green beans, and the fully opened blooms can be chopped or shredded before adding to soup or salad. You can leave the plant in the same container for two seasons. Divide the plants and repot after the second summer.

Nasturtiums are a favorite among food gardeners, not only for their sweetly fragrant, colorful blooms but also for their succulent leaves that carry a slightly spicy bite. They can substitute for watercress in any recipe. Poke the large seeds into an eight-inch pot of growing mix and keep well watered. Once the plants are about six inches tall, feed them lightly with a balanced organic fertilizer. Water the pots when the soil begins to dry out. Plants will grow slowly during summer heat and put on a show late in the season. In cool summer areas, they bloom continuously.

Japanese Flower Soup

When I was growing and selling organic produce, one of my best customers was a chef who made this soup using edible flowers I grew for him. I am proud to share the recipe from the now-defunct Annie's restaurant in Knoxville, Tennessee.

YIELD: **4 SERVINGS**

4 cups **dashi** (page 228)

2 **scallions**, trimmed, cut into 3-inch pieces

1 clove **garlic**, peeled

1 1-inch piece of fresh **ginger**, peeled

1 **star anise**

¼ cup **red miso**

2 **scallions**, trimmed and sliced diagonally into 1-inch pieces

½ cup loosely packed **edible flowers** in season

1. Place the dashi in a saucepan and add the 3-inch scallion pieces, garlic, ginger, and star anise. Bring to a boil, reduce the heat, and simmer gently, covered, for 15 minutes. Strain the dashi, discarding the solids, and return it to the pan. Place the miso in the bowl of a ladle, immerse the ladle into the broth, and use a spoon to stir the miso into the broth from the ladle. If you merely drop the miso into the broth, it will be difficult to incorporate it into the soup.

2. To serve, ladle the soup into bowls and garnish with the 1-inch scallion pieces and the edible flowers.

GINGER

People are always surprised when I suggest ginger as a homegrown crop, but it is, in fact, easy to grow and well-adapted to container cultivation. The best time to plant is in late winter. Choose a plump, healthy specimen from the grocery store. Asian markets are likely to have the freshest roots. Select a container at least four times larger in diameter than the width of the rhizome you are planting. Fill the container three-quarters full with a good, well-drained potting mix containing plenty of compost. Place the rhizome on top of the mix with its eyes pointing upward. Cover with more potting mix and water well. Place the container in a plastic bag in indirect light until green shoots appear. (This can take a month.) Then remove the bag and water well. Keep the plant in bright, indirect light and never allow the soil to dry out. Growing plants need protection from wind and should be brought indoors any time the temperature is headed below 50°F. The ideal growing temperature is between 75°F and 85°F. After all danger of frost has passed, transplant the ginger to a sixteen-inch pot or shallow tub, and place in full sun. Feed every three weeks with a soluble organic fertilizer. After the weather heats up, the plants will grow rapidly.

Harvest ginger roots when the leaves begin to turn yellow. A plant started in a pot in January should be ready to harvest late in September. Dump out the container and separate the rhizomes, cut the stems back to about an inch, and spread the harvest in a warm, dry place for a few days to allow the skin to toughen and cure. The color will change from yellow-green to tan. The best way to preserve the harvest is by freezing. Simply peel the rhizomes, cut into usable-size chunks, and drop them into a freezer container.

Winter Squash Soup with Asian Flavors

YIELD: **4 TO 6 SERVINGS**

Oil for the baking pan

1 medium **acorn squash**

2 tablespoons **vegetable oil**

1 cup chopped **onions**

2 cloves **garlic**, minced

2 teaspoons minced fresh **ginger**

4 cups **chicken stock**

2 **star anise**

1 tablespoon **soy sauce**

A few grinds of fresh **white pepper**

Salt

2 **scallions**, white and green parts, sliced thinly on the diagonal

Cilantro oil (page 241)

1. Oil a 9 x 12-inch baking pan. Preheat the oven to 400°F. Cut the squash in half lengthwise and scoop out the seeds. Place the halves cut side down in the baking pan and roast until the skin begins to brown. A sharp knife should meet no resistance when inserted into the thickest part of the squash flesh. Start checking after twenty minutes, although the exact baking time will depend on the age and size of the squash. When the squash is done, remove from the oven and allow it to cool. Scrape the flesh from the skin into a bowl, discarding the skin. Reserve the flesh while you continue with the recipe.

2. In a large saucepan set over medium heat, add the oil and heat until it ripples. Add the onions and cook, stirring occasionally, until they are translucent. Add the garlic and ginger and continue cooking, stirring frequently, for 1 or 2 minutes. Add the chicken stock and star anise, together with the reserved squash. Bring to a boil, reduce the heat, and simmer 15 minutes. Add the soy sauce. Taste and add freshly ground white pepper and salt as needed. Remove the saucepan from the heat and allow the soup to cool for 15 minutes. Remove the star anise and discard.

3. Transfer the soup to a blender jar and purée, in batches if necessary. Return the puréed soup to the pan and heat through. Serve at once, garnished with the scallions and a few drops of cilantro oil.

NOTE: *If using an immersion blender, it is not necessary to cool the soup before blending. For a heartier soup, add crumbled bacon, minced ham, cheese, cooked spinach, or cooked pasta to suit your fancy.*

Vegetable and White Bean Curry with Rice

This ginger-infused curry makes use of a variety of garden vegetables that will be in season when your ginger crop is ready to harvest. If making the curry with older, stored ginger, reduce the amount by about 25 percent.

YIELD: **4 SERVINGS**

1 cup chopped **onions**

2 tablespoons **butter**

¼ cup finely diced **red bell pepper**

¼ cup finely chopped **scallions**

¼ cup finely diced **carrots**

1 teaspoon minced **garlic**

1 tablespoon minced **ginger**

¼ teaspoon **sweet paprika**

1 teaspoon **curry powder**

1 cup diced **potatoes** (*white or sweet*)

1 cup peeled, seeded, diced **tomatoes**

2 cups ½-inch pieces **green beans**

¼ cup diced yellow **summer squash**

1 cup **vegetable stock**

Steamed **rice** to serve

Lime wedges

Fresh **cilantro**, chopped

1. Place the onions and butter in a large, heavy-bottomed pot and place over medium heat. When the butter sizzles, stir the pot well, cover, and reduce the heat to low. Cook gently until the onions are soft but not browned, about 5 minutes.

2. Add the red pepper, scallions, carrots, garlic, and ginger, and continue to cook, covered, 5 more minutes. Add the paprika, curry powder, and potatoes. Cover and cook an additional 5 minutes. Add the tomatoes and ½ cup water, stirring to scrape up any browned bits on the bottom of the pot. Add the beans, squash, and stock and bring to a boil. Adjust the heat and cook gently, partially covered, until the potatoes are tender, about 5 minutes. Serve with rice and a lime wedge, garnished with chopped cilantro.

LEMONGRASS

Lemongrass is a vigorous plant that is a cinch to grow during hot, humid weather. It needs a large container to support its root system, but a single sixteen-inch pot should produce an abundant harvest. Find lemongrass at an Asian market, or you can purchase plants at a well-stocked garden center. Lemongrass is sold as stems with most of the foliage removed. Each stem has a bulbous base. You may see tiny roots or root buds sticking out from the base. When planted, the basal portion quickly roots. Simply insert the stem about an inch into a small pot of damp growing mix, supporting it with a plant stake. When roots protrude from the drain hole in the pot, you are ready to transplant to a large container outdoors, but wait until all danger of frost has passed.

Lemongrass grows rapidly. Plants should be watered frequently. They normally colonize stream banks and other moist locations. Feed them every two weeks with a balanced soluble fertilizer solution. Wear heavy gloves and a long-sleeved shirt to protect your skin from the sharp, serrated edges of the leaves when harvesting. Select stems whose base is about half an inch in diameter, and cut away from the main clump with a sharp knife. Trim the stalk to eight or ten inches. Stems will keep well under refrigeration for a week or two, or you can chop and freeze them. Lemongrass can also be dried successfully.

Raw Vegan Thai Curry Soup

This soup is best when made with a young coconut. You can find them at Asian markets and specialty stores. The coconut looks like a white cylinder that has been sharpened to a point on top. It takes some effort to remove the husk and open the coconut inside, but the results are worth it. If this seems like too much trouble, use canned coconut water and substitute fresh-frozen, unsweetened coconut.

YIELD: **4 SERVINGS**

3 cups **coconut water**

3 cloves **garlic**

1 piece **ginger root**, about 2 inches long, peeled

2 stalks **lemongrass**, trimmed and chopped

¼ cup **soy sauce**

½ teaspoon **curry powder** (*not Madras style*)

½ cup **coconut meat**, chopped

1 **shallot**, peeled and sliced thinly

½ **carrot**, finely shredded

1 inner stalk of **celery** with leaves, thinly sliced

1 red **Thai chili pepper**, seeded and sliced into thin rings

1 **scallion**, white and green parts, sliced thinly on the diagonal

A few leaves of fresh **cilantro**

1. Place the first six ingredients in a blender jar and liquefy. Transfer to a bowl and place in the refrigerator to chill overnight. Strain the soup through a fine sieve to remove fibrous material. Serve in chilled bowls, garnished with the remaining ingredients.

Grilled Lemongrass Pork Kebabs with Slaw

YIELD: **4 SERVINGS**

1 pound boneless **pork loin**, trimmed of all visible fat

1 stalk **lemongrass**, trimmed and chopped, more if you like

2 cloves **garlic**, minced

1 tablespoon **soy sauce** *(see note)*

2 tablespoons **vegetable oil**

8 **bamboo skewers**

2 cups finely shredded **cabbage**

2 teaspoons **salt**

½ cup finely shredded **carrots**

¼ cup thinly sliced **red radishes**

2 tablespoons **rice vinegar**

1 tablespoon **lime juice**

1 tablespoon **sugar**

½ teaspoon **sesame oil**

1. Cut the pork loin into bite-size cubes. Place the pork in a resealable plastic bag and add the chopped lemongrass, garlic, soy sauce, and vegetable oil. Seal the bag and marinate the pork in the refrigerator at least 8 hours or overnight.

2. Soak the bamboo skewers in water for at least 30 minutes. Prepare the grill.

3. Drain the pork, discarding the marinade. Thread the pork cubes on the skewers. Set aside while you prepare the slaw.

4. In a large bowl, mix the cabbage with the salt. Let stand 30 minutes, then rinse and drain thoroughly. Add the carrots and the radishes to the cabbage. In a small bowl, mix the vinegar, lime juice, sugar, and sesame oil. Pour over the vegetables and stir to combine.

5. Grill the skewered pork cubes over medium-high heat until they are well marked and browned, about 2 to 3 minutes per side. Test for doneness by cutting into one cube. There should be no pink coloration at the center.

6. Remove the skewers from the grill and serve immediately on a plate accompanied by the slaw.

NOTE: Use an Asian fish sauce instead of the soy sauce for a gluten-free dish or use a gluten-free soy sauce. You could substitute mushrooms and other vegetables for some or all of the pork. If you use both, double the amount of marinade and marinate the pork and vegetables in separate plastic bags. Good selections include leeks trimmed and cut into 1-inch pieces, small quartered onions, chunks of summer or winter squash, and squares of bell pepper, any color.

RASPBERRY

Raspberries have only recently joined the ranks of plants truly suitable for container growing. Newly developed varieties will grow and produce a crop in a sixteen-inch container. These include Raspberry Shortcake and Joan J, both of which offer the added benefit of being thornless. Old standards, such as Heritage and Latham, can also be grown in containers, but productivity is reduced compared with plants grown in the ground. That said, a large, built-in planter on a deck or patio in full sun would be an ideal location for a couple of standard raspberry plants.

Regardless of type, raspberries need well-drained soil that remains evenly moist and should be fertilized with a balanced organic fertilizer when growth begins in early spring. The new miniature types should be cut to the base in autumn after a couple of frosts kill the foliage, sending them into dormancy. Standard varieties require a different pruning schedule. After the frost, remove all the canes that have produced fruit, allowing the new, un-fruited canes that developed the previous summer to dominate the container. The new canes will bloom the following season, after which they too should be removed and discarded. Standard varieties grown in a container should be divided and replanted every four to five years.

Raspberry Hand Pies

Unabashedly making use of refrigerated commercial pie crust, this recipe avoids having to divide and re-roll the crust to achieve individual size pies.

YIELD: **4 HAND PIES**

1 pint fresh **raspberries**

1¾ cup granulated **sugar**

1 whole **clove**

1 9-inch refrigerated **pie crust**

1. Place the raspberries and the sugar into a heavy-bottomed pot. Stir gently to combine and refrigerate overnight.

2. The next day, bring the raspberries to room temperature. Drop the clove into the pot. Set the pot over medium heat and cook, stirring occasionally, until the mixture comes to a slow boil. Continue cooking, stirring constantly until the mixture is thickened. Take care not to let it burn. When the mixture drops slowly from the spoon, remove the pan from the heat and allow it to cool. The raspberries should have the consistency of thick jam. Pick out and discard the clove.

3. Preheat the oven to 350°F.

4. Unroll the pie crust on a work surface. Spoon some of the raspberry jam into four mounds spaced evenly around half of the pie crust. Leave a 1-inch border at the edges and between each mound of jam. Brush the edge of the crust and the spaces between the mounds of jam with water. Fold the other side of the crust over the jam, pressing down at the edges and in between the mounds to seal the dough.

5. With a chef's knife, cut between the mounds to create four hand pies. Press down on the edges with a fork to ensure a good seal. Transfer the pies to a parchment-lined baking sheet and bake until golden brown, about 20 minutes.

Raspberry, Jicama, and Pecan Salad with Raspberry Vinaigrette

Tart-sweet raspberries, juicy jicama, and crunchy pecans team up in this simple summertime salad.

YIELD: **2 SERVINGS**

½ pint **raspberries**

2 tablespoons **extra virgin olive oil**

2 teaspoons **red wine vinegar**

¼ teaspoon **salt**

⅛ teaspoon ground **white pepper**

2 cups **mixed salad** greens

½ cup peeled and shredded **jicama** *(or carrot)*

¼ cup **pecans**, toasted *(page 244)*

1. Wash and pick over the raspberries. Select two tablespoons of them for the dressing, keeping the remaining ones for the salad. Drain the salad raspberries on paper towels to allow them to dry thoroughly.

2. In the jar of a blender, combine the reserved berries, oil, vinegar, salt, and pepper. Blend to a smooth emulsion.

3. Arrange the salad greens on two chilled plates. Top them with some of the jicama, raspberries, and pecans. Drizzle the dressing over all and serve at once.

ROSEMARY

An ideal plant for container growing, rosemary is equally at home in an herb bed. Prostrate forms that look good cascading over the edge of a pot are popular, as are the more numerous upright ones. Look for Barbecue, which produces lots of long, straight stems ideal for use as skewers. Other popular ones are Salem and Arp. The latter is particularly cold tolerant. Rosemary seedlings exhibit considerable variation in their characteristics, so it is best to purchase plants propagated by cuttings from known cultivars.

Mix ground limestone with your regular potting mix. Use a teaspoon of limestone per twelve-inch-diameter pot. Grow the plants in full sun and keep them well watered. A wilted plant may not recover. Cut sprigs as you need them for the kitchen. Rosemary takes so well to pruning that it can be used for topiary. Plants can be moved indoors for the winter if you can supply a sunny window and good air circulation. Reduce watering for indoor plants, but do not allow the growing medium to dry out completely.

Skillet Chicken with Rosemary

This recipe can be made with any cut of chicken or a mixture. I prefer the deeper flavor of boneless, skinless thighs because they have a good ratio of light to dark meat. If you use boneless breasts, reduce the simmering time to 15 minutes to avoid making them tough. Pound breasts to a uniform thickness between two sheets of plastic wrap so they will cook evenly and quickly.

YIELD: **4 SERVINGS**

½ teaspoon **paprika**

½ teaspoon **salt**

¼ teaspoon ground **black pepper**

¼ teaspoon **onion powder**

¼ teaspoon **garlic powder**

⅛ teaspoon **cayenne pepper**

4 boneless, skinless **chicken thighs**

2 tablespoons **unsalted butter**

¼ cup chopped **onions**

¼ cup chopped **celery**

2 tablespoons chopped **bell pepper**, any color

1 teaspoon fresh or dried **rosemary** leaves

1 cup **chicken stock**

Hot cooked **rice**

Chopped fresh **parsley** to garnish

1. Combine the paprika, salt, pepper, onion powder, garlic powder, and cayenne in a small bowl. Sprinkle the chicken with half the seasoning mix and rub it in with your fingers. Reserve the remaining mix in the bowl. Cover the chicken with plastic wrap and place in the refrigerator for at least one hour or overnight.

2. Set a large skillet with a lid over medium heat. Add the butter. When the foam subsides, add the chicken pieces. Cook, turning once, until they are browned, about 4 minutes per side. After turning the chicken the first time, add the onions, celery, bell pepper, and rosemary. Stir the vegetables occasionally as the chicken finishes browning. After the chicken is browned on both sides, stir the remaining seasoning mix into the stock and pour into the skillet. Reduce the heat, cover the skillet, and cook gently for 30 minutes. Remove the lid, raise the heat, and reduce the liquid in the skillet by about half.

3. For each serving, set a piece of chicken on a bed of rice and spoon some of the pan sauce over it. Garnish with the chopped parsley.

NOTE: Steamed fresh summer squash is a splendid accompaniment for this dish.

Oven-Dried Tomato Bruschetta with Rosemary Oil

YIELD: **8 APPETIZERS**

½ cup loosely packed **parsley** leaves

4 to 5 homemade oven-dried **tomatoes**, about half a cup *(page 232)*

3 gloves **garlic**, peeled

6 whole fresh **basil** leaves, each about 1½ inches long

2 tablespoons grated **Parmigiano-Reggiano cheese**

1 tablespoon **extra virgin olive oil**

8 slices of **bread**, about ¼ inch thick, cut from a crusty baguette on the diagonal

Rosemary oil *(page 240)*

1. Combine the parsley, dried tomatoes, garlic, and basil in the bowl of a food processor. Pulse to mince. Add the cheese and olive oil. Pulse to combine. Do not reduce to a paste. The dish may be completed up to this point one day in advance. Refrigerate in a covered container. Bring to room temperature before use.

2. Spread the bread slices on a parchment-lined baking sheet and toast under the broiler until lightly browned. Remove from the oven, flip the bread with tongs, and drizzle with the rosemary oil. Use about ¼ teaspoon oil per slice. Return the bread to the oven until it is lightly browned on top. Remove and allow to cool. Distribute the tomato mixture among the slices, drizzle with another drop of rosemary oil, and serve.

NOTE: You may substitute an equal quantity of commercially oil-packed sundried tomatoes for the homemade ones. In that case, omit the olive oil and substitute 1½ teaspoons of the oil in which the tomatoes are packed. Do not reduce the amount of rosemary oil.

STRAWBERRY

Strawberries have long been container garden subjects, so much so that the "strawberry jar" is ever-present in garden centers. Plant breeders have created new varieties even more suited to small-scale container growing. Some of these have traits that make them decorative as well as useful, with large, colorful flowers and variegated foliage. All are grown in the same way.

While technically perennials, strawberry plants should be treated as annuals by the backyard grower, unless you are prepared to devote considerable space to the production of new plants each season. After the first season, productivity declines significantly. Purchase plants from a certified disease free source, and plant them in twelve-inch pots or hanging baskets. Any commercial growing mix will do. Mix in a tablespoon of balanced organic fertilizer with each pot of soil. Alternatively, you can feed the plants with soluble fertilizer every two weeks from emergence until the first blooms appear. Stop feeding when you see blooms, or the harvest will be reduced. The modern, container-ready varieties will produce a few berries all season and then a large flush as the weather cools at the end of summer. Old standard varieties may be either June bearing with a single large crop near the summer solstice, or everbearing with the same pattern of production as the container types.

Strawberry Shortcake

Designed for cooks who seldom bake, the fake shortcake in this recipe
is fat free.

1 pound **strawberries**,
rinsed and drained

⅓ cup **sugar**

3 cups all-purpose **flour**

3 tablespoons **sugar**

1½ tablespoons
baking powder

1½ teaspoons **salt**

1 12-ounce bottle **beer**

⅔ cup **heavy cream**

2 tablespoons
powdered sugar

1 teaspoon
vanilla extract

1. Stem the strawberries, cut them in half if they are large, and place them in a bowl with ⅓ cup sugar. Stir to combine and place in the refrigerator.

2. Grease a loaf pan. Preheat the oven to 375°F. Place the dry ingredients in a mixing bowl and combine well with a wire whisk. Whisk in the beer, mixing until you have a uniform batter. Pour the batter into the pre-pared loaf pan, place in the oven, and bake until the top is golden brown, 45 to 60 minutes. Remove from the oven and allow to cool. Invert the pan over a wire rack and turn out the loaf. Cool completely on the wire rack.

3. Just before serving, place the cream in a chilled bowl. Whisk with a wire whisk until the cream just begins to thicken. Add the sugar and vanilla extract and whisk a few strokes more. The cream should have the consis-tency of hollandaise sauce.

4. Cut 1-inch-thick slices from the loaf and place on serving plates. Top with the strawberries and cream. Serve at once.

Salad of Baby Lettuce, Early Peas, and Strawberries

The ingredients for this salad should be available at around the same time if you grow them in your garden.

YIELD: **2 SERVINGS**

½ cup **shelled early peas**

1 cup freshly picked **strawberries**, stemmed

2 cups loosely packed **baby lettuce leaves**

2 tablespoons **sour cream**

1 tablespoon **lemon juice**

¼ teaspoon **salt**

¼ teaspoon **pink peppercorns**, crushed in a mortar

Toasted seed topping (*page 252*)

1. Bring a small saucepan of water to a boil, drop in the peas, and cook for 3 minutes. Drain the peas in a colander, then refresh them under cold running water and drain again. Set aside. Pick out two strawberries for the dressing and set aside. Slice the remaining berries in half if they are large. Arrange the lettuce leaves on each of two chilled salad plates. Top with the strawberries and scatter the peas over them.

2. In a blender jar, combine the reserved strawberries, sour cream, lemon juice, salt, and crushed pepper corns. Blend until smooth. If the dressing seems too thick, blend in a little milk or cream. Pour the dressing over the salads, garnish with a sprinkling of the seed topping, and serve.

THYME

Thyme is perhaps the best choice for a container herb garden. Most cultivars are naturally compact and take well to pruning and division. The most useful form is French thyme, which produces long, straight stems from which it is easy to strip the leaves. You will also find creeping, or English thyme, thymes with various citrus notes, thymes with variegated leaves, and thymes that are more decorative than culinary in their appeal. They are all easy to grow.

A single thyme plant will grow satisfactorily in an eight inch pot, but a group of several plants in a larger planter looks great sitting on the patio or at the windowsill. To commercial potting mix, add one part sand or perlite per three parts mix. After placing the plants, fill the container almost to the top with growing mix, leaving room for a half-inch layer of fine gravel. This will help retain moisture and prevent soil from splashing on the leaves. If your garden center does not have something suitable, check with an aquarium shop for the gravel. Thyme is drought tolerant, but should not be allowed to wilt. Mixing two teaspoons of balanced organic fertilizer into each eight-inch pot supplies all the nutrients needed for a season of growth. Harvest the leaves as you need them. The plants respond well to regular pruning.

Chicken and Thyme Dumplings

The key to these light, fluffy dumplings is to incorporate the milk with a minimum of stirring. Too much mixing will make the dumplings heavier. Traditionally, chicken and dumplings is made with a whole chicken, but a simpler modern approach is to use chicken thighs, which have plenty of flavor and a good balance of both white and dark meat.

YIELD: **6 TO 8 SERVINGS**

3 to 4 pounds **chicken thighs** *(with bone and skin)*

6 cups cold **water**

½ cup diced **celery**

2 teaspoons **salt**

1 **bay leaf**

1 tablespoon fresh **oregano leaves** *or* 1 teaspoon dried oregano

¼ teaspoon freshly ground **black pepper**

2 cups all-purpose **flour**

1 tablespoon **baking powder**

1 teaspoon **salt**

1½ teaspoons fresh **thyme leaves** *or* ½ teaspoon dried thyme

3 tablespoons **vegetable shortening**

1 cup **milk**

1. Place the chicken thighs in a large pot or Dutch oven, add the water, and set the pot over medium-high heat. When the water comes to a boil, reduce the heat, skim off any scum that has risen to the surface, and add the celery, salt, bay leaf, oregano, and black pepper. Cover the pot, adjust the heat to a slow simmer, and cook until the chicken is very tender, 30 to 45 minutes. Using tongs, remove the chicken to a plate to cool. Cover the stock and keep it warm. Debone the chicken, reserving the meat and discarding bones and trimmings. The chicken can be prepared up to this point one day in advance. Instead of keeping the stock warm, plunge the pot into a sink full of ice water to cool it rapidly, then store it, covered, in the refrigerator. Store the boned chicken in the refrigerator in a separate covered container.

2. It may be tempting to remove the fat that accumulates at the surface of the stock when it cools. However, it is traditional to leave the fat in. The final result will not taste as good without it.

3. Measure the stock and add water to bring the volume to 6 cups, if needed. Set the stock on the stove and bring it to a simmer. While the stock warms, make the dumplings.

4. In a mixing bowl, combine the flour, baking powder, salt, and thyme, using a wire whisk. You can also sift the ingredients together if you prefer. Using a pastry blender, cut the shortening into the flour until it resembles coarse meal. Add the milk, stirring to incorporate it with a few quick strokes.

5. Raise the temperature of the broth to a rolling boil. Dip a spoon into the boiling broth, and then use it to drop a teaspoonful of the dumpling batter into the pot. If the spoon is dipped into the broth each time, the batter will not stick to it. When all of the batter has been added, reduce the heat, cover the pot, and cook gently for 12 to 15 minutes, or until all of the dumplings are floating. Gently stir the reserved chicken meat into the broth and serve at once.

Slow Cooker Beef Stew with Beer

2 tablespoons **unsalted butter**

2 tablespoons **flour**

¼ teaspoon freshly ground **black pepper**

2 pounds lean **beef chuck**, cut into ¾-inch cubes

½ cup thinly sliced **onions**

1 bottle **beer**, preferably a rich craft brew

1 clove **garlic**, minced

1 teaspoon fresh **thyme** leaves

½ teaspoon **brown sugar**

½ teaspoon **cider vinegar**

1. Melt the butter in a large skillet over medium heat. Place the flour and pepper in a paper bag. Working in batches, add the beef cubes to the bag and shake to coat the beef. Remove with tongs, place in the skillet, and brown on all sides. Repeat until all the beef is browned.

2. While the first batch of beef is browning, place the onions in the bottom of a slow cooker. As the beef is browned, use tongs to transfer it to the slow cooker atop the onions. When all the beef is browned and in the slow cooker, combine the remaining ingredients, pour into the cooker, cover, and cook on high for 2 hours.

3. This dish is excellent with any roasted root vegetable, or a combination. I like to make it at the end of the season when I have winter squash, carrots, and turnips available, but any combination will be delicious. Chopped fresh parsley, dill, or basil would also complement the dish.

CHAPTER 3

Gardening in Raised Beds

If you have a sunny outdoor space, you can grow enough vegetables for both seasonal cooking and preserving by installing raised growing beds. Although there are some drawbacks, as I will enumerate later, raised beds help eliminate many of the problems that sometimes plague beginning vegetable gardeners.

Raised beds have excellent drainage. Where the native soil is either dense, heavy clay that tends to drain too slowly, or a loose, sandy soil that drains too

rapidly, it may be cheaper and less work to construct raised beds rather than try to improve the native soil.

Raised beds have few weeds, and those that do manage to sprout are easy to pull. You can control many plant diseases and insects by removing and replenishing the growing mix in the beds every few years. Most gardeners find raised beds are more comfortable to work in, also.

On the downside, vegetables grown in raised beds will be less productive than those grown in the ground with proper spacing. Raised beds tend to warm up more slowly in spring and cool down more quickly in autumn, in effect shortening the growing season. Perhaps the biggest drawback is the time and expense necessary to build and fill the beds initially.

Nevertheless, when all is taken into consideration, raised beds are the best option for small-scale vegetable production when space or soil conditions will not allow for in-ground beds.

Where and How

Locate your vegetable beds so they will receive the maximum amount of sunshine. You will need a path at least two feet wide for access between beds and a nearby water source. Your best bet is to sketch out the design of your garden before you begin. It is easy to make changes on paper, but not so when construction has begun.

A bed three feet wide or more will require access paths on both sides, as most people cannot comfortably reach beyond three feet. The length is arbitrary. Many gardeners build beds that are eight feet long simply because lumber in that length is easier to handle. The choice of materials is up to you. Naturally rot-resistant woods, such as cedar and cypress, are preferred. Composites offer the greatest durability and the highest initial cost. Metal is also costly and can be difficult to work with for the inexperienced. Pressure-treated lumber offers an inexpensive option, but many people are concerned about the contamination of vegetables with preservative chemicals. I do not consider this a significant risk, and all of my raised beds are made from pressure-treated pine.

KALE

Kale will serve as our introduction to the cabbage family. This group of vegetables has been in the spotlight recently because they are rich in vitamins, minerals, and beneficial phytochemicals. Also known as cole crops or brassicas, the entire group was derived from an Old World plant similar to modern kale.

Dwarf cultivars of kale can be produced successfully in a large container, but this and the other cabbage family crops need the added space of a raised bed in order to make the harvest worth the effort of growing them.

Kale is a cool season crop that can be sown in early spring or late summer. Spring sowings should be selected from fast-maturing cultivars, as you want the crop to mature before the onset of summer heat. Sow the seeds in groups of three or four, spacing the groups six inches apart each way. When germination is complete, after about two weeks, thin the seedlings to only one per spot. Feed them at this point with a soluble fertilizer solution, and repeat the feeding every two weeks. Keep the bed evenly moist but not soggy. You should be able to begin harvesting leaves after about two months of growth.

In some regions of the country, cabbage butterflies (*Pieris rapae*) will devastate any of the cabbage family crops if measures are not taken to control them. See the section on management of this pest in Chapter 6.

Caldo Verde

This traditional Iberian stew has many variations and can be modified to suit your taste.

YIELD: **2 SERVINGS**

¼ pound fresh **kale**

2 ounces garlic-seasoned smoked **pork sausage**, such as Spanish (*not Mexican*) chorizo, andouille, *or* kielbasa

2 medium **potatoes**

3 cups **water**

1 teaspoon **salt**

¼ cup **Spanish olive oil**

Freshly ground **black pepper**

1. Wash, trim, and finely shred the kale. Reserve. Slice the sausage into rounds about ¼-inch thick. Film a skillet with a little oil and fry the sausage pieces until lightly browned. With a slotted spoon, transfer the sausages to paper towels to drain. Reserve.

2. Peel the potatoes and cut them into chunks. In a large saucepan, combine the water, salt, and potatoes, bring to a boil, and simmer until the potatoes are tender, about 15 minutes. Remove the potatoes with a slotted spoon, reserving the liquid in the pan. Transfer them to a bowl and mash with a fork, leaving a few chunks. Return the potatoes to the saucepan with the kale, olive oil, and a few grinds of pepper. Bring to a boil and simmer for 3 minutes. Add the reserved sausage and continue to cook just until heated through. Serve the caldo verde with a crusty, country-style bread.

BEET

Beets offer the double pleasure of edible greens as well as their sweet, earthy roots. Rich in healthful phytochemicals, beets grow best when the weather is cool but will nevertheless produce a crop during summer heat. Gardeners with a long growing season can plant beets sequentially from early spring to late summer for a continuous supply. Beets also store well and can be preserved successfully at home without too much work.

Direct seed beets into your growing bed about a month before the last spring frost in your area. Drop the large seeds on the surface of the growing medium, spacing them about two inches apart each way. Cover with one-quarter inch of growing medium, water well, and expect germination in two to three weeks. If conditions are not right, the first planting may not germinate. If this happens, simply replant. When true leaves have appeared on the seedlings, thin them to stand four inches apart each way. This will produce the best quality roots. If you are growing them mostly for greens, you can leave the spacing at two inches.

Beets do not require especially fertile soil, but they do need a slightly alkaline pH to perform best. Add lime, bone meal, or wood ashes to the growing area at least a month before planting. Keep the beet bed well watered. Maturity time is typically a little over two months.

Borscht: Two Variations

It is said that every Russian household has its own recipe for borscht. Here are some of my own takes on this delicious beet soup.

YIELD: **4 SERVINGS**

Borscht I

1 medium **beet**, roasted (*page 243*) and diced

1 medium **onion**, diced

1 **carrot**, diced

1 medium **Russet potato**, peeled and diced

2 cups **vegetable stock**

Salt

Freshly ground **black pepper**

½ cup coarsely grated **stale bread**

Borscht II

One recipe borscht (*above*)

1 cup **water**

Salt

Freshly ground **black pepper**

Sour cream

Dill *or* other fresh herb, finely minced

Borscht I:

1. Combine the vegetables and stock in a saucepan and bring slowly to a boil. Simmer, partially covered, until the potato is very tender. Taste and season with salt and pepper. Stir in the bread and continue to cook until the soup is thickened. If the soup becomes too thick, add additional vegetable stock or water. Serve at once or use as the base for the variation below.

Borscht II:

1. Cool the soup from the previous recipe to room temperature, or refrigerate overnight. Transfer to the jar of a blender and add 1 cup water. Blend until smooth. Cover and chill until very cold. Taste and adjust the seasoning. Serve cold in chilled bowls, topped with a dollop of sour cream and a sprinkling of fresh herbs. Dill goes especially well, but parsley, cilantro, chives, or basil will be fine.

Beet Canapés

The idea for combining beets with strawberries came from the legendary Blackberry Farm and appears in one of the splendid cookbooks by Sam Beall, *The Foothills Cuisine of Blackberry Farm.* I took the idea and came up with this easy appetizer.

YIELD: **4 SERVINGS**

4 slices homemade-style **whole wheat bread**

¼ cup **mascarpone cheese**

2 medium **beets**, roasted *(page 243)*

Freshly ground **black pepper**

8 pickled **strawberries** *(page 234)*

1. Cut each slice of bread in half crosswise to make 8 pieces. Spread each piece of bread with some of the mascarpone, dividing it evenly.

2. Slice the roasted beets crosswise into ¼-inch-thick slices. Save the end pieces for another use, and place a slice on top of the mascarpone on each appetizer.

3. Grind a little black pepper over the canapés. Top each canapé with a pickled strawberry and serve.

NOTE: You could also make this with pickled beets.

LEEK

These large, mild-flavored relatives of the onion are often expensive at the grocery store. They are easy to grow but require some planning and effort on the gardener's part. Your trouble will be rewarded with a crop of sweet, tasty leeks—better than you can buy.

Leeks take a long time to reach harvestable size, so they must be started early. Finding transplants in the market is often not easy, but you can start your own if you have a sunny window. Alternatively, you can start plants outdoors beginning in mid-summer and grow them as a fall crop.

Fill a six-inch pot with growing medium, water it thoroughly, and scatter leek seeds on top. Cover them with about one-quarter inch of growing medium and place in a warm, sunny spot. Expect germination in about ten days. When the seedlings are an inch tall, start feeding them every two weeks with soluble fertilizer solution. Keep them in the same pot until they are almost a foot tall and many plants are as thick as a drinking straw. About a month before the last expected frost in your area, knock the clump of plants out of the pot and separate them, using the largest and most vigorous ones as transplants. Clip off the roots to about two inches long and set them in your growing beds, spacing them six inches apart each way. Bury the roots and the lower two inches of the plant in the growing medium. Keep the bed irrigated when rainfall is insufficient, and continue to feed the plants every two weeks. When they have doubled in diameter, pile up additional soil around them, burying the lower end by at least two inches. Repeat this procedure when they have doubled in diameter again. Thereafter, let them grow until they have reached the size you prefer. Harvest as needed for the kitchen. They will keep well under cool, moist conditions.

Heirloom Potato and Baby Leek Vichysoisse

This version of vichysoisse utilizes delicately flavored baby leeks. Pull smaller specimens to make room for the other leeks to grow, and turn them into this soup, using whatever potatoes you have on hand. I particularly like this soup made with Russian Banana potatoes, but you can substitute at will.

YIELD: **2 TO 3 SERVINGS**

2 cups peeled, chunked **potatoes**

3 **baby leeks**, each about ½ to ¾ inch in diameter, carefully washed and coarsely chopped

½ cup **sour cream**

½ cup **vegetable** or **chicken stock**

¼ teaspoon freshly ground **white pepper**

1 teaspoon **kosher salt**, or to taste

Pinch of ground **mace**

¼ cup finely chopped **parsley**, **chives**, or a combination

1. Place the potatoes in just enough water to cover. Bring to a boil and cook 5 minutes. Add the chopped leeks, reduce the heat, and simmer until the potatoes are tender, about 15 minutes longer. Remove from heat and allow to cool.

2. Transfer the potatoes and leeks to a food processor and purée. Add sour cream, chicken stock, white pepper, mace, and salt. Process to combine.

3. Transfer to a covered container and chill at least 2 hours. Thin with a little more chicken stock if needed. Top each serving with a sprinkling of minced herbs.

Winter Gazpacho

I love gazpacho, but having good fresh tomatoes and cucumbers in winter can be a challenge. To satisfy my gazpacho craving, I invented this soup with ingredients that are available outside the main gardening season. Substitute canned roasted peppers if you cannot find good ones in the market. The soup will be better with your own home-canned or frozen produce, of course. And since it's for winter dining, serve it hot.

YIELD: **4 SERVINGS**

2 tablespoons **unsalted butter**

2 **leeks**, white and light green parts quartered lengthwise and thoroughly rinsed, chopped

1 clove **garlic**, minced

2 cups canned **whole tomatoes** with their juices

2 cups **chicken** or **vegetable stock**

2 tablespoons **tomato paste**

1½ tablespoons chopped fresh **parsley** leaves

1½ teaspoons dried **basil** leaves, crumbled

Salt

Freshly ground **black pepper**

1 red, yellow, or orange **bell pepper**, roasted (page 243), skinned, seeded, and diced

2 **scallions**, chopped

¼ cup **sour cream**

1. Melt the butter in a soup pot and sauté the leeks with the garlic for 5 minutes. Add the tomatoes, stock, tomato paste, and herbs, along with salt and pepper to taste, and bring to a boil. Reduce the heat and simmer 15 minutes.

2. Ladle the soup into bowls and garnish with the diced peppers, scallions, and sour cream.

Winter Vegetables in Rich Chicken Broth

Winter vegetables tend to be sweet. The acidity of the tomatoes balances the sweetness and enhances the flavor of the broth. The broth is enriched by cooking a chicken breast and some aromatic vegetables in it. Use the chicken breast to make Trader Vic's Chicken Salad (page 183).

YIELD: **4 SERVINGS**

4 cups **chicken broth**, preferably homemade

½ **carrot**, in 2 pieces, each about two inches long

4-inch stalk of **celery**, in 2 pieces

Inner green leaves of 2 **leeks**, chopped

1 large clove of **garlic**, peeled, but left whole

1 boneless, skinless **chicken breast** fillet

1 cup diced, peeled **butternut squash**

White part of a **leek**, chopped

½ cup diced **carrot** (*preferably yellow or purple*)

½ cup **parsnip**, diced, cored

¼ cup **radishes**, trimmed, diced

1 sprig fresh **rosemary**

½ teaspoon **salt**

Freshly ground **black pepper**

½ cup **canned tomatoes**, chopped

1 slice **wheat bread**, crusts removed, torn into small pieces

Freshly ground **white pepper**

Chopped fresh **parsley** leaves

1. In a large saucepan, combine the chicken broth, carrot, celery, leek leaves, garlic, and chicken breast. Bring to a boil, reduce the heat, and simmer gently for 30 minutes, skimming off any scum that appears. Using a slotted spoon, remove the chicken breast to a plate, reserving it for another use. Strain the stock into a heatproof bowl, discarding the vegetables, and return it to the saucepan.

2. Add the remaining ingredients, bring to a boil, reduce the heat and simmer, covered, for 30 minutes or until the vegetables are tender when tested with a dinner fork. Remove and discard the rosemary. Taste and adjust the seasoning. Keep the soup warm while you prepare the garnish.

3. Combine the tomatoes, bread, and white pepper in a small bowl. Stir well. Ladle the soup into bowls, add a dollop of the tomato sauce, and garnish with some chopped parsley.

BROCCOLI

Broccoli is a member of the large cabbage clan, bred for its clusters of flower buds. One of the most nutritious crops you can eat, broccoli is not easy to grow in warm summer areas. In these locations, broccoli does best as a fall crop.

Home gardeners may want to purchase started plants from a reputable garden center, as stress during early life will reduce the productivity of mature broccoli. If you want to try your hand at starting plants from seed, start them in July for a fall crop. Sow three seeds in each of several four-inch pots, covering them with one-quarter inch of growing medium. Water well and keep evenly moist throughout development of the seedlings. Outdoors in summer, this may mean watering several times a day. When most of the seeds have germinated, select the best one in each pot and cut the others off at ground level. Transplant seedlings to the raised bed about sixty days before you expect to harvest, spacing plants on twelve-inch centers. When the plants are a foot tall, sprinkle a tablespoon of balanced organic fertilizer around the base of each one. Apply a two-inch layer of mulch to protect the shallow roots from heat and to conserve moisture. Irrigate as needed to keep the soil evenly moist but not soggy.

Infestation by the cabbage butterfly (*Pieris rapae*) is a serious problem where the pest occurs. Recommendations for control of this insect, as well as snails and slugs, another common broccoli problem, are found in Chapter 6.

Harvest broccoli while the head is dark green without a trace of yellow. Small side shoots, each with a miniature head, will form after you remove the main head. Freshly harvested broccoli keeps a week under refrigeration. It also freezes well.

Jade Green Broccoli

An ancient Chinese restaurant dish, this remains one of the best ways to serve fresh broccoli. You can use the same technique with cauliflower, cabbage, bok choy stems, or a combination of all these cool season vegetables.

YIELD: **2 SERVINGS**

1 teaspoon **brown sugar**

1 tablespoon **cornstarch**

1½ tablespoons **soy sauce**

½ cup **water** or vegetable stock

2 tablespoons **vegetable oil**

Pinch of **salt**

1 clove **garlic**, minced

1 pound fresh **broccoli**, in bite-size pieces

2 tablespoons **dry sherry**

1. Combine the sugar, cornstarch, soy sauce, and water in a small bowl and set aside. Heat a wok or skillet until it is hot, and add the oil and salt. Reduce the heat, add the garlic, and then the broccoli, and stir fry for 2 minutes. Add the sherry and cover the pan. Cook an additional 2 minutes. Uncover, add the sauce ingredients, and stir until the sauce thickens. Serve immediately over rice or noodles.

Broccoli Steamed with Bay Leaves

Here is a recipe with a more interesting flavor than plain steamed broccoli. You could also use the same technique for other vegetables, or a mixture.

YIELD: **2 TO 4 SERVINGS**

1 cup **water**

1 pound fresh **broccoli** florets and diced stalks, about 2 cups

3 large **bay leaves**

½ teaspoon **salt**

Freshly ground **black pepper**

3 tablespoons **extra virgin olive oil**

1. Bring the water to a boil in a saucepan that will hold the broccoli in one layer. Add all ingredients except the olive oil, reduce the heat, and simmer slowly, covered, for 10 minutes, turning the broccoli once. Remove the broccoli from the pan with tongs, place on a plate, and keep warm. Discard the bay leaves. Raise the temperature and reduce the pan liquid to about three tablespoons. Serve the broccoli drizzled with the pan sauce and the olive oil.

NOTE: Substituting vegetable or chicken stock for the water gives even more depth of flavor to the broccoli.

CABBAGES

Cabbages are another form of the same botanical species as broccoli, *Brassica oleracea*. The familiar heads may be green or red, and the leaves are deeply crinkled in savoy cabbage. Generally considered to be easier to grow than broccoli, cabbage nevertheless needs proper care to produce a decent crop. As has been mentioned regarding the other members of this group, the cabbage butterfly is a serious pest where it occurs. See the recommendations for controlling it in Chapter 6.

Cabbage seeds should be started in small pots, either indoors under strong light or outdoors after all danger of frost is past. Home gardeners may want to rely on the local garden center for spring cabbage plants, unless you have ideal conditions for starting seeds yourself. Outdoors in summer, you can easily start a few plants for a fall harvest. Sow a few seeds on the surface of small pots of growing medium, covering them about one-quarter inch deep. Water thoroughly and place in a warm, bright location. They should germinate within two weeks. When true leaves have formed, remove all but the best-looking plant in each pot. Feed them at this point with soluble fertilizer and again every two weeks. Transplant them to their permanent location when they have three pairs of true leaves. Space plants a foot apart each way. Keep the bed well-irrigated if rainfall is insufficient. They should receive an inch of water per week. Uneven moisture may cause the heads to split. Harvest when the heads have reached the size typical of the variety you have planted. Smaller, faster-maturing cultivars perform best in small-space gardens.

Coleslaw Brass Rail-Style

The coleslaw recipe devised in 1958 by Frank J. Kotsianas for his Brass Rail Restaurant in downtown Knoxville, Tennessee, was published and later reprinted by the *Knoxville News-Sentinel.* As a result, it became a staple on many tables in the Tennessee Valley region. Inevitably, people developed their own interpretations. Here is mine.

YIELD: **6-8 SERVINGS**

1 medium head **cabbage**, chopped

½ cup chopped **pickled jalapeno peppers**

2 tablespoons chopped fresh **parsley**

1 tablespoon **sugar**

½ teaspoon **salt**

3 tablespoons **red wine vinegar**

2 tablespoons **extra virgin olive oil**

1. Toss all ingredients in a large bowl until well mixed. Refrigerate until ready to serve.

Virginia Peanut Coleslaw

This recipe takes traditional coleslaw ingredients and combines them with Asian flavors for a decidedly different take. The slaw goes well with seafood dishes and grilled chicken.

YIELD: **4 SERVINGS**

2 tablespoons **cider vinegar**

2 tablespoons **mayonnaise**

2 tablespoons chopped **green onions**

2 tablespoons chopped fresh **cilantro**

2 teaspoons **sesame oil**

1 teaspoon **sugar**

1 teaspoon prepared **horseradish** (*not horseradish sauce*)

½ teaspoon grated fresh **ginger root**

¼ teaspoon **salt**

⅛ teaspoon **cayenne pepper**

2 cups shredded **cabbage**

⅓ cup oil-roasted, salted **Virginia peanuts**

1. Combine all ingredients except the cabbage and peanuts in a bowl or jar and shake or beat thoroughly with a fork until well combined. Pour the dressing over the cabbage, cover, and refrigerate at least 1 hour or overnight. Add the peanuts just before serving.

CAULIFLOWER

Gardeners in warm summer areas find cauliflower to be a challenge. Where it can mature during cool, moist, sunny weather, it performs at its best. Cauliflower is another *B. oleracea* type, and its culture is identical to that described for broccoli. Take great care if you grow your plants from seed. Any setback that affects the seedlings is likely to prevent head formation when the plant matures. Also, be prepared for pest control as described for the other members of this group.

Given that the flavor of homegrown cauliflower is exceptionally good, I recommend lavishing a lot of attention on one or two plants rather than trying to produce a bumper crop. For example, cover each plant individually with floating fabric to keep out pests.

Plant breeders have produced cauliflower varieties that are suited to either spring or fall cultivation. Because head production depends upon day length, the plants will succeed only during the season for which they were bred.

Gratin of Cauliflower

A classic presentation for cauliflower, this simple dish lets the flavor of the vegetable shine through.

YIELD: **2 SERVINGS**

2 cups **cauliflower** florets, thawed if frozen, steamed 5 minutes if fresh

1 tablespoon **unsalted butter**

½ cup **vegetable** or **chicken broth**

¼ teaspoon dried **thyme** leaves or ½ teaspoon fresh leaves

Salt

Freshly ground **black pepper**

2 tablespoons fine dried **bread crumbs**

2 tablespoons shredded **Parmigiano-Reggiano cheese**

1. Preheat the oven to 350°F.

2. Generously butter a shallow gratin dish large enough to hold the cauliflower in one layer. Arrange the florets in the bottom of the dish. Pour the chicken broth over them and sprinkle with the thyme, salt, and pepper.

3. Place the dish in the oven and bake for 15 minutes or until most of the liquid has evaporated and the cauliflower is fork tender.

4. Combine the bread crumbs and cheese in a small bowl. Remove the dish from the oven and then sprinkle the top with the crumb mixture.

5. Turn on the broiler and broil the gratin until the top is lightly browned, about 2 minutes.

Cauliflower and Potato Salad

Adding cauliflower to potato salad increases the nutritional value and adds a new flavor dimension to the dish.

YIELD: **4 SERVINGS**

2 tablespoons **extra virgin olive oil**

2 teaspoons **red wine vinegar**

½ teaspoon **salt**

¼ teaspoon freshly ground **black pepper**

2 pounds waxy **boiling potatoes,** washed but unpeeled

2 cups **cauliflower** florets, in bite-size pieces

½ cup chopped **scallions,** white and green parts

½ cup chopped **sweet pickle**

½ cup **mayonnaise,** more if desired

¼ cup chopped **parsley**

1 teaspoon Dijon **mustard**

Ground **paprika**

1. Combine the first four ingredients in a large mixing bowl, whisking to emulsify. Bring a large pot of water to a boil, add the potatoes and cook, regulating the heat to keep the water at a gentle boil, until the potatoes offer little resistance when pierced with the tip of a knife, about 20 minutes. Drain the potatoes in a colander and allow them to cool. When the potatoes are cool enough to handle, peel them, cut them into bite-size pieces, and toss them with the dressing mixture while they are still warm.

2. Bring another pot of water to a boil, drop in the cauliflower, and cook, regulating the heat to maintain a gentle boil for 3 minutes. Drain the cauliflower in a colander, rinse well under cold water, and drain again. Add the cauliflower to the bowl with the potatoes.

3. In a mixing bowl, combine the remaining ingredients. Fold this mixture into the vegetables, adding more mayonnaise for a thinner consistency. Refrigerate overnight to allow the flavors to marry. Serve the salad garnished with a dusting of paprika.

COLLARDS

Collards are another version of cabbage, and the recommendations for growing any of the other members of this group apply equally to it. Long associated with Southern cooking, collards have enjoyed recent popularity as a nutritious superfood. While they are more heat tolerant than their cousins, gardeners in hot summer areas will have better luck growing them as a fall crop.

Sow seeds directly in the garden in mid- to late July, covering them with one-quarter inch of growing medium. Sow three or four seeds in clumps, spacing them a foot apart each way. Keep the bed well watered and expect germination within two weeks. When true leaves have developed, remove all but the sturdiest plant in each clump. Sprinkle a tablespoon of balanced organic fertilizer around the base of each plant after thinning. For large, hefty leaves, remove every other one when the plants are six inches tall, leaving them spaced two feet apart.

You can harvest individual leaves as soon as they reach a nice size of about six inches long, not counting the stem. You can leave them until they are twice that size, if you prefer. Plants will continue to produce new growth well into cold weather. Feed them every two weeks to encourage more leaf development. Collards are subject to damage from cabbage butterflies and, to a lesser extent, snails and slugs. See the recommendations for controlling these pests in Chapter 6.

Southern Style Collard Greens

This Southern staple is about as traditional as it gets. You can order Benton's bacon online if you want authentic flavor, but the dish will be almost as good with any top-quality smoked bacon.

YIELD: **2 TO 4 SERVINGS**

A big bunch of **collard greens**, woody stems removed and the leaves cut into 1-inch ribbons

3 strips **smoked bacon**, such as Benton's, chopped

1 cup **water** *or* **chicken stock**

Freshly ground **black pepper**

Cider **vinegar** for serving

1. Cook the bacon slowly in a large saucepan until most of the fat has been rendered and the bacon is crisp. Remove with a slotted spoon to a plate lined with paper towels and reserve. Heat the bacon fat until it is almost smoking, add the collards, and sauté. Adjust the heat as needed to prevent burning. When the collards are wilted, add the stock, salt, and as much pepper as you like. Cover the saucepan and cook until the collards are tender, about 10 minutes. Uncover and continue to cook gently, allowing the liquid to evaporate somewhat. Taste and adjust the seasoning as needed. Serve the collards warm, or cool to room temperature, cover, and refrigerate up to 2 days. Reheat gently before serving. Pass cider vinegar so diners can add as much as they like. This dish is traditionally served with cornbread to soak up the delicious juices, or "pot likker."

NOTE: For even greater authenticity, pass homemade hot pepper vinegar with the collards. Prick any sort of small hot peppers with a toothpick and pack into a clean glass bottle or small jar. Fill the jar with vinegar and allow to sit in the refrigerator for a few days before using.

Cayettes with Collards

Cayettes are a cross between a hamburger and a meat loaf. The ground meat is held together by strands of vegetables rather than breadcrumbs.

2 teaspoons **olive oil**

⅓ cup chopped **onion**

3 **scallions**, white and green parts, chopped

1 clove **garlic**, minced

4 ounces, about 2½ cups, well-washed **collards**, stemmed and shredded

1 **egg**, well beaten

¼ pound **ground beef**

¼ pound **ground pork**

¼ teaspoon **salt**

Pinch of freshly ground **black pepper**

Grating of fresh **nutmeg**

1. Heat the oil in a skillet, add the onions and scallions, and cook, stirring, until the vegetables are softened, about 1 minute. Add the garlic and collards and continue to cook, stirring occasionally, until the collards are wilted. Take the skillet off the heat and set it aside to cool.

2. Oil a baking pan. Preheat the oven to 375°F. When the collards are cool, combine them with the remaining ingredients, mixing well. Form the mixture into four patties and place them in a single layer in the baking pan. Bake for 25 minutes.

3. The cayettes may be eaten hot with your favorite sauce or condiment, or you can allow them to cool, then refrigerate and eat them cold the next day with mustard and horseradish.

CORN

Traditionally, fresh sweet corn has been the pride of the backyard gardener, primarily because its peak of flavor was so fleeting. A few decades ago, the conventional wisdom was to set water on to boil before going out to harvest the corn, as the time from stalk to plate was to be minimized at all costs. Plant breeders found a way to increase the window of time during which corn remains usable by manipulating the amount of sugar stored in the seeds. Thus, today we have sugar-enhanced and supersweet hybrid corns that remain sweet and tasty for as much as a week after harvest.

Corn needs long, warm, sunny days to produce a crop. Plants with a compact growth habit are essential for production in limited space. Corn should be planted in blocks, rather than in rows, as block planting aids in pollination. Corn is wind-pollinated, although the gardener can assist the process by jostling the stalks now and then when they have produced male flowers, or tassels, on top. The female flowers are, of course, the ears, with their protruding silks that catch the pollen grains.

Corn should be planted in groups of three seeds, spaced a foot apart each way in the bed. I suggest planting at least twenty-five square feet in order to have a worthwhile harvest. Corn benefits from added nitrogen and should receive regular feeding with a balanced organic fertilizer every two weeks from the time the plants are three or four inches tall. That is also the size at which they should be thinned, leaving the strongest plant to grow in each spot. Corn is drought tolerant, but should never be allowed to wilt.

When the silk has turned brown, the ears will be near harvest time. Carefully pull back the husk on an ear and press a kernel with your thumbnail. If the juices are milky and sweet, the corn is ready to pick. If the juice is clear, replace the husk and check again in a few days. In traditional corn varieties, such as Golden Bantam or Silver Queen, the sweet stage is brief, lasting only two or three days.

Sweet Corn Soup

Although you can make this soup with out-of-season corn from the grocery store, it soars to new heights with fresh corn from the garden.

YIELD: **4 SERVINGS**

4 to 6 ears of fresh **corn** *(if they are smallish, go with the larger number)*

2 quarts **water**

1 small **yellow onion,** trimmed but unpeeled, cut into quarters

1 **carrot,** trimmed and cut into 2-inch pieces

1 whole clove **garlic,** unpeeled

2 tablespoons **unsalted butter**

¾ cup chopped **onions**

¾ cup chopped **red bell pepper**

½ cup **heavy cream**

1 teaspoon **salt**

Freshly ground **black pepper**

1 tablespoon shredded fresh **basil** leaves

1. Shuck and silk the corn, trim off any damaged kernels, and place it in a large pot. Add the water, bring to a boil, then reduce the heat and simmer 3 minutes. Remove the ears with tongs, reserving the water in the pot. When the ears are cool enough to handle, cut the corn from the cobs into a bowl. Reserve.

2. Break the cobs in halves or thirds and return them to the pot with the onion, carrot, and garlic. Again bring the liquid to a boil, reduce the heat, and simmer slowly until the liquid is reduced by half.

3. Strain the corn stock, discarding the solids, and keep it warm and covered while you complete the soup.

4. In a large saucepan, heat the butter. When the foam subsides, add the onions and bell pepper and cook, stirring occasionally, until the onions are translucent. Add the reserved corn kernels and cook, stirring occasionally, until some of the vegetables begin to brown. Add the reserved corn stock, bring to a simmer, and cook for 10 minutes. Stir in the cream, salt, and a few grinds of black pepper. Do not allow the soup to boil after the cream has been added. Taste and adjust the seasoning as needed. Serve hot, garnished with the basil leaves.

Edamame Succotash

This recipe offers an update on an age-old Native American dish using an ancient ingredient from the other side of the world. "Succotash" is derived from a Narragansett word meaning "broken corn kernels." In the South, almost any dish with corn and beans together may be called succotash.

YIELD: **2 SERVINGS**

1 tablespoon **olive oil**

½ cup shelled **edamame**, frozen and then thawed, *or* fresh and blanched

½ cup fresh **corn kernels**, *or* frozen and thawed

¼ cup chopped **red onion**, plus additional for garnish

¼ cup **red bell pepper**, in ¼-inch dice

½ cup **vegetable stock**, homemade or canned

¼ teaspoon dried **thyme**, *or* 1 teaspoon fresh thyme leaves

Salt

Freshly ground **black pepper**

Chopped fresh **parsley** for garnish

1. Heat the oil in a small skillet over medium-high heat. Add the onions and cook gently, stirring once or twice, until they are softened, about 2 minutes. Add the remaining vegetables and cook, stirring occasionally, until the onions are translucent, about 2 minutes. Pour in the vegetable stock and add the thyme, a pinch of salt, and a few grinds of pepper. Reduce the heat and simmer until the edamame are tender, about 10 minutes. Remove from the heat and keep warm or serve immediately. Garnish with chopped red onion and parsley. This dish is a perfect accompaniment to tonkatsu-style pork cutlets (recipe follows).

Thawed frozen lima beans can be substituted for the edamame, if necessary.

Tonkatsu-Style Pork Cutlets

This is a great way to prepare boneless pork loin chops for a variety of dishes.

2 boneless
pork loin chops,
each about
½-inch thick

1 clove **garlic**,
minced

1 tablespoon **soy
sauce**

⅓ cup **rice flour**

1 **egg**

⅓ cup **panko** *or*
bread crumbs

Canola oil for
shallow frying

1. Slash the fat at the edge of the chops about every half inch, barely cutting through the fat layer. Place the chops in a shallow dish and sprinkle with the garlic and soy sauce. Refrigerate until ready to use, up to 3 hours. Bring to room temperature before continuing.

2. Remove the chops from the marinade, discarding the liquid. Place the rice flour, egg, and panko in each of three shallow bowls. Beat the egg until the white and yolk are combined. One at a time, dip each chop into the rice flour, turning until lightly coated. Dip the coated chop into the egg, allowing the excess to drain off before transferring the chop to the panko. Turn the chop until well-coated with panko and transfer to a rack set over a plate. Prepare the other chop in the same manner. Place the rack with the breaded chops in the refrigerator for at least 1 hour, or overnight if you wish.

3. In a heavy skillet, preferably cast iron, pour ¼ inch of canola oil. Place the skillet over medium-high heat, and heat the oil until a crumb of panko dropped into it sizzles and turns brown. Carefully place the prepared pork chops into the oil, one at a time, and cook, turning once, about 4 minutes on each side, or until the coating is golden brown. Regulate the heat to prevent the coating from scorching.

4. When the chops are done, transfer them to a wire rack over a tray lined with paper towels. Keep warm until ready to serve.

5. For a vegetarian version, use portabello mushrooms instead of the pork chops. Drizzle them with a little oil during the marinating process and proceed as directed. If you do not like the black spores portabellos produce, use a melon baller to remove this portion of the cap before placing the mushrooms in the marinade.

Sweet Corn Pudding

Sweet corn pudding is a Southern classic, and there are few better ways to dress up sweet corn for company. This recipe can be easily multiplied. It travels well and tastes good at room temperature, making it a frequent choice for potluck suppers.

YIELD: **2 SERVINGS**

3 ears fresh sweet **corn**, such as Ambrosia

¼ to ½ cup **heavy cream**

Salt

White pepper

Butter

1. Generously butter an oval gratin dish. Preheat the oven to 325°F.

2. Scrape the corn off the cob with a paring knife, holding the knife with the edge toward the center of the cob. You should do this over a large bowl to catch splatters. The scraped corn will have lots of milky juice and not many kernels will remain whole.

3. Combine the corn with enough cream to give the mixture the texture of a wet batter, about ¼ cup cream per cup of corn. Season with a pinch of salt and several grinds of white pepper.

4. Transfer the corn to the prepared gratin dish. Dot the top with butter. Bake for 1 hour, or until almost all the liquid is gone and the pudding is browning at the edges. Serve immediately.

Fresh Corn Chowder with Tortilla Shreds

YIELD: **4 SERVINGS**

¾ teaspoon **paprika**

½ teaspoon **garlic powder**

½ teaspoon dry **mustard**

½ teaspoon **black pepper**

¼ teaspoon **white pepper**

¼ teaspoon dried **thyme** leaves

¼ teaspoon dried **basil** leaves

½ teaspoon **salt**

2 **corn tortillas**

Vegetable oil for frying

1 cup **corn kernels**

½ cup **water**

¼ cup dry **white wine**

½ cup, or more, **vegetable stock**

2 tablespoons **olive oil**

¾ cup chopped **onions**

¾ cup chopped **celery**

¾ cup chopped **bell pepper** (*any color*)

1½ cups **vegetarian tomato bullion** (*page 230*)

2 tablespoons chopped fresh **cilantro**

1. Combine the first eight ingredients in a small bowl. Reserve. Prepare the tortilla shreds by cutting the tortillas into narrow strips, about ¼ inch wide. Pour enough vegetable oil in the bottom of a skillet to cover it to a depth of ¼ inch. Heat over medium heat until the oil ripples. Drop the shreds, a few at a time, into the oil. Cook a few seconds, until light golden. Remove the shreds with a slotted spoon, drain on paper towels, and sprinkle while hot with ½ teaspoon of the seasoning mixture.

2. In a saucepan, place the corn kernels with the water over medium-high heat. Bring to a boil, reduce the heat, and simmer for 5 minutes. Drain the kernels in a sieve, reserving the liquid in a bowl. Add the wine to the corn liquid, together with enough vegetable stock to yield a total of 1½ cups. Reserve.

3. Heat the olive oil in a saucepan and sauté the onions until translucent. To the onions, add half of the remaining spice mixture plus the celery and bell peppers. Sauté until the onion is golden. Add the corn, vegetarian tomato bullion, and the reserved corn liquid mixture. Simmer the soup for 10 minutes. Serve garnished with chopped cilantro and some of the tortilla shreds.

NOTE: Leftover tortilla shreds make a great snack or can be used to garnish other dishes. Try making them with red or blue corn tortillas. If fresh corn is out of season, substitute an 11-ounce can of whole-kernel corn. Tortilla chips broken into bite-size pieces can be substituted for the tortilla shreds.

Karibbean Kebabs

This is the recipe that appears on the cover of this book. The sweetness of ripe bell peppers pairs perfectly with pineapple and pork. Serve these kebabs with rice and a side of crisp coleslaw. While there is technically no corn in the ingredients, these kebabs pair so deliciously well with summer corn, making a complete meal for any barbecue.

YIELD: **4 SERVINGS**

3 tablespoons **sunflower oil**

1 tablespoon freshly squeezed **lime juice**

1 tablespoon minced fresh **parsley**, plus more for garnish

1 teaspoon minced fresh **oregano**

1 teaspoon minced fresh **basil**

1 teaspoon unsulfured **molasses**

½ teaspoon ground **coriander**

½ teaspoon **salt**

¼ teaspoon ground **black pepper**

1 pound boneless **pork loin**

½ of a fresh **pineapple**

1 **red bell pepper**

1 **yellow bell pepper**

1 **red onion**

1. In a small bowl, combine the first nine ingredients, stirring to combine well. Divide the mixture between two resealable plastic bags.

2. Cut the pork loin into one-inch cubes and place them in one of the bags with the marinade. Cut the pineapple into one-inch chunks and place them in the second bag. Refrigerate both bags at least three hours, or overnight. Bring to room temperature before continuing.

3. Remove the stems and seeds from the bell peppers and cut them into squares about one inch on each side. Peel and trim the onion and cut it lengthwise into eighths, keeping the pieces attached at the root end. (This can be done the day before you plan to serve the dish. Store the vegetables in a covered container in the refrigerator.)

4. Soak bamboo skewers in cold water for at least 30 minutes before you begin to cook. Prepare your grill for cooking. Remove the pork from the marinade, discarding the liquid. Remove the pineapple from its marinade, retaining the liquid for basting the kebabs.

5. Thread the vegetables, pineapple, and pork on the soaked skewers, dividing the food evenly and arranging it attractively. Grill the kebabs over moderate heat, turning and basting them until the pork is done and the vegetables are marked, about 20 minutes total. Cut into a piece of pork to check. It should not be pink at the center. If so, cook a few minutes longer. Brush the kebabs with the last of the pineapple marinade just before you remove them from the grill. Serve at once.

Mâque Choux

The origins of this dish, not to mention the name, are somewhat obscure. Some say the name derives from the Creole word for corn (mâque) and the French word for cabbage (choux). However, others claim the name derives from the Native American word for corn stewed with tomatoes. Chef Paul Prudhomme, in *Chef Paul Prudomme's Louisiana Kitchen,* offers no derivation for the name but does state that every Cajun family has a preferred recipe. In researching recipes, I found the only constants to be corn and onions. Substitutions, therefore, are fine.

YIELD: **6 TO 8 SERVINGS**

4 tablespoons **vegetable oil** *or* bacon drippings

½ cup finely chopped **onions**

¼ cup finely chopped **green bell pepper**

1 clove **garlic**, minced

4 cups **corn kernels**, fresh *or* frozen *(thawed)*

½ cup peeled, seeded, and diced **tomatoes,** *or* canned diced tomatoes in sauce

½ cup **chicken broth** *or* water

½ teaspoon **salt**

¼ teaspoon **black pepper**

¼ teaspoon ground **white pepper**

⅛ teaspoon **cayenne pepper**

Diced, cooked **smoked sausage,** such as Andouille

Cooked small **shrimp** *(optional)*

Minced fresh **parsley, chives/green onions** for garnish *(optional)*

1. In a 12-inch skillet, preferably cast iron, heat the fat until it begins to ripple and add the onions. Reduce the heat and cook, stirring occasionally, until the onions are soft. Add the bell peppers and corn. Cook, stirring occasionally, until the onion is translucent. Add the tomatoes, broth, and seasonings. Bring to a simmer, adjust the heat, and cook until almost all of the liquid has evaporated. If using, add sausage or shrimp. Toss to combine and heat through. Garnish with the herbs and serve at once.

FIELD PEAS

This group of legumes originated in Asia, made its way to Africa, and arrived in the United States with enslaved people during the colonial period. Tolerant of drought and poor soil, field peas, like other legumes, have been selected and re-selected over the years to yield an amazing variety of colors, tastes, and textures. They may be known as field peas, crowder peas, lady peas, cowpeas, red peas, or black-eyed peas, but all are grown in the same way.

Sow the seeds after the weather has warmed up in late spring, spacing them six inches apart each way and pressing them into the growing medium about an inch deep. Keep the bed well watered until the seeds germinate, after which they are fairly drought tolerant. Allow them to grow without further attention apart from occasional watering until the pods are fully filled out and the seeds have colored up. Open a pod to check. Or, if you prefer, leave them to dry on the plants. When the pods are thoroughly dry, harvest them all. Place the pods in an old pillowcase and bash it around on a convenient wall or rock, then separate the peas by dumping everything out on a rimmed baking sheet and allowing the wind to blow the chaff away.

Tennessee Caviar

One reason for the popularity of little brown field peas is that they can be cooked without prior soaking. This dip is essential tailgating fare.

YIELD: **8 TO 12 SERVINGS AS PART OF A BUFFET**

1 cup dried **field peas**

1 clove **garlic**, peeled

1 **bay leaf**

3 grinds of **black pepper**

6 cherry **tomatoes**, chopped

Pinch of **salt**

½ cup frozen **whole kernel corn**, thawed

¼ cup diced **red bell pepper**

¼ cup minced **green onions**

¼ cup bottled mild **taco sauce**

2 tablespoons chopped fresh **cilantro**

1 tablespoon fresh **lime juice**

Pinch of **salt**

Pinch of **garlic powder**

1. First, cook the field peas. Place the peas in a medium saucepan and rinse well under cold water. Discard any peas that float to the top. Drain well. Add water to cover the peas by about an inch. Set the pan over medium heat and add the garlic, bay leaf, and black pepper. Bring to a boil, reduce the heat, and simmer until the peas are tender, about an hour. Test for doneness by removing a few peas with a spoon. Blow on them. If the skins split, they are done. You can also taste for doneness. Remove the pan from the heat and allow it to cool for 30 minutes. Remove and discard the garlic and bay leaf. Remove and drain one cup of the peas, reserving the remainder for another use.

2. Place the chopped tomatoes in a strainer over a small bowl. Sprinkle with salt. Allow to drain 10 minutes.

3. Combine the cup of field peas and the drained chopped tomatoes with the remaining ingredients. Stir well and refrigerate, covered, at least 1 hour and for up to 3 days. Serve with tortilla chips.

Hoppin' John

No one seems to know where this traditional dish of field peas and rice got its name. Using both fresh and powdered onions and garlic and adding the seasoning blend in two stages creates layers of flavor in the dish. Benton's bacon comes in extra-long slices. If you cannot find it, use 5 strips of any good smoked bacon.

YIELD: **8 SERVINGS**

1¾ cups dried **black-eyed peas**

3 strips good quality **smoked bacon**, such as Benton's, chopped

1 cup chopped **onions**

2 cloves **garlic**, minced

1 tablespoon chopped **jalapeno pepper**, fresh or pickled

1½ teaspoons fresh **oregano** leaves, *or* ½ teaspoon dried

½ teaspoon **salt**

½ teaspoon **garlic powder**

½ teaspoon **onion powder**

¼ teaspoon ground **black pepper**

⅛ teaspoon **cayenne pepper**

2 cups **water**

3 cups hot **cooked rice**

Chopped fresh **scallions** for garnish

1. Wash, sort, and soak black-eyed peas overnight in water to cover. When ready to prepare the dish, drain them well.

2. In a large, heavy pot over medium heat, cook the bacon slowly until it is crisp and has rendered its fat. While the bacon is cooking, combine the oregano, salt, garlic powder, onion powder, black pepper, and cayenne in a small bowl, stirring well to combine. Remove the bacon with a slotted spoon and place on paper towels to drain. When it is cool enough to handle, crumble the bacon. Cook onion in the bacon fat until it is transparent. Add the garlic, jalapeno, and half the seasoning mix and cook 2 more minutes. Add the water, the reserved bacon, the remaining seasoning mix, and the soaked black-eyed peas.

3. Cover and cook about 30 minutes, or until the peas are tender. Combine the peas with the hot cooked rice and serve immediately, garnished with the scallions.

MELONS

Melons demand warm weather, a fertile growing medium, and considerable space. Recently developed cultivars take up less room than their conventional ancestors, but nevertheless you should be prepared to devote about twenty-five square feet to each planting. From this, you should expect anywhere from only one to perhaps five or six melons, depending upon the cultivar and your growing conditions.

In the center of the bed you are devoting to melon cultivation, build up a mound of growing medium about eight inches in diameter and half as high. Bury two tablespoons of balanced organic plant food in the center of the hill, a few inches below the surface. Plant five seeds in the hill, spacing them evenly and pressing them into the soil about an inch. Water the bed well and expect germination in a week or so. The plants should grow rapidly. When each seedling has a pair of true leaves, remove the two smaller plants and leave three to grow. You can allow the plants to sprawl, but the fruit will remain in better condition if you provide a sturdy trellis for the vines to climb. Nylon netting or a series of strings work best. When fruits form, you will need to fashion each one a "hammock," using a strip of cloth tied to the trellis support. Different varieties of melons mature at different rates, with larger fruits taking the greatest time to mature. As a general rule, the fruit will slip easily from its stem when fully ripe.

Chilled Melon Soup

Refreshing on a sultry August day, you can make melon soup with any melon.

1 cup cubed **melon**,
any variety

½ cup **coconut water**,
fresh or canned

2 **strawberries**

2 teaspoons **sugar**

2 teaspoons finely shredded
lemon verbena leaves

1. In a blender or food processor, purée all the ingredients except the lemon verbena. Transfer the soup to a covered container and chill at least 2 hours or overnight. Serve the soup very cold, garnished with the lemon verbena leaves.

NOTE: You may substitute finely grated lemon zest if you don't have lemon verbena in the garden.

Salad with Melon and Crisp Tennessee Prosciutto

Benton's country ham has been called Tennessee prosciutto because of its fine flavor. Its savory, salty punch pairs well with the cool, soft sweetness of melon. Substitute Italian prosciutto for the Benton's, if you must.

YIELD: **2 SERVINGS**

1 small slice Benton's **country ham**

2 teaspoons **safflower oil**

2 cups **mixed salad greens**

1 cup **melon**, any variety, in bite-size chunks

Juice of half a **lemon**

1 teaspoon **agave nectar**

1 teaspoon minced fresh **basil** leaves

Pinch of **salt**

Freshly ground **white pepper**

1. In a small skillet, cook the country ham in the oil over medium heat, turning occasionally, until it is crisp and lightly browned. Transfer the ham to a work surface and chop it into small bits. Reserve. Pour the drippings from the skillet into a small heatproof bowl and reserve. This can be done several hours ahead of serving.

2. Divide the greens between two chilled salad plates. Top with the melon. Add the lemon juice, agave nectar, basil, salt, and pepper to the cooled drippings. Whisk to combine. Pour the dressing over the salads and garnish with the reserved country ham bits.

OKRA

Another vegetable traditionally associated with the American South, okra has received renewed attention in recent years, thanks to the efforts of dedicated chefs striving to keep Southern food at the forefront of culinary trends. It is a member of the hibiscus family, related to cotton and the ornamental hibiscus shrubs found in garden centers. The large, showy flowers give way to elongated pods that are eaten in a variety of ways. Okra requires heat but is not fussy about soil. The plants are drought tolerant but should receive an inch of water per week during the growing season.

Plants can be started in small pots and transplanted, but most people sow the seeds of okra directly in the ground. In a raised bed, space them a foot apart each way. Ten to twenty plants will provide a good picking of okra every few days when they mature. At planting time, sprinkle a tablespoon of balanced organic fertilizer over every four square feet of growing area. Further feeding should not be required. Keep the bed moist until the plants emerge. Thin out any sickly ones after all have at least one pair of true leaves. When pods begin to appear, keep them picked to encourage further production. Most varieties have the best quality when the pods are three to four inches long. Some cultivars can get much larger than this without becoming tough, however. Okra could not be easier to preserve. Just wipe the pods with a kitchen towel, drop them into freezer bags, and freeze. If you prefer, you can slice them for cooking, but this can also be done after they are thawed.

John's Creole Style Gumbo

Not only does this recipe feature the best vegetables and herbs of high summer, all the other ingredients are at your favorite grocery store or farmer's market. The recipe involves making a Creole-style roux. Follow the directions carefully for best results.

YIELD: **6 SERVINGS**

½ pound fresh medium **shrimp,** preferably wild-caught Gulf *or* Atlantic shrimp

1 **bay leaf**

1 clove **garlic,** unpeeled

3 tablespoons **vegetable oil**

3 tablespoons **flour**

¼ cup chopped **onions**

¼ cup chopped **green bell peppers**

¼ cup chopped **celery**

2 tablespoons **garlic**

1 teaspoon **Creole seasoning** *(page 252)*

1 teaspoon **salt**

¼ cup peeled, seeded, and diced **tomatoes**

Freshly ground **black pepper**

3 cups **seafood** *or* **chicken stock**

3 **bay leaves**

½ teaspoon **Worcestershire sauce**

2 to 3 dashes **hot sauce**

¼ teaspoon dried **thyme** *or* ¾ teaspoon fresh thyme leaves

2 ounces **Andouille sausage,** chopped into ½-inch pieces

1 cup fresh **okra,** sliced crosswise into ½-inch-thick slices

1 tablespoon finely chopped fresh **oregano** leaves

1 tablespoon finely chopped fresh **basil** leaves

Steamed **rice**

3 **scallions,** white and green parts, chopped

2 **hard-boiled eggs** *(optional)*

(Continued on page 149)

1. Peel and devein the shrimp, reserving the shells for the stock. Store the shrimp in the refrigerator. Place the shells in a saucepan with the bay leaf and garlic clove and cover with cold water. Cover, bring to a simmer, and cook 5 minutes. Strain, reserving the stock and discarding the solids.

2. In a large, heavy-bottomed pot over medium-high heat, heat the oil until it ripples. Add the flour. Stirring constantly with a wire whisk, reduce the heat and cook the roux until it becomes the color of mahogany, a rich red-brown. Have patience and take care not to get the roux on your skin. It is extremely hot. Regulate the heat so the roux barely bubbles as you cook it, taking care not to let it burn. When the roux is approaching the desired color, carefully add the chopped onions, bell peppers, and celery. Continue stirring until the roux stops getting darker, avoiding the steam that will be produced from the vegetables. Add the garlic, Creole seasoning, salt, a few grinds of pepper, tomatoes, the reserved shrimp broth, the stock, bay leaves, Worcestershire sauce, hot sauce, and thyme. Bring to a simmer and cook 8 to 10 minutes, stirring occasionally. Stir in the Andouille and okra. Simmer 20 minutes.

3. Meanwhile, steam the rice, chop the scallions, and peel the eggs.

4. Add the shrimp, oregano, and basil to the gumbo. Simmer 10 minutes, or until the shrimp are pink. Taste and adjust the seasoning as needed. Gumbo is traditionally served in a wide, shallow bowl, as with some pasta dishes. Mound rice in the center of the bowl, ladle the gumbo over it, and garnish with the chopped scallions. Top with half a boiled egg.

Fried Okra
(aka Cajun Popcorn)

Frying okra could not be simpler because it makes its own "breading" when it is sliced, releasing a gelatinous juice that browns up nicely. If you want to really show off, bread the okra as described in the appended note.

YIELD: **2 SERVINGS**

1 pound fresh **okra**

3 tablespoons **vegetable oil** *or* bacon drippings

Salt

Creole seasoning (*page 252*)

1. Avoid wetting the okra. Wipe off any debris with a clean kitchen towel. Slice the okra crosswise into ½-inch slices. Place the fat in a heavy skillet, preferably cast iron, and heat it over medium heat until a light haze forms over it. Add the sliced okra all at once, and stir to coat it well with the oil. Regulate the heat so the okra sizzles but does not burn. Continue cooking, stirring occasionally, until all of the okra pieces have some browned areas. With a slotted spoon, transfer the okra to a paper towel-lined bowl to drain. While the okra is hot, sprinkle it with as much salt and Creole seasoning as you like. Serve.

NOTE: *To bread the okra, pour a beaten egg over the sliced okra and toss well to coat. Using a slotted spoon, remove the okra from the egg, allow it to drain well, and transfer it to a bowl with ½ cup cornmeal to which you have added a teaspoon of Creole seasoning. Toss to coat the okra well, then dump the bowl into a colander to get rid of all the smaller pieces of coating. Fry the okra in batches in hot fat until the coating is golden brown, turning occasionally. Drain on paper towels and add more Creole seasoning if desired.*

Okra Karen

Here is another way to fry okra, this time with summer vegetables and a Philippine-style adobo sauce. Feel free to add or substitute whatever vegetables you have on hand. Peppers, celery, broccoli, or other crunchy types work best. The recipe name honors the friend who suggested this method for preparing okra.

YIELD: **4 SERVINGS**

½ pound small, perfect **okra pods**, wiped clean but left whole

1 small **yellow onion**, peeled, quartered, and separated into segments

1 small **summer squash**, sliced diagonally into ½-inch slices

2 teaspoons **vegetable oil**

1 tablespoon chopped **garlic**

2 large **bay leaves**

2 tablespoons **soy sauce**

1 tablespoon **white vinegar**

1 tablespoon **water**

1. Place the prepared vegetables in a bowl. Put the garlic and bay leaves in a small bowl. In a second small bowl, combine the liquids. Have everything near the stove when you begin.

2. Set a wok or a large skillet over medium heat. When the wok is hot, add the oil and heat until it develops a light haze above it. Add the vegetables all at once and stir fry for 1 minute. Add the garlic and bay leaves and stir fry for 30 seconds. Add the remaining ingredients and continue to cook, stirring occasionally, until the liquid is almost evaporated. The vegetables should be crisp-tender. Serve at once with rice.

SUMMER SQUASH

Productive, versatile, and easy to grow, summer squashes offer plenty of possibilities to both the gardener and the cook. Straight or bent, flying-saucer-shaped, bi-colored, huge or tiny, the various types of summer squashes are all selections from two or three wild squash species. All thrive on warm, sunny weather and abundant moisture. Where insect pests are a problem, they can be grown under a row cover.

Sow the large seeds where the plants are to grow, placing five seeds in a spot, and separating the hills two feet apart each way. Bury two tablespoons of balanced organic fertilizer in the middle of each hill. The seeds should germinate within two weeks, and the plants will grow rapidly. When they all have a pair of true leaves, pinch off the two smaller plants and leave the other three to grow. Only a few summer squashes produce climbing vines. Those need a suitable trellis of strings or nylon netting. The other varieties can be allowed to sprawl. Compact cultivars make the best use of space in a raised-bed garden. With a few exceptions, summer squashes need insect pollinators. Plants grown under cover must be uncovered when blooms appear to allow pollinator access. Pick fruits early and often. Leaving fruits to mature on the plant will reduce or stop production.

Fall Garden Salad with Parmesan Peppercorn Dressing

With a dressing inspired by the house dressing at Bayou Bay restaurant in Knoxville, here is a composed salad that takes advantage of fall vegetable bounty. Vary the ingredients to accommodate whatever is available from your garden or farmer's market. Making this with Singing Brook cheese from Blackberry Farm and homemade purple basil vinegar raises it to a whole new level, but it will be delicious with any good vinegar and parmesan, too.

YIELD: **2 SERVINGS**

Salad

Arugula, **lettuce** *or* other leaves, washed and spun dry

Alfalfa sprouts

Heirloom **tomato**, sliced

Sugar snap peas

Summer **squash**, trimmed and cut into matchsticks

Cucumber, peeled, seeded, and diced

Mint, **parsley**, *or* **basil** leaves, *or* a combination

Dressing

3 tablespoons **mayonnaise**

3 tablespoons grated **Parmesan** cheese

1 teaspoon **cider vinegar** *or* other vinegar

1 teaspoon freshly ground **black pepper**

⅛ teaspoon **garlic powder**

1. Combine the dressing ingredients in a small bowl and set aside. Arrange the salad on chilled plates and drizzle with the dressing.

Lemon Basil Zucchini

Garden-fresh summer squash benefits from simple preparation. You can make this into a raw dish by omitting the oil and cooking the squash; just salt it lightly and then dress it with the other ingredients.

YIELD: **4 TO 6 SERVINGS**

2 teaspoons **canola oil**

4 medium **zucchini**, trimmed and sliced into rounds

¼ cup fresh **basil**, torn into bits

Zest of 1 **lemon**, grated

1. Heat the oil in a large skillet over medium heat. Add the zucchini and cook until lightly browned on one side. Flip the slices with a spatula and cook until the second side is lightly browned, about 2 to 3 minutes. Sprinkle with the basil and lemon zest and serve at once.

NOTE: This recipe works equally well with any other variety of summer squash.

Fried Corn with Zucchini

This dish goes particularly well alongside seafood with a touch of sweetness, such as scallops, shrimp, or lobster, and with pork. For a vegetarian meal, pair fried corn with a bean dish.

YIELD: **2 SERVINGS**

2 tablespoons **vegetable oil**

Fresh **corn kernels**, cut from two ears, about 1½ cups

1 medium **zucchini**, trimmed and sliced into ¼-inch thick rounds

2 teaspoons minced fresh **tarragon**

Salt

Freshly ground **black pepper**

1. Heat the oil in a heavy cast iron skillet and sauté the onion until it is translucent. Add the corn and cook, stirring occasionally, until it begins to brown and sticks to the bottom of the skillet. Add the zucchini, stirring and tossing to prevent further sticking. Continue cooking until the squash begins to brown and most of the corn has browned lightly. Remove from the heat, stir in the tarragon, and season with salt and pepper. Serve immediately as a side dish.

Summer Squash Casserole

When I was a kid, this casserole appeared on the table once or twice a week when squash was in season, yet we never got tired of it. Make the casserole with any type or combination of summer squash you happen to have. In my neck of the woods, it is a must-have with roast pork loin.

YIELD: **6 SERVINGS**

2½ pounds **summer squash**

2 cups **bread crumbs**, from two slices day-old homemade-style white bread

2 tablespoons diced **onion**, more if you prefer

¼ cup **brown sugar**

1 clove **garlic**, peeled and mashed to a paste

½ teaspoon **salt**

¼ teaspoon freshly ground **black pepper**

4 tablespoons (*½ stick*) **unsalted butter**, melted

2 **eggs**, lightly beaten

1. Trim the squash and cut it into uniform, bite-size chunks. In a large saucepan, place the squash in enough water to cover. Bring the water to a boil, reduce the heat, and simmer gently until the squash is tender when pierced with the point of a knife. The time required will depend upon the type of squash and the size of the chunks. Drain the squash and then place on a clean surface, such as a rimmed baking sheet. Set a clean cutting board or another baking sheet on top of the squash and weigh it down with canned goods or other heavy objects. Let sit for 10 minutes. This technique helps to remove remaining moisture, resulting in a fluffier finished casserole.

2. Transfer the squash to a food processor and coarsely chop, or chop it by hand. Place the squash in a large mixing bowl with bread crumbs, brown sugar, garlic, salt, and pepper. Pour the melted butter over the mixture and toss to combine. Add the eggs and mix well. Turn the mixture into a greased casserole dish. Bake at 350°F for 35 to 40 minutes, or until lightly browned on top.

SWEET POTATOES

The sweet potato is a member of the morning glory family, a native of the New World that has spread far and wide. Rich in vitamins and high in complex carbohydrates, sweet potatoes produce a good crop to store for out-of-season use. Properly stored, they will keep at least six months. Besides the familiar orange-fleshed sweet potatoes, there are yellow, white, and purple varieties. The different varieties vary somewhat in flavor, texture, and moisture content, but all are grown basically the same way. For small-space gardens, compact varieties like Puerto Rico make sense. Sweet potatoes are very productive in warm climates, so you don't need a huge patch to yield a reasonable harvest.

Purchase sweet potato plants from your local garden center, where they will appear at the proper planting time for your area. You can also start plants from a saved root if you begin in mid-winter and grow the plants in a bright, warm indoor location. Wait until a month after your last frost date before planting sweet potatoes outside. Set them in a rich, organic growing medium, allowing about three feet between plants. Keep them well watered but do not fertilize, as this may reduce the number of roots produced. As the plants grow, you can harvest a few leaves now and then. They are delicious when prepared like spinach. Wait as long as possible to harvest at the end of the season, but do not allow frost to touch the leaves, or the keeping quality of the roots will be impaired. Dig all the potatoes at once, spread them on newspapers in a cool, dry spot for a week, and then gently rub off any debris clinging to them. They will keep in baskets in a warm, dry, dark location for months.

Sweet Potato Mascarpone Gnocchi

Don't let the length of this recipe put you off. This dish is simple and foolproof, yet fancy enough for guests.

YIELD: **4 SERVINGS AS AN APPETIZER OR SMALL PLATE**

¼ pound roasted **sweet potato**, skin removed (*2 small sweet potatoes*)

¼ cup **mascarpone cheese**

2 tablespoons finely grated **Parmigiano-Reggiano cheese**

1 **egg**, well beaten

¼ teaspoon **salt**

¼ teaspoon ground **black pepper**

¼ cup all-purpose **flour**, divided

6 tablespoons **unsalted butter**, in all

Salt and freshly ground **black pepper**

1 teaspoon minced fresh **rosemary** leaves

¾ teaspoon finely grated **Parmigiano-Reggiano cheese**

1. In a mixing bowl, mash the roasted sweet potato with the cheeses until they are well combined. Add half the egg, reserving the remainder for another use. Stir to combine. Add the salt, pepper, and 2 tablespoons of the flour. Stir gently until the flour is incorporated. Add the remaining flour, a tablespoon at a time, until the dough just comes together. You may not need all the flour, depending upon how dry the sweet potatoes were to begin with. Cover the bowl with plastic wrap and refrigerate at least 8 hours or overnight.

2. Bring the dough to room temperature. Heat a large pot of salted water until it comes to a boil. Place 1 tablespoon of butter in a small skillet over low heat. Heat the oven to 180°F. Warm the serving plates in the oven.

3. When the water is boiling, regulate the heat so it remains at a gentle boil, and increase the heat under the butter if it is not yet melted and separating. Using 2 teaspoons, form pieces of dough into small dumplings and drop them into the boiling water, 5 or 6 at a time. Maintain the heat so that the water continues to boil gently. When all of the gnocchi have floated to the surface, wait 1 minute, then remove them with a slotted spoon, drain well, and transfer to the melted butter. The butter should be warm enough to sizzle when the gnocchi are dropped in. Cook the gnocchi until they are golden brown on the bottom, turn, and brown the other side. Transfer the browned gnocchi to a serving plate, return it to the oven to stay warm, and repeat with the remaining dough. You should have enough dough for four batches, or about 2 dozen gnocchi. Wipe out the skillet between batches, if necessary, to prevent over-browning.

4. When all of the gnocchi are browned and ready to serve, heat the remaining 2 tablespoons of butter in a clean skillet. When it has begun to separate, add the minced rosemary, a pinch of salt, and a few grinds of pepper. Stir over medium heat until the foam subsides, and then pour over the gnocchi, distributing the rosemary butter evenly among the plates. Sprinkle each serving with a dusting of Parmegianno-Reggiano and serve.

Instead of the rosemary butter and cheese garnish, you may wish to serve the gnocchi with the pecan sorghum brown butter sauce that follows.

Pecan Sorghum Brown Butter Sauce

Use this as an alternative to the rosemary butter and cheese garnish, and you turn the gnocchi dish into a light dessert or an accompaniment for roast pork or ham.

YIELD: **2 SERVINGS**

2 tablespoons **butter**

2 tablespoons **sorghum syrup**

⅛ teaspoon **ground cinnamon**

Pinch of **salt**

1 tablespoon chopped **pecans** *(preferably the native variety)*

1. After preparing the gnocchi and placing them on warm serving plates, melt the butter in a small skillet over medium heat. As soon as the foam subsides, stir in the sorghum syrup, cinnamon, and salt. Stir to combine, and then drizzle the sauce over the warm gnocchi. Garnish with the chopped pecans.

Sweet Potatoes Stuffed with Winter Greens

YIELD: **4 SERVINGS**

While this is not a traditional Southern side dish, the combination takes some traditional Southern ingredients to gourmet heights.

½ cup **balsamic vinegar**

4 shapely, uniform **sweet potatoes**, washed and trimmed

2 cups **mixed winter greens**, such as dandelions, mustards, endive, etc., washed and spun dry

Vegetable oil

1 tablespoon **extra virgin olive oil**

¼ cup chopped, cooked **lean country ham**

1. Preheat the oven to 325°F. Place the vinegar in a small saucepan and simmer over medium heat until reduced to ¼ cup. Reserve. As you trim the washed potatoes, dry each one with paper towels and coat with oil to prevent darkening. Place potatoes in a small baking pan and roast for 20 minutes. Pierce each potato with a fork and continue cooking until they are tender, another 20 to 25 minutes. Remove the sweet potatoes from the oven, split them lengthwise, and place on serving plates. Place some of the greens between the halves of each potato, top with some of the ham, drizzle the balsamic reduction over all, and serve immediately.

Sweet Potato Casserole
with Marshmallows

This recipe makes enough for a crowd as part of a dinner celebration.
You want to end up with about 6 cups of roasted potato. If your potatoes look
as though they will need a lot of trimming, cook an extra pound.

YIELD: **6 OR MORE SERVINGS**

3 pounds white-fleshed **sweet potatoes**, scrubbed and trimmed

Vegetable oil for the baking pan

½ stick **butter**, melted

½ cup **brown sugar**

⅛ teaspoon ground **cinnamon** (*more if desired*)

½ to 1 cup **miniature marshmallows**

1. Place the scrubbed sweet potatoes in an oiled baking pan, turning them to coat with the oil. Place the pan in a preheated 375°F oven and roast until the potatoes are tender. The point of a knife should meet no resistance all the way to the center of the largest potato. Start checking after the first 25 minutes or so, depending upon how large the potatoes are. Total cooking time will be about an hour. When they are done, remove them from the oven and cool to room temperature. They will keep fine at room temperature overnight, or they can be used immediately. They will be easy to peel after roasting.

2. Reduce the oven temperature to 350°F. Peel the potatoes, trim out any dark spots or blemishes, and slice them into a large bowl. Have the melted butter ready. Start mashing the potatoes, sprinkle with the sugar and cinnamon, and keep mashing until thoroughly combined. This can take a while but gets easier as you go along. Drizzle in the butter a little at a time and keep mashing until you have a uniform mixture. Transfer to a buttered, 10-inch deep-dish pie plate and cover the top with a single layer of miniature marsh-mallows. Press down gently on the marshmallows. Bake until the marshmallows are nicely browned, about 45 minutes.

NOTE: Use the leftovers. Cover the pie plate with foil and refrigerate. The following day, remove from the refrigerator, bring to room temperature, transfer to a preheated 350°F oven, and bake until the marshmallows melt into the potatoes, about 30 minutes. Uncover and serve.

Sweet Potato Salad

2 pounds **sweet potatoes**

2 tablespoons **canola oil**

1 **cooking apple**

1 **navel orange**

1 cup **walnuts**

½ cup chopped **scallions**, white and green parts

¼ cup chopped **cilantro** or Italian parsley

¼ cup **apple cider vinegar**

2 tablespoons minced **shallots**

2 tablespoons **brown sugar**

2 tablespoons fresh **orange juice**

½ teaspoon **dry mustard** (such as Colman's)

½ teaspoon **salt**

¼ teaspoon freshly ground **black pepper**

½ cup **extra virgin olive oil**

1. Preheat the oven to 425°F. Line a rimmed baking sheet with heavy-duty aluminum foil. Peel the sweet potatoes and cut them into bite-size pieces. Place them in a bowl, add the canola oil, and toss until the potatoes are well coated. Spread the potatoes in a single layer on the baking sheet, transfer to the oven, and roast until the edges of the cubes begin to brown, about 20 minutes. They should be barely fork tender when done. Test one with a fork and cook a little longer, if needed.

2. While the potatoes are roasting, core the apple and cut into bite-size pieces. Place the pieces in a bowl and toss with a few drops of vinegar to keep them from darkening.

3. Peel the orange and cut the sections from the membranes, working over a bowl to catch the juice. Reserve the segments and juice separately. One orange should provide more than enough juice for the recipe.

4. Place the walnuts in a dry skillet. Set the skillet over high heat and toast, stirring frequently, until the walnuts begin to brown. Remove from the heat and transfer to a heat-proof bowl to stop cooking. When cool, chop the walnuts into smaller pieces.

5. Combine the sweet potatoes, apples, orange segments, walnuts, and parsley in a bowl. In a small bowl, combine the vinegar, shallots, brown sugar, orange juice (use any remaining juice for another purpose), dry mustard, salt, and pepper. Whisk until thoroughly combined, then whisk in the olive oil in a stream and continue whisking until emulsified. Pour the vinaigrette over the salad, stir to combine, and refrigerate until ready to serve.

Sweet Potato Pie

I prefer making this with white-fleshed sweet potatoes, such as O'Henry, but it will be equally delicious with regular yellow or even purple sweet potatoes. Use your favorite pie crust recipe, or purchase one from the grocery.

YIELD: **1 9-INCH PIE**

1⅓ cups mashed cooked **sweet potatoes**

1 9-inch **pie shell**, unbaked

2 **eggs**

¼ cup **brown sugar**

½ cup **white sugar**

1 5 ounce can **evaporated milk**

3 tablespoons **unsalted butter**, melted

1 teaspoon pure **vanilla extract**

¼ teaspoon ground **cinnamon**

A grating of fresh **nutmeg**

1. Prepare the mashed sweet potatoes. Drizzle a little canola oil in the bottom of a baking pan large enough to hold the potatoes in one layer. Wash and trim the potatoes, placing each one in the baking pan as you go. Shake the pan to roll the potatoes around and coat them with the oil. Place the pan in a preheated 350°F oven and bake until a knife inserted in the thickest potato meets no resistance, about 30 to 45 minutes. Remove from the oven and leave at room temperature until cool enough to handle. Using a spoon, scrape the flesh from the potatoes into a bowl. Use immediately or cover and refrigerate up to three days.

2. Chill the pie shell until ready to fill. Preheat the oven to 350°F. In a mixing bowl, beat the eggs with the sugars until light. Add the milk, butter, vanilla, and spices. Whisk well, then whisk in the mashed sweet potatoes until smooth.

3. Pour the filling into the chilled crust, cover the edges with foil, and place in the oven for 30 minutes. Remove the foil, return to the oven, and bake until a paring knife inserted in the center comes out clean, about 25 to 30 minutes longer. Cool the pie completely on a wire rack before serving with whipped cream. If baked more than 2 hours before serving, cover and refrigerate.

TOMATOES, INDETERMINATE

For the greatest variety of sizes, shapes, colors, and tastes, indeterminate tomatoes are the hands-down choice for backyard gardens. Indeterminate tomatoes do not cease growing as determinate tomatoes do but instead keep getting bigger, producing additional blooms and fruit throughout the season. Among the indeterminate group are many modern hybrids as well as treasured heirlooms. Inexperienced gardeners should begin growing the hybrids, as they have much more resistance to common tomato diseases than the heirlooms do. Once you have some experience with tomatoes, you can try the heirlooms. You should have the best luck with heirlooms that are already popular in your region of the country. These old-fashioned plants were often perpetuated by gardeners who found them to be especially well-adapted to a certain locale.

Although you can start tomatoes from seed at home, you will need to do this after the weather warms up, unless you have a very bright indoor light source. Tomatoes, especially when small, do not thrive with anything less than full sunshine. Beginners are therefore urged to purchase plants from a garden center. The staff should be able to discuss the characteristics of the varieties they offer.

If you start seeds yourself, sow two or three in each of several four-inch pots of growing medium. They will germinate within two weeks. When true leaves are present, remove all but the sturdiest-looking plant. Feed them with a soluble fertilizer solution at this time, and again every two weeks until the first blooms appear. They should be transplanted to their permanent spot in the garden when they have two to three pairs of true leaves. Do not leave them in pots any longer than necessary. Space plants eighteen to twenty-four inches apart in growing beds, and provide a sturdy support to which you can tie the vines. Indeterminate tomatoes can reach as high as eight feet or more.

Fried Green Tomato Napoleons

Want to know a dirty little secret? Fried green tomatoes were not all that popular, even in the South, until the advent of Fannie Flagg's novel *Fried Green Tomatoes at the Whistlestop Café*. Nevertheless, you see them referred to as a Southern "classic," as if they were Robert E. Lee's favorite. This recipe, easily doubled, is good enough for company but comes together quickly for a weeknight dinner.

YIELD: **2 SERVINGS**

2 **green tomatoes**, each about the size of a baseball

Salt and freshly ground **black pepper**

Cornbread mix for dredging (*I use the White Lily brand*)

4 tablespoons **canola oil**

2 ounces fresh **goat cheese**

2 handfuls of fresh **field greens**, washed well and spun dry

Green dressing (*page 24*)

Sriracha *or* other hot sauce (*optional*)

1. Slice the tomatoes into uniform slices about ⅜-inch thick, discarding the end pieces. You should have 6 nice slices. Arrange the slices on a plate or tray and sprinkle lightly with salt and a few grinds of black pepper, turning to season both sides. Heat the oil in a large, heavy skillet until its surface ripples. Dip the tomato slices in the cornbread mix, coating them well on both sides. Shake off the excess and fry in batches in the hot oil until golden, turning once, about 4 minutes per side. Transfer the cooked tomatoes to a rack set over paper towels and keep warm. When all of the tomatoes are cooked, assemble the dish onto two warmed plates. Place a tomato slice in the center of the plate and top with a tablespoon of goat cheese and a second tomato slice. Repeat with the remaining cheese and tomatoes. Surround the tomato napoleons with field greens and drizzle the green dressing over all. Spice it up with Sriracha sauce if desired.

Pepper Crusted Pork Provençal

Tomatoes combine with other Mediterranean flavors to create a vibrant sauce for the pepper crusted pork. If you cannot find the mixed peppercorns, use any that are available, regardless of the color.

YIELD: **4 SERVINGS**

2 tablespoons mixed **peppercorns**
(green, black, white, and red)

1 whole **pork tenderloin**

½ teaspoon **salt**

1 tablespoon **Dijon mustard**

2 tablespoons **olive oil**

1 cup chopped **onions**

½ cup thin strips of **red bell pepper**

½ cup thin strips of **yellow bell pepper**

2 teaspoons minced **garlic**

1 **bay leaf**

1 teaspoon sweet **paprika**

¼ cup dry **white wine**

1 cup peeled, seeded, and diced **tomatoes**

¼ cup small ripe **olives**, such as Niçoise *or* Coquillo, pitted

Freshly ground **black pepper**

1 tablespoon chopped fresh **basil**

2 tablespoons minced fresh **parsley**

1. Preheat the oven to 400°F. Crush the peppercorns in a mortar, or place them between sheets of plastic wrap and crush with the bottom of a heavy skillet. You want coarse particles of pepper, not a powder. Pat the tenderloin dry and sprinkle it with the salt. Brush the tenderloin all over with the mustard, then roll it in the peppercorns to coat thoroughly. Place the tenderloin on an oiled rack in a baking pan. Set the pan in the oven to cook while you prepare the sauce.

2. In a large saucepan, heat the oil over medium heat and add the onions. Cook, stirring occasionally, until the onions are soft, about 4 minutes. Add the peppers and cook, stirring occasionally, until the onions are translucent. Add the garlic, bay leaf, and sweet paprika and cook, stirring often, until the onions have barely begun to brown, another 2 or 3 minutes. Pour in the wine and the tomatoes and stir, scraping up any browned bits from the bottom of the pan. Adjust the temperature, bring the sauce to a simmer, and cook, uncovered, until it is slightly thickened, about 15 minutes. Stir in the olives, basil, and a few grinds of black pepper. Taste and adjust the salt, if needed. Cover the sauce and keep it warm.

3. When the tenderloin is done, remove it from the oven and transfer to a carving board. Slice the tenderloin into medallions, transferring them to heated serving plates and distributing the slices evenly. Top with the sauce and garnish with the parsley.

NOTE: *If you desire, mound mashed potatoes or steamed rice on the serving plate before plating the pork and sauce.*

Yellow Tomato and Bacon Jam

Besides being good on biscuits, this jam can be used to add flavor to steamed vegetables. Try it with crackers and cheese, too.

2½ ounces **smoked bacon** *(about 3 strips)*

½ cup finely diced **sweet onion**

10 ounces **yellow cherry tomatoes**, halved

¼ cup **dark brown sugar**

2¼ teaspoons **apple cider vinegar**

1 sprig of fresh **thyme**

½ teaspoon **salt**

A few grinds of **black pepper**

Dash **hot pepper sauce**

1. Cook the bacon in a skillet over medium-low heat until it is crisp and browned. Transfer the bacon to a plate lined with paper towels. Place a tablespoon of the rendered bacon fat in a small saucepan, reserving the remainder for another use. Set the pan over medium-low heat and cook the onions in the bacon fat, stirring occasionally, until they are caramelized, about 15 minutes. Add the tomatoes, sugar, vinegar, salt, pepper, and hot sauce. Bring to a boil. Reduce heat and cook, stirring occasionally, until thickened to your satisfaction. Crumble the bacon and add it near the end of the cooking time.

2. Transfer the jam to a small jar, cool, and refrigerate or freeze. Keeps refrigerated for 1 week or frozen for 6 months.

TURNIPS & TURNIP GREENS

The turnip is a cool-season member of the brassica clan that produces edible greens and roots. Easy to grow and productive, turnips are enjoying a new round of popularity as gardeners and cooks rediscover vegetables that like cold weather.

Sow turnips directly in your raised beds as soon as the growing medium can be worked in spring. If you are growing them primarily for greens, sow thickly, allowing only an inch or two between seeds. The greens can be cut back hard and will resprout multiple times. Fertilize lightly after each harvest of leaves.

For root crops, space the plants out a bit. Thin them to stand six inches apart each way after true leaves appear. Harvest only one or two leaves from each plant. Root crops need only one feeding, when the plants are about two inches tall. Use any soluble fertilizer solution. Turnip roots are best when small, around the size of a golf ball up to billiard ball diameter. Larger specimens are likely to be tough and harshly flavored.

Turnip Greens Oshitashi

This Japanese dish is typically made with spinach, but turnip greens bring a different flavor and work just as well.

YIELD: **2 SERVINGS**

1 large bunch
turnip greens

1 tablespoon
safflower oil

1 tablespoon
cider vinegar

1 teaspoon
soy sauce

¼ teaspoon
sesame oil

1 tablespoon
sesame seeds

1. Rinse the turnip greens well, and pick over them to remove any yellowed or otherwise unusable leaves. Arrange the greens so the stems are all in one direction, as with a bouquet of flowers. Bring a large pot of water to a rolling boil. Holding the turnip greens by the stems, immerse them in the water for 45 seconds. Remove the greens and hold them under cold running water to stop the cooking and set the bright green color. Drain thoroughly. Lay the bundle of greens on a tray lined with paper towels and cut off the uncooked stems. Using the paper towels as an aid, roll up the greens into a roll about an inch in diameter. Squeeze gently to dry the greens and help them hold together in the roll.

2. Carefully unroll the greens on a work surface. Trim the ends of the roll neatly and then slice it into 1-inch slices. Arrange the slices on each of two serving plates. In a small bowl, combine the remaining ingredients. Whisk with a fork to emulsify the liquids, pour the dressing over the appetizers, and serve.

Mixed Turnip Mash

The flavor of Japanese white turnips is delicate and sweet, making them a great choice for this dish. For maximum contrast, use a yellow-fleshed potato, such as Yukon Gold.

YIELD: **2 SERVINGS**

1 cup peeled and coarsely chopped **turnips**

1 cup peeled and coarsely chopped **carrots**

1 cup peeled and coarsely chopped **potatoes**

3 tablespoons **milk**, divided

1 tablespoon **butter**, divided

¾ teaspoon **salt**, divided

Freshly ground **white pepper**

Ground **mace**

1. You will need three small saucepans, or you can make each of the mashes one at a time and keep in small bowls until ready to combine them at the end. The recipe assumes you have three saucepans.

2. Place each of the vegetables in a separate saucepan, cover with cold water, and bring to a boil. Adjust the heat and cook until the vegetables are tender. This will take about 6 minutes for the potatoes and about 5 minutes for the turnips and carrots. Test by mashing a piece against the side of the pan with a fork. It should mash easily. When the vegetables are done, drain them thoroughly. To each vegetable, add 1 teaspoon of butter and 1 tablespoon of milk. Mash each vegetable with a fork until you have a uniform texture. If the mash seems too dry, dribble in a little more milk. Season each vegetable with ¼ teaspoon of salt. Add nothing else to the turnips. Add a few grinds of white pepper to the potatoes, and add a pinch of mace to the carrots. Stir these seasonings in to combine.

3. Transfer the vegetables to a large bowl and gently fold them together using a rubber spatula. You want the individual colors and textures of the vegetables to be visible in the final mix rather than combining them into a uniform blend. Keep the mash warm in a low oven until you are ready to serve.

WINTER SQUASHES

This group of cucurbits includes pumpkins, gourds, and other squashes that are left to mature before they are harvested. Most are good keepers, with flesh that is rich in vitamins and carbohydrates. One or two hills of winter squash should provide all you will need for storing over winter, unless you really love squash.

After all danger of frost is past and the weather is warm and settled, sow the large seeds where the plants are to grow. Most winter squashes need 90 days or more of warmth to mature a crop. Sow five seeds per hill in small hills placed three feet apart each way. At planting time, bury two tablespoons of balanced organic fertilizer underneath the hill. Germination will occur in a week to ten days. When the plants all have a pair of true leaves, remove the two weakest ones and leave three to grow. The vines can be left to sprawl, but the fruit will be cleaner and more nearly perfect if you provide a sturdy trellis for the plants to climb. Compact varieties are also available that do not require a trellis. These are ideal for limited-space gardens.

Allow the squash to mature until the skin is tough enough not to be pierced by your thumbnail. The skin should also develop the color characteristic of the type, ranging from deep green through orange and yellow to tan. Remove the fruits with about an inch of stem still attached. Do this as late in the season as possible, but before the first hint of frost. Fruits will keep in a warm, dry place for about six months.

Winter Squash Pickle

We don't often think of making pickles with winter squash, but these should convince you it is worthwhile to do. They can accompany a variety of dishes in addition to the one on the following page.

YIELD: **2 CUPS**

2 cups ½-inch cubes of peeled, seeded **winter squash**

2 teaspoons **kosher salt**

4 whole fresh **sage leaves**

¼ cup **sorghum**

½ cup **cider vinegar**

¼ cup **apple juice**

1. Combine the squash and salt in a bowl. Stir well, then cover and allow to sit at room temperature for 4 hours. Drain well in a colander, rinse under cold water, drain again, and pat dry with kitchen towels.

2. Combine the remaining ingredients in a large saucepan. Bring to a simmer, stirring constantly. Add the squash, return to a simmer, and cook gently for 5 minutes. Cool to room temperature, cover, and refrigerate up to a month. Allow 2 days for the flavors to develop before using.

Winter Squash and Shrimp Bisque for Company

I got the idea for this dish from a review of Eleven Madison Park, as reported in the *New York Times Magazine*. One average-sized winter squash should be enough for both the pickles and the bisque.

YIELD: **4 SERVINGS**

2 tablespoons **unsalted butter**

2 cups ½-inch cubes of peeled, seeded **winter squash**

¼ cup sliced **celery**

2 pieces **ginger**, each about the size of a quarter and ⅛ inch thick

1 clove **garlic**, peeled and smashed

2 tablespoons all-purpose **flour**

1 tablespoon **sherry vinegar**

½ cup peeled, seeded, and diced ripe **tomatoes**

4 cups **shrimp stock** *(recipe follows)*

¼ cup **tarragon leaves**

1 tablespoon **sour cream**

½ teaspoon **salt**

Juice of ½ a **lime**

Sriracha sauce to taste

4 slices **bacon**

12 ounces medium **shrimp**, preferably wild-caught, peeled, and deveined *(about 20)*

1 teaspoon **unsalted butter**

Squash pickles *(page 173)*

Toasted seed topping *(page 252)*

For the stock:

Shells from 12 ounces **shrimp**

1 **shallot**, chopped

1 stalk **celery** with leaves, chopped

1 clove **garlic**, smashed

(Continued on page 175)

1. A few days ahead of time, make the squash pickles. Cut a medium winter squash in half lengthwise. Remove the seeds. Peel one half and cut into cubes for the pickles. Peel and cube the other half and store in a covered container in the refrigerator until you are ready to complete the dish, for up to one week.

2. Peel and devein the shrimp a few hours ahead, using the shells for the stock and reserving the prepared shrimp, covered and refrigerated, preferably on ice.

3. Two hours or less before serving, cook the bacon over medium heat until crisp. Drain the bacon on paper towels and reserve. Pour off the fat from the skillet, reserving any browned bits, and set the skillet aside for cooking the shrimp just before serving.

Shrimp Stock:

1. Put the shrimp shells in a large saucepan or stock pot. Cover with two quarts of cold water. To the stockpot add the shallot, celery with leaves, and garlic. Bring the stock to a simmer over medium heat, then lower the heat and cook slowly until reduced by half, about 1 hour. Strain and use immediately, or cool to room temperature and store covered in the refrigerator until ready to use. Stock will keep in the refrigerator for 3 days or in the freezer for 1 month.

2. To complete and serve the bisque, melt the butter in a large saucepan or Dutch oven over medium heat. Add the squash, celery, shallot, ginger, and garlic. Cover the pan, lower the heat, and steam the vegetables slowly until they are soft, about 15 minutes. Stir in the flour and cook for 5 minutes. Add the vinegar and tomatoes and stir to incorporate. Cook slowly for 3 minutes, then add the stock. Simmer gently for 30 minutes. Add the tarragon, cover, and remove from the heat. Allow to steep for 5 minutes. Whisk in the sour cream. Strain the bisque through a fine-mesh sieve into a heatproof bowl. Add the lime juice, salt, and Sriracha sauce to taste. Keep warm on the back of the stove over a pan of hot water.

3. Heat the skillet in which you cooked the bacon over medium-high heat and add the teaspoon of butter. When the foam subsides, drop in the shrimp and cook, turning once, until they are pink and cooked through, about 30 seconds per side.

4. Ladle some squash bisque onto a heated plate. Top with some of the shrimp, a slice of bacon, crumbled, and a sprinkling of the seeds. Serve the squash pickles on the side.

Winter Squash Ravioli with Vegetables in Broth

Make this dish with frozen ravioli (recipe on following page) when the other vegetables are in season, or substitute whatever vegetables you happen to have available and make the dish at any time.

YIELD: **2 SERVINGS**

¼ cup one-inch pieces of **haricots verts**

4 **asparagus** stalks, cut into one-inch pieces, tips reserved separately

1 ear of fresh **white sweet corn**

6 **winter squash ravioli** (*page 177*)

2 medium firm ripe **tomatoes**, peeled, seeded, and coarsely chopped

2 **scallions**, white and green parts, chopped

4 leaves of fresh **basil**, shredded

1 teaspoon minced fresh **tarragon** leaves

2 cups **vegetable stock**

1. Bring a pot of water to a boil. Add a teaspoon of salt and the haricots. Boil 1 minute. Add the asparagus stems and continue cooking for two minutes. Add the asparagus tips. Cook 1 minute, then drain the vegetables in a colander. Rinse well under cold running water, drain, and reserve. Bring another pot of water to a boil. Drop in the ear of corn, and cook for five minutes. Drain. When the corn is cool enough to handle, stand it in a bowl and cut off the kernels. Reserve.

2. Bring a large pot of water to a boil. Add a tablespoon of salt and the ravioli. Cook 3 minutes, or until the ravioli float. Remove the ravioli with a slotted spoon, drain briefly, and transfer them to two serving bowls.

3. Meanwhile, heat the vegetable stock over medium heat. Add the tomatoes and scallions, a pinch of salt, and a few grinds of black pepper. Simmer while the ravioli are cooking. When the ravioli are done, add the prepared vegetables to the broth and warm until just heated through. Ladle the broth over the ravioli, sprinkle with the fresh herbs, and serve.

Winter Squash Ravioli

Wonton skins make perfect ravioli and can be used with a variety of fillings. The completed ravioli may be frozen on waxed paper on a baking sheet and stored in plastic bags in the freezer, where they will keep for three months.

½ cup roasted **winter squash** pulp *(page 244)*

¼ cup **mascarpone cheese**, softened

10 grinds of **white pepper**

5 grinds of **black pepper**

$\frac{1}{16}$ teaspoon of ground **mace**

30 **wonton wrappers**

1. Cream the first five ingredients together in a small bowl. This makes enough filling for 15 ravioli.

2. Lay out 15 of the wonton wrappers on a sheet pan covered with waxed paper. Place approximately 1 rounded teaspoon of the filling in the center of each wrapper. Seal the ravioli one by one. Wet your finger and moisten all four edges of the ravioli. Place another wonton wrapper on top of the one with the filling. Press down gently so that the filling spreads out a little and you are able to align the edges of the pasta. Seal the edges together by pressing them firmly with your fingers. You may need to remoisten here and there if they refuse to stick. Repeat until each of the ravioli is sealed.

3. Cover the prepared ravioli with another sheet of waxed paper. Place the sheet pan in the freezer overnight. The following day, remove the ravioli from the freezer, transfer to a reclosable storage bag, and return to the freezer.

4. To cook the ravioli, bring a large pot of water to a boil and add a tablespoon of salt. Drop in the frozen ravioli and cook gently for 3 minutes or until they float. Remove with a slotted spoon, drain, and serve with your favorite sauce.

Shrimp-Stuffed Butterbush Squash with Seafood Tomato Sauce

Burpee's Butterbush winter squash makes loads of perfect little butter-nuts with deep orange flesh. For this recipe, cut off the neck of the squash about three-quarters of an inch above the enlarged portion. Use the neck for another purpose. Wrapped in plastic wrap, it will keep several days in the refrigerator. You can also substitute acorn squash for the Butterbush.

YIELD: **2 SERVINGS**

The larger end of a **Butterbush squash**

1 teaspoon **vegetable oil**, approximately

1 package herb-seasoned **wild and long grain rice mix**, prepared according to package directions

1 tablespoon **coconut oil**

½ cup chopped **onions**

½ cup chopped **celery**

½ cup chopped **green bell pepper**

¼ teaspoon **garlic powder**

Freshly ground **black pepper**

½ cup toasted **green pepitas**, divided

8 large **wild Carolina shrimp**

¼ cup diced **celery**

¼ cup diced **shallots**

1 **bay leaf**

1 tablespoon **butter**

2 tablespoons minced **shallots**

1 tablespoon **all-purpose flour**

1 cup **shrimp stock**

½ cup **tomato sauce**

¼ teaspoon dried **tarragon** leaves *or* ¾ teaspoon fresh leaves

¼ cup fresh green **peas** *or* asparagus tips

1 tablespoon **butter**

(Continued on page 179)

1. Prepare the squash. Preheat the oven to 400°F. Cut a thin slice off the blossom end so the squash will stand upright. Set the squash on a cutting board and split it in half lengthwise. Using a melon baller or spoon, scoop out all the seeds and pulp. Brush the squash with oil inside and out. Place it skin side up in a baking pan. Set the pan in the middle of the oven and bake 15 minutes. Using tongs, turn one of the pieces over and check for doneness. It should be barely tender when pierced with a fork. If necessary, cook a few more minutes, checking frequently. When the squash is done, remove the pan from the oven and allow to cool.

2. Prepare the stuffing. You will not need all of the wild rice mix. Cover the remainder and store in the refrigerator. It reheats easily in the microwave and makes a good side dish on its own or dressed up with fresh-cooked vegetables.

3. Melt the coconut oil in a small skillet and cook the onions, celery, and bell pepper until the onions are translucent. Transfer to a bowl with 1 cup of the rice mixture, and add the garlic powder and several grinds of black pepper. Mix in ¼ cup of the toasted pepitas. Reserve.

4. Prepare the shrimp. Peel and devein the shrimp, reserving the shells in a small saucepan and discarding the veins. Cover and store the peeled shrimp in the refrigerator, preferably in a plastic bag on ice. To the reserved shells, add the celery, shallot, and bay leaf together with enough water to cover them. Bring to a simmer, reduce the heat, and cook gently, covered, for 30 minutes. Strain the stock into a heatproof bowl, discarding the solids. Reserve.

5. To make the sauce, melt the tablespoon of butter in a small saucepan over medium heat. Add the minced shallots and cook, stirring occasionally, for 2 minutes. Add the flour, stir to incorporate, and cook, stirring occasionally, for 1 minute. Add the shrimp stock, increase the heat, and continue to cook, stirring constantly, until the mixture is thickened and bubbling. Reduce the heat. Stir in the tomato sauce, tarragon, peas or asparagus, and salt and pepper to taste. Cook gently for 5 minutes. Remove the sauce from the heat and keep warm, covered.

6. Preheat the broiler. Melt another tablespoon of butter in a small skillet set over medium heat. Add the shrimp and toss, cooking them until they barely turn pink. Remove from the heat.

7. Fill the cavities of the squash with the rice mixture. Top each squash with four of the shrimp. Drizzle any pan juices from the shrimp evenly over the squash halves. Place the filled squashes on heatproof plates and run under the broiler for 1 minute, or until the shrimp begin to char in a spot or two. Remove from the oven, top with a generous portion of the tomato sauce, and serve immediately.

Traditional Thanksgiving Dressing

This recipe has been in my family for at least 100 years.

YIELD: **8 SERVINGS**

4 tablespoons **unsalted butter**

½ cup chopped **onion**

½ cup chopped **celery**

1½ cups **chicken broth**

1 teaspoon **salt**

1 teaspoon rubbed **sage**

1 teaspoon fresh **thyme** leaves

½ teaspoon dried **oregano** leaves

Freshly ground **black pepper**

6 cups crumbled day-old **cornbread** (*1 12-inch skillet*)

1. Preheat the oven to 350°F. Grease a 9 x 12-inch rectangular baking pan. Melt the butter in a large pot over medium heat and cook the onions and celery, stirring occasionally, until the onions are translucent but not browned, about 3 minutes. Add the broth and bring just to a simmer.

2. Meanwhile, in a large bowl, combine the other ingredients and stir well. Stir the dry ingredients into the pot. Gently stir the pot until all the dry ingredients are moistened. Turn the dressing into the prepared baking pan, gently spreading it into an even layer. Bake uncovered for 30 minutes.

NOTE: Stirring too vigorously or packing the dressing into the baking pan too firmly will result in a heavy, cake-like texture.

CELERY

A member of the large and useful parsley family, celery grows best in cool summer regions, although gardeners in the South and Southwest can successfully produce a crop if plants are started early enough. Celery seedlings are weak and slow-growing; therefore, they must be started indoors about three months before the last frost date. Move into the garden when the frost danger is past and the weather is mild. Sow the tiny seeds on the surface of small pots of growing medium and keep well watered. It may take three weeks for the seedlings to appear when the room temperature is around 65 to 70°F. When the seedlings have feathery true leaves, snip off all but the strongest plant in each pot. Feed with a soluble fertilizer solution at this point. When the plants are six inches tall, they are ready for their permanent spot in the garden. If the weather gets hot quickly where you live, try to place celery where it will receive some shade during the hottest part of the day. Space plants eight inches apart each way.

Celery is a bog plant and must have abundant moisture throughout the growing season. A growing medium rich in organic matter will give the best results, and it need not be exceptionally fertile. A small amount of balanced organic fertilizer sprinkled around the plants at transplant time is all the food they will need. Celery's main pest is slugs. See the section on controlling them in Chapter 6.

Harvest individual celery stalks from the outside of the bunch as you need them for the kitchen. As the weather warms up, harvest the entire plant, cutting it off at ground level with a sharp blade. Celery will keep well in a plastic bag in the refrigerator.

Celery Soup with Sweet Potatoes and Blue Cheese

The person who tested this recipe admitted she was at first skeptical, but became convinced that this soup is delicious after making it. Substitute peeled, chopped celery root for the celery for a slightly different flavor profile.

YIELD: **4 SERVINGS**

1 tablespoon **butter**

⅓ cup thinly sliced **onion**

1 cup chopped **celery**

2 cups **chicken stock**

¼ cup **heavy cream**

½ teaspoon **salt**

⅛ teaspoon freshly ground **black pepper**

1 cup cubed **sweet potato** *(preferably the white-fleshed variety)*

2 teaspoons **butter**

¼ cup crumbled **blue cheese**

Chervil leaves for garnish

1. Melt the butter in a soup pot over medium heat. Add the onion, cover, reduce the heat, and sweat until the onion is soft, about 3 minutes. Add the celery and continue to cook, covered, until it is softened, another 5 minutes. Add the stock, bring to a simmer, cover, and cook until the vegetables are very tender, 15 to 20 minutes.

2. While the soup simmers, bring a small pan of water to a rolling boil. Drop in the sweet potato cubes and boil 3 minutes. Drain in a colander and rinse quickly under cold water. Drain thoroughly and reserve.

3. Remove the soup from the heat and allow to cool at least 15 minutes. Transfer to a blender and purée. If you purée the soup with an immersion blender, no cooling period is necessary. Strain the soup back into the saucepan and place over low heat. Stir in the cream, salt, and pepper, and heat through. Do not allow the soup to boil. Taste and adjust the seasoning if needed. Keep warm while you finish cooking the potatoes.

4. Melt the 2 teaspoons of butter in a small skillet. Pat the potatoes dry with kitchen towels. When the foam subsides in the skillet, add the potatoes. Cook, turning occasionally, until the potatoes are nicely browned, about 6 minutes.

5. Ladle the soup into warmed bowls. With a slotted spoon, remove the potatoes from their skillet and distribute them evenly among the bowls. Similarly distribute the blue cheese, garnish with chervil leaves, and serve the soup at once.

Trader Vic's Chicken Salad

Trader Vic's has been around for eighty years. This recipe came to me from a friend who received it from a woman who claimed she refused to leave the restaurant until the chef yielded the recipe. It is doubtful, therefore, that this is the authentic dish, but who knows? Visit a Trader Vic's location and decide for yourself. Like all good chicken salads, this one gets plenty of crunch from celery.

YIELD: **4 SERVINGS**

1 skinless, **boneless chicken breast fillet**, poached and cubed, about ¾ cup

½ cup chopped **scallions**, white and green parts

½ cup diced **water chestnuts**

½ cup **mandarin orange** segments

½ cup diced **celery**

½ cup **mayonnaise**

¼ cup **sour cream**

1½ teaspoons **soy sauce**

Freshly ground **black pepper**

Packaged **chow mein noodles**

Fresh **cilantro**, chopped

1. Combine the chicken, scallions, water chestnuts, mandarin oranges, and celery in a large bowl. In a separate small bowl, combine the mayonnaise, sour cream, soy sauce, and a few grinds of pepper. Stir to combine, then pour over the chicken mixture. Toss gently to combine. Refrigerate until ready to serve.

2. Scatter some chow mein noodles on a baking sheet and place them in a preheated 350°F oven for a few minutes to crisp. Watch carefully and do not let them become too brown.

3. Serve the salad in individual bowls, topped with some toasted noodles and garnished with chopped cilantro.

Potato Stacks with Celery Sauce

As a first course or small plate, this dish would be appropriate for dinner guests. It comes together quickly and can star as a weeknight entrée, too.

YIELD: **2 SERVINGS**

1 large **baking potato**

1 tablespoon **safflower oil**

6 stalks **celery**, chopped

1 cup chopped **onion**

1 cup **vegetable stock**

1 **bay leaf**

6 **parsley** stems, chopped

6 whole **black peppercorns**

¼ teaspoon **salt**

1 tablespoon **safflower oil**

2 cups sliced **mushrooms**, any variety

½ cup chopped **onion**

1 clove **garlic**, minced

1 tablespoon **olive oil**

Minced fresh **parsley** for garnish

(Continued on page 185)

1. Bring a large saucepan of water to boil. Peel the potato and cut it crosswise into slices about ¼ inch thick. Drop the slices into the boiling water, adjust the heat, and simmer for 12 minutes. Drain the potatoes in a colander, rinse them under cold water to stop the cooking, drain again, and allow to cool. Reserve.

2. Heat one tablespoon of safflower oil in a saucepan over medium heat. Add the celery and onion, stir well, cover, and cook over low heat until the onions are soft, about 5 minutes. Add the stock, bay leaf, parsley stems, peppercorns, and salt. Bring to a simmer and cook gently, covered, until the vegetables are very tender, about 20 minutes. Remove the bay leaf. Cool the sauce for 15 minutes then transfer it to a blender jar and purée. If you use an immersion blender, there is no need to cool the sauce. Strain the sauce through a fine sieve, discarding any fibrous matter. Cover the sauce and keep it warm.

3. Preheat the oven to 375°F. Line a baking sheet with parchment.

4. In a small skillet, heat another tablespoon of safflower oil over medium heat. Add the mushrooms and onion and sauté until the onions are tender and any juices released by the mushrooms have almost evaporated. Add the garlic and continue to cook 1 minute longer. Remove the mushrooms from the heat and keep warm.

5. Spread the potato slices in an even layer on the prepared baking sheet. Brush with some of the olive oil. Place the sheet in the oven and bake for 6 minutes. Turn the slices with a spatula, brush with more olive oil, and return the sheet to the oven. Bake for an additional 6 minutes, or until golden brown on top.

6. To serve, place a potato slice in the center of a warmed serving plate. Top with some of the mushrooms and then another potato slice. Repeat with additional mushrooms and a third potato slice. Ladle the celery sauce over the potato stacks and garnish with minced parsley.

DILL

Dill is not only useful in the kitchen; its flowers are decorative in the garden and attract pollinators. Planting dill near other vegetables is thought by many to help deter insect pests. Growing dill could not be simpler. Just scatter the seeds where you want plants to grow. Do this around the frost date in your area, and the plants will appear when the time is right. The young seedlings have fine, feathery foliage, and they grow quickly once established. If you want seeds, let the plants get large enough to bloom. You can also harvest small amounts of foliage without harming them. If you primarily want the foliage, you can begin harvesting as soon as the plants are about a foot tall. Again, do not take too much—no more than 20 percent of the foliage from any one plant. Dill will grow in a container in a sunny window, but you are unlikely to get blooms that way. You can, however, get a jump on the season by planting dill indoors. Lightly harvest the leaves until all danger of frost is past, at which time you can transplant the herb to a garden bed.

The seeds of dill will change color from green to tan as they mature. Harvest the entire flower head when most of the seeds have changed. Drop the heads upside-down into a paper bag. Hang the bag to dry where it's warm and airy, and the seeds should fall off the stems. If not, encourage them by crushing the stems gently. Both dried stems and seeds carry good dill flavor.

Dilled Green Tomatoes or Green Beans

This recipe is a great way to use up the end-of-the-season tomatoes or beans. Select only perfect vegetables for the best quality pickles. Freshly picked homegrown dill produces a flavor that is impossible to duplicate with dried dill. These pickles brighten up winter dinners with their summery tang.

YIELD: **2 TO 3 PINTS**

Small, green hard **tomatoes** no larger than two inches in diameter *or* mature, well-filled green beans

A batch of Universal **Pickling Solution** (*page 233*)

Fresh, whole **garlic cloves**, peeled

Dill seeds *or* dill flower heads, fresh or dried

Bay leaves

Whole small **hot red peppers**, fresh or dried

1. Tomatoes can be used whole if they are as small as a golf ball. If larger, halve or quarter them. Just make sure there is no trace of ripening or they may become mushy. Beans should be washed and then blanched in boiling water for 3 minutes. Drain, then plunge into cold water to stop the cooking and set their color. Drain thoroughly before continuing.

2. Bring the pickling solution to a boil, remove from heat, and keep hot.

3. Pack the vegetables into clean, hot pint jars, adding along with them one garlic clove, one bay leaf, one teaspoon of dill seeds (or one head of dill), and one whole pepper per jar. Cover with pickling liquid, leaving ¼ inch of head space. Apply lids and process 15 minutes in a water bath, or store in the refrigerator without processing. Wait at least 2 weeks for the flavor to fully develop before consuming.

SAGE

Sage adds a special, savory note to many dishes, notably sausages, Thanksgiving dressing, and recipes using winter squash or sweet potatoes. Numerous varieties of sage can be found in garden centers in spring. Some of these are more decorative than flavorful. It is wise to taste a leaf to make sure the flavor is not too assertive. Better cultivars for the kitchen may be labeled as culinary sage to distinguish them from other types. A dwarf culinary form also exists, but it is not easy to find.

Different varieties of sage may exhibit different levels of winter hardiness. Sometimes plants are evergreen, but they may also be killed to the ground by harsh weather. Sage responds well to hard pruning and should be cut back in late winter before new growth emerges. Grow sage in any well-drained location. It makes a good companion for other Mediterranean herbs, such as rosemary and thyme. Like them, it needs only average moisture and little fertilizer. I typically sprinkle a couple tablespoons of balanced organic fertilizer on my herb bed in early spring each year, and then pay no further attention to the plants, other than pruning to keep them tidy.

Brown Butter and Sage Sauce

This extremely simple but delicious sauce goes great with pasta, sweet potatoes, winter squash, and carrots. Multiply the ingredients for the number of diners you are serving.

YIELD: **1 SERVING**

1 tablespoon **butter**

2 **sage leaves**, shredded thinly

Pinch of **salt**

½ teaspoon **lemon juice**

1. In a small skillet, heat the butter over medium heat until the foam subsides. Watching carefully, cook the butter until browned bits appear and a nutty fragrance develops. Add the sage and salt, stir well, and remove from the heat. Add the lemon juice and serve immediately.

TARRAGON

Genuine French tarragon does not produce seeds and must therefore be grown from cuttings. It is one of the most useful and prolific herbs you can grow. Start with a plant or two from your local garden center, setting them into well-drained soil of average fertility. You can create a growing bed just for the Mediterranean herbs, if you have room, for tarragon thrives under conditions similar to those needed by rosemary, thyme, oregano, and sage. Watering is required only if the soil begins to dry out completely. Add a small amount of fertilizer to the bed in early spring, but do not overdo it. Too much nitrogen will lead to rampant growth and poor flavor in tarragon and its companion herbs. Although several of these herbs remain in leaf all winter, tarragon will die to the ground after frost arrives.

After a couple of years, your tarragon clump will need dividing. Replant a portion from the outer edge of the clump and use the remainder for another bed or as a gift to a friend.

Gouda Mac 'n' Cheese with Fresh Tarragon

The ultimate comfort food gets all dressed up with gouda and fresh tarragon. Perfect as a side for anything from barbecue to veggie burgers, this mac is company good.

YIELD: **6 TO 8 SERVINGS**

Butter for the dishes

1½ cups **whole wheat pasta**

2 tablespoons **butter**

2 tablespoons all-purpose **flour**

2 cups **whole milk**

2 cups shredded raw-milk **Gouda-style domestic cheese**

1 teaspoon minced fresh **tarragon leaves**

¼ cup fine dry **bread crumbs**

2 tablespoons grated domestic **Parmesan cheese**

1 tablespoon **butter**, melted

1. Preheat the oven to 350 °F. Grease a 2-quart casserole dish and a large, heatproof bowl using dabs of vegetable oil. Set aside.

2. Bring a large pot of water to a rolling boil and add a tablespoon of salt and the pasta. Cook 9 minutes. Drain the pasta and transfer to the oiled bowl. Reserve.

3. In a saucepan over medium heat, melt the butter. Whisk in the flour and cook, whisking, to produce a roux, about 3 minutes. Add the milk slowly and continue to stir until you have a smooth, bubbling Bechamel sauce. Add the cheese and continue to stir until it melts. Stir in the tarragon. Pour the sauce into the bowl with the pasta, mix well, and transfer to the prepared casserole.

4. In a small bowl, combine the breadcrumbs and Parmesan. Stir in the melted butter, then transfer the topping to the surface of the casserole. Bake until brown and bubbly, about 30 minutes.

NOTE: For a Southern take on the Italian classic arancini, chill leftover mac 'n' cheese overnight. Cut into small squares. Dip the squares in flour, then in beaten egg, and finally in dry breadcrumbs or panko. Coat the squares well on all sides. Place on a rack and chill for at least one hour before cooking. Fry the squares in hot fat until golden, and serve with your favorite hot sauce.

Marinated Cheese with Tarragon Vinegar

Infuse cheese with herbal flavors and create a sensation at your next dinner party. This dish could be part of an antipasto platter.

YIELD: **4 SERVINGS**

1 cup cubes of any firm, **white cheese**, such as feta, Monterey jack, *or* white cheddar

¼ teaspoon dried **basil** leaves, *or* 1 teaspoon chopped fresh basil

¼ teaspoon dried **oregano** leaves, *or* 1 teaspoon chopped fresh oregano

¼ teaspoon dried **thyme** leaves, *or* 1 teaspoon fresh thyme leaves

¼ teaspoon dried **hot pepper flakes**, more if desired

Freshly ground **black pepper**

½ cup **extra virgin olive oil**

3 tablespoons **tarragon vinegar** *(page 242)*

1. In a suitable container with a fitted cover, toss the cheese cubes with the herbs, pepper flakes, and a few grinds of black pepper. In a small bowl, combine the oil and tarragon vinegar. Whisk to emulsify and pour over the cheese, turning to coat the cheese well with the dressing. Cover the container, place in the refrigerator, and allow to marinate overnight or up to 3 days before serving.

CHAPTER 4

The Edible Landscape

Expanding your food garden to include in-ground outdoor growing spaces affords you the greatest opportunity for increased diversity and productivity for all crops. All of the vegetables mentioned in the previous sections will grow well in properly-prepared garden beds. The plants mentioned in this section can also, in some cases, be grown in raised beds or containers but will do much better if grown in the ground.

Some people turn their entire property into a food-producing space. That is a great idea if you have the time and energy to devote to the project. You can probably produce all the fruits, herbs, and vegetables you require, provided you dry, can, and/or freeze a substantial amount of the bounty.

Many gardeners may choose to include only one or two of the plants discussed in this chapter. It is worthwhile to consider that all these food crops have features that can be integrated into existing landscapes. For example, a dwarf fruit tree can stand in for any other small-stature tree, such as a Japanese maple or dogwood. A patch of asparagus, its feathery foliage waving yellow-gold upon the autumn breeze, can take the place of a clump of ornamental grasses.

New Issues

Gardening in the ground raises a few new issues not presented by either container or raised-bed cultivation. In particular, you will need to examine the condition of the existing soil, decide on appropriate amendments, if any, and make preparations at the right time for planting in your location. In other words, an in-ground garden needs more careful planning than a smaller-scale garden.

It is neither necessary nor desirable to use only one approach to growing food. Most avid gardeners have some plants growing in containers, some in raised beds, and an in-ground patch of strawberries or rhubarb somewhere on the property. As with any large home-based project, the key is to choose a combination of techniques that makes sense for the types of food crops you want to grow. For example, if I wished to grow only fine-quality tomatoes, I would probably use only raised beds outdoors. If I wanted only a few herbs, I would use pots on the deck. However, if I wanted cherries, I would put the trees in the ground.

BLACKBERRIES

Like all other bramble fruits, blackberries bloom and produce fruit only on one-year-old growth. Blackberries should be grown with a trellis arrangement that allows you to separate the previous year's canes from the current year's. Two rows of posts with two parallel wires running along each side is the simplest approach. You tie the first year's canes to one side's wires and the following year's canes to the opposite side, alternating with each subsequent year.

Prepare the blackberry bed in fall or late winter prior to setting out plants in spring. If the soil is too sandy or contains heavy clay, add organic matter to improve the water retention properties. Spread a balanced organic fertilizer at the rate recommended by the manufacturer on the bed about a month before you set out plants. Plants in nursery containers should be set at the same level as the plant was growing in the container. Bare root plants should be set so the crown, where roots and stems converge, is just below the soil surface. Dig a hole large enough to accommodate the root ball, after loosening the roots and spreading them out. Set the plant in the hole, firm the soil well, and water thoroughly. Keep the bed irrigated if rainfall is less than one inch per week during the growing season.

The second year after planting, blooms will appear in spring on the old canes. Shortly thereafter, new canes will appear. Separate the new canes and tie them to one side of your trellis. In fall, after at least two frosts have occurred, cut all of the two-year canes down to the ground. They will never bloom again. You want to encourage the plant to produce more canes next spring. After pruning, apply two inches of loose, organic mulch over the bed. Each spring when new growth is emerging, feed the bed with balanced organic fertilizer.

Blackberry Cobbler

Cobblers are easy to make. Other summer fruits can be substituted for the blackberries.

1½ cups all-purpose **flour**

1½ teaspoons **baking powder**

¾ cup **lard**

3 tablespoons **ice water**, approximately

6 cups **blackberries**

1½ cups **sugar**

4 tablespoons **butter**

1. Butter a 9 x 9-inch baking pan.

2. Combine the flour, baking powder, and salt in a mixing bowl. Cut in the lard with a pastry blender or two knives until the mixture resembles coarse crumbs. Using a dinner fork, toss the mixture with the ice water, adding it a little at a time until the dough comes together in a ball.

3. Roll the dough in plastic wrap and chill at least one hour.

4. Divide dough in two pieces, with about two-thirds for the bottom of the pan. Roll this piece out between two pieces of plastic wrap. Peel off the top plastic and use the other as an aid in handling the dough. Line the baking pan, including the sides. Keep the remaining dough piece wrapped in plastic in the refrigerator until you need it.

4. Wash and pick over the blackberries carefully, then drain them thoroughly on kitchen towels. Blot any excess moisture. Transfer the berries to a bowl and toss with the sugar until a few berries are bruised and some juice appears. Spoon the mixture into the unbaked crust and then dot the top with the butter.

5. Roll out the remaining crust, cover the berries, and cut slits to allow steam to escape. Bake at 325°F for 1 hour or until golden brown.

LEMON VERBENA

This subtropical shrub is not reliably winter hardy north of Zone 8. It is a bit unwieldy for container cultivation, unless you have a greenhouse to winter it. I therefore recommend planting it outdoors and growing it as an annual in areas where it will not survive winter cold. In a single season, a small plant from the garden center will grow to a four-foot-diameter shrub, with more leaves than you can probably use.

Lemon verbena has a unique lemon flavor with floral undertones that go beautifully with fruits and cheeses. It retains flavor well when dried and can be used for a refreshing tea. Not fussy about soil type, it does not do well with constantly moist soil. Irrigate only if rainfall is insufficient. Plants grow rapidly and produce a lot of leaves, and thus benefit from biweekly applications of soluble fertilizer solution. Harvest the leaves as you need them. Near the end of the season, cut the entire plant and use the leaves to make jelly, or dry them for future use. In long-summer areas, the plants may produce white or pale lavender flowers that are flavorful and can be used as a garnish.

Fresh Fruit with Lemon Verbena Syrup

Sugar syrup provides an excellent medium for extracting flavor from herbs, zest, or spices. Lemon verbena gives syrup a flavor that goes especially well with fresh fruit.

YIELD: **APPROXIMATELY 1 CUP SYRUP**

1 cup **sugar**

1 cup **water**

1 cup loosely packed **lemon verbena leaves**

Fresh fruit

1. Place the sugar and water in a saucepan. Set the pan over medium heat, cook, and stir until the sugar dissolves. Bring the liquid to a simmer and cook 1 minute.

2. Remove the pan from the heat, add the lemon verbena, and cover the pan. Allow to cool to room temperature and then refrigerate overnight.

3. The following day, strain the syrup, discarding the lemon verbena. The syrup will keep in the refrigerator for a week. Serve it drizzled over any fresh seasonal fruit.

NOTE: You can use this same recipe to make herb syrups from mint, lemongrass, or basil, among others. Simply substitute one cup of loosely packed herb for the lemon verbena.

Steamed Lemon Verbena Fish

This recipe can easily be multiplied to serve additional diners.

2 6-ounce filets of firm-fleshed **white fish**, such as flounder, grouper, sea bass, or halibut

8 **lemon verbena leaves**

4 slices fresh **ginger**, each about the size of a quarter

6 whole **coriander seeds**

½ teaspoon **sesame oil**

¼ teaspoon **kosher salt**

Freshly ground **black pepper**

1. Preheat the oven to 375°F.

2. Lay out two sheets of heavy-duty aluminum foil on a work surface. Place a fish filet in the center of each piece of foil. Top the fish with the lemon verbena leaves, ginger, coriander, and sesame oil, dividing the ingredients equally. Sprinkle everything with the salt and a few grinds of pepper. Bring the sides of the foil up to the center and fold the edges together. Fold the ends over to seal the packets.

3. Place the packets on a baking sheet, set in the oven, and cook for 15 to 20 minutes. Open the packets, lift the fish out with a spatula, and transfer it to serving plates. Drizzle the juices from each packet over the fish, discarding the solids.

OREGANO

Although oregano will grow in a pot, its tendency to spread makes it better suited to an in-ground herb garden. It is not fussy about soil type, although it prefers a well-drained, slightly sandy soil with only a little organic matter. Wet roots will rot, so the plant should be irrigated only if the soil is dry to the touch when you insert your forefinger to the first joint. Locate the plants where they will receive full sun. Oregano is a good companion for the other Mediterranean herbs: rosemary, thyme, sage, and tarragon.

Oregano comes in a number of cultivars and selections, with some of them being more decorative than flavorful. Many cooks prefer Greek oregano for its distinctive aroma and tall, straight stems from which the leaves are easy to strip. For best results, start your patch with plants of a named cultivar. Although they cost less, seedlings vary considerably in flavor. It is a good idea to taste a bit of leaf to make sure you get what you were hoping for. An established oregano patch is relatively carefree. If you live in a warm location, plants will likely bloom at the end of the season. At this time, the flavor becomes harsh. It is best to let them bloom and then shear the plants off at ground level. They will remain relatively short through the cold months and then return reinvigorated the following spring.

Chicken Minestrone

Summer vegetables and oregano team up in this flavor-packed soup.

YIELD: **4 SERVINGS**

2 boneless, **skinless chicken breasts**

3 cups **chicken stock**

½ cup diced **carrots**

½ cup diced **zucchini** *or* other summer squash

½ cup diced **green beans**

½ cup diced **scallions**

½ cup peeled, seeded, and diced **tomatoes**

1 **bay leaf**

1 tablespoon chopped fresh **oregano**

2 tablespoons fine **egg noodles** *or* small pasta

1 tablespoon chopped fresh **parsley**

1. Place the chicken breasts and the stock in a medium saucepan. Set the pan over medium heat, bring to a simmer, and cook, regulating the heat as necessary, until the chicken is fully cooked, about 25 minutes.

2. Using tongs, remove the chicken to a plate. Add all the vegetables, bay leaf, and oregano to the stock in the saucepan. Bring to a boil, adjust the heat, and simmer 20 minutes.

3. Meanwhile, chop the chicken into bite-size pieces. Add the chicken and egg noodles to the stock. Cook until the noodles are done, about 6 minutes, depending upon the type of noodle or pasta used.

4. Ladle the soup into bowls and garnish with chopped parsley.

Greek Salad Pizza

Among the better ideas from the Tomato Head Restaurant in Knoxville, Tennessee, is a pizza topped with ingredients you might find on a Greek-style salad. Here is my version of this pizza. For two servings, you need a ball of dough about the size of an apple.

YIELD: **2 SERVINGS**

Pizza dough
(*page 246*)

Olive oil

1 cup baby **spinach** leaves

½ cup **arugula** leaves

1 firm, ripe **tomato**, cored and thinly sliced

1 small **red onion**, trimmed, thinly sliced, and separated into rings

6 pitted **Kalamata olives**, chopped

2 teaspoons **red wine vinegar**

1 tablespoon chopped fresh **oregano** leaves

½ cup crumbled **feta cheese**

1. Preheat the oven to 500°F. Position a rack in the top half of the oven.

2. On a foil-lined baking sheet, pat out the dough to form a circle about 12 inches in diameter.

3. Brush the dough with olive oil. Sprinkle the spinach and arugula leaves evenly over the surface of the dough. Top the leaves with slices of tomato and onion rings. (Depending upon your preference, you may not want to add all these vegetables.) Sprinkle the Kalamata olives evenly over the vegetables, followed by the vinegar and oregano. Finally, top the pie with the feta cheese. Drizzle another teaspoon or two of olive oil over the pizza.

4. Bake until the top is brown and bubbly, about 10 to 15 minutes.

SAFFRON

The world's most expensive spice, saffron is actually fairly easy to grow. You need a good-sized patch to make the effort worth the trouble, but if you can spare about twenty-five square feet in a sunny, well-drained spot, you can grow your own. Saffron is the anthers, or male flower parts, of a species of autumn-blooming crocus. The bulbs are widely available and are planted in summer, when they are dormant. Set them about six inches apart and three inches deep. They can be over-planted with summer blooming annual flowers, as long as the annuals do not need too much water. Keeping the bed too wet in summer will rot the saffron bulbs.

When the foliage pokes through the soil in late summer, remove the overplanting to give the saffron all the room. When the blooms appear, use tweezers to pluck the anthers, three from each flower. The saffron can be used immediately or dried for future use. It will dry successfully simply lying in a plate on the counter, covered with a cloth to protect it from dust. Like its spring-blooming cousins, saffron will benefit from an application of bone meal each year after the plants bloom.

Pennsylvania Dutch Chicken Turnover

Deep-dish chicken pie is a Pennsylvania Dutch specialty, and saffron often turns up in recipes for it. Here is a recipe that is better suited to a smaller household and a weeknight meal. For even quicker results, use a refrigerated pastry crust.

YIELD: **2–3 SERVINGS**

Crust

1 cup all-purpose **flour**

½ teaspoon **salt**

6 tablespoons **butter**

3 tablespoons **lard**

3 tablespoons **ice water**, or a little more

Filling

2 boneless, **skinless chicken breast fillets**

2 cups **chicken stock**

1 **bay leaf**

¼ teaspoon **saffron** threads

1 tablespoon **warm water**

2 tablespoons **butter**

¼ cup chopped **onion**

½ cup sliced **celery**

½ cup sliced **carrots**

2 tablespoons **flour**

1 tablespoon chopped fresh **parsley**

½ teaspoon **salt**

Freshly ground **black pepper**

(Continued on page 205)

1. Chill all the ingredients for the crust, along with the bowl, for at least an hour before you begin.

2. Make the crust by combining the flour and salt in a bowl. With a pastry blender, cut in the butter and lard until the mixture resembles coarse crumbs. Using a fork, toss the mixture with the ice water until the dough forms a ball. Wrap the dough in plastic wrap and refrigerate for at least 30 minutes while you make the filling.

3. For the filling, place the chicken breasts, the stock, and the bay leaf in a saucepan. Bring to a boil, adjust the heat, and simmer, covered, for 25 minutes. Remove the chicken, reserving the broth, and allow it to cool. Discard the bay leaf. When the chicken is cool enough to handle, cut it into cubes and set aside.

4. Crumble the saffron into a small bowl. Add the warm water and stir to extract the flavor. Set aside.

5. Melt the butter in a saucepan set over medium heat. When the foam subsides, add the onion and cook, stirring occasionally, until they have softened, about 2 minutes. Add the celery and carrots and cook until the onions are translucent, about 3 minutes more. Stir in the flour and cook, stirring, until the fat and flour are well combined. Slowly add one cup of the reserved chicken stock and cook, stirring, until the mixture comes to a boil. It will be thicker than gravy. Add the saffron and water, parsley, salt, pepper, and reserved chicken. Stir to combine, then set aside to cool slightly.

6. Preheat the oven to 350°F. Remove the pastry dough from the refrigerator and roll it out into a circle about 9 inches in diameter. Spoon the filling onto one half of the pastry circle, leaving a 1-inch margin around the edge. Brush the edge of the circle with water, fold over the pastry to enclose the filling, and pinch the edges to seal. With a sharp knife, cut three slits into the top of the pastry. Carefully transfer the turnover to a parchment-lined baking sheet.

7. Bake for 25 to 30 minutes, or until golden brown. Cut into slices and serve hot.

NOTE: *Use leftover chicken broth to make gravy for the dish, if you like.*

ASPARAGUS

A member of the lily family, asparagus has been consumed by humans for centuries. It is said that when Augustus Caesar wanted quick action, he demanded results "in as little time as it takes to cook asparagus." Although you have to wait two years to harvest your first spears, an asparagus patch is well worth the wait if you enjoy the unique flavor of this vegetable. A half dozen plants in a twenty-five-square-foot bed will produce enough for two to enjoy as an occasional treat. For a bumper crop, you will need at least 100 square feet, or about thirty plants. Purchase asparagus crowns from a garden center. You can start plants from seeds, but the seedlings are delicate and slow growing. Purchasing crowns not only ensures healthy plants, but you gain a year. Seedlings require three years to harvest, crowns only two.

Asparagus likes rich, well-drained soil in full sun. Prepare the bed well and the asparagus will reward you for decades to come. Dig down a foot and spread a layer of good compost on the bottom of the hole. Add two tablespoons of balanced organic fertilizer, and mix it and the compost into the soil. Set the asparagus plants with their roots spread out in a natural manner so that the crown is about three inches below the surface. Refill the hole, firming the soil well and taking care not to damage the crowns. Water thoroughly to settle the soil and to eliminate any air pockets. When the shoots begin to produce feathery foliage, feed them again by sprinkling another tablespoon of organic fertilizer around the base of the plants. Do not harvest during the first season. The following spring you can begin to harvest, cutting spears below the soil line. Take care to avoid cutting into the crown.

Asparagus "Rockefeller"

The recipe for Oysters Rockefeller, created at Antoine's in New Orleans, remains a secret. Numerous versions have been published, though none can claim authenticity. I have adapted the idea of sumptuous toppings from that famous creation for a dish of asparagus set on a savory rice cake.

YIELD: **4 SERVINGS**

Prepare a day or two in advance:

1 pound **asparagus**

1 **onion**, chopped

1 stalk **celery**, chopped

1 **bay leaf**

1 box herb-seasoned **wild rice mix**

Rice cakes

1 cup cooked **wild rice mix**

¼ cup chopped **walnuts**, toasted (*page 244*)

¼ cup **pepitas**, toasted

1 tablespoon all-purpose **flour**

¼ teaspoon granulated **garlic**

1 **scallion**, white and green parts, finely chopped

Pinch of dried **thyme**

Salt

Freshly ground **black pepper**

1 **egg**

2 tablespoons **milk**

Oil for frying

"Rockefeller" Sauce

½ cup frozen **peas**, thawed

1 teaspoon **unsalted butter**

1 cup **heavy cream**

¼ teaspoon dried **tarragon** leaves, crumbled (*or ¾ teaspoon fresh*)

Freshly ground **white pepper**

2 teaspoons **unsalted butter**

Shredded **Parmesan cheese**

Poached **eggs**, 1 or 2 per serving

2 tablespoons finely chopped fresh **parsley**

(*Continued on page 208*)

1. Rinse the asparagus and snap off the bottom ends. Set the stalks upright in a jar, with the root ends in about an inch of water, until you are ready to cook them. A pinch of sugar added to the water will improve the flavor.

2. Place the asparagus bottom ends, onion, celery, and bay leaf in a saucepan and cover with water. Bring to a simmer, adjust the heat, and cook 30 minutes. Strain the stock, discarding the solids after pressing down on them to extract all the flavor.

3. Return the stock to the heat and bring it to a boil, drop in the asparagus stalks, and cook gently for 3 minutes.

4. Remove the pot from the heat and add a cup of cold water to stop the cooking. Set the pot in an ice water bath to cool it quickly to room temperature. Cover and refrigerate the asparagus in the stock until you are ready to use it.

5. Cook the wild rice mix according to the label directions. Cool it in the pan, fluff with a fork, and store covered and refrigerated until you make the rice cakes.

Final preparation and assembly:

Rice Cakes:

1. Combine the rice, nuts, flour, garlic, scallion, and thyme in a bowl. Season to taste with salt and pepper.

2. In a small bowl, beat the egg with the milk until well combined. Pour over the dry ingredients and mix well with a wooden spoon. Cover the bowl with plastic wrap and place it in the refrigerator to chill, at least 1 hour.

3. Preheat the oven to 200°F. Place a large, heavy skillet over medium heat and coat the bottom well with oil. Form the rice mixture into patties and fry a few at a time, turning once, until they are nicely browned on both sides. Transfer the patties as they are cooked to a baking sheet lined with paper towels and place in the oven to keep warm.

"Rockefeller" Sauce:

1. In a small saucepan, melt the butter. Add the peas, stir until just heated through, and then add the cream, tarragon, and white pepper. Cook gently until slightly thickened. Taste and add salt if needed. Keep the creamed peas warm until you are ready to serve.

2. In a small skillet, melt 2 teaspoons of butter over low heat. Add some of the previously cooked asparagus and toss to reheat.

3. Place one or two rice cakes on a heated serving plate. Top each cake with some of the asparagus, followed by some of the creamed peas. Sprinkle with parmesan cheese and top with poached eggs. Garnish with chopped parsley and serve immediately.

Asparagus Wrapped with Tennessee Prosciutto

Thinly sliced country ham has been dubbed Tennessee prosciutto by aficionados. When you try it, you will understand why.

YIELD: **2 SERVINGS**

8 fresh **asparagus spears**

1 center slice Tennessee **country ham**, preferably Benton's

Freshly ground **black pepper**

2 tablespoons **Coca-Cola** *(regular, not diet)*

1. Grease a baking dish. Preheat the oven to 375°F.

2. Holding an asparagus spear in one hand, bend back the stalk near the bottom until it snaps off. Save the bottom ends for the stock pot. Cut the ham into strips about ½ inch wide and 6 inches long. Wrap each spear with a strip or two of ham, beginning below the tip and wrapping the spear in a spiral. As each spear is wrapped, place it with the ends of the ham on the underside in the prepared baking dish. Sprinkle the asparagus with a few grinds of black pepper.

3. Place the dish in the oven and cook until the ham begins to brown, about 10 minutes. Remove the pan from the oven.

4. Taking care to avoid the steam, pour the Coca-Cola over the asparagus and return to the oven for another 2 or 3 minutes, or until the liquid has almost evaporated. Serve immediately as a first course.

BLUEBERRIES

Blueberries are native to North America. Their wild cousins, from which domesticated blueberries were developed, are known as huckleberries. Gardeners who wish to grow blueberries should choose plants adapted to their location. Highbush blueberries are native to mountainous areas and do best where summers are cool. They make the largest and most productive bushes. Lowbush and rabbiteye blueberries are better adapted to warm-summer areas. Recently, container-size blueberries have been introduced to the home-gardening market and are proving popular. These diminutive hybrids can be grown throughout most of the United States.

All blueberries require strongly acidic, organically rich soil. Because few other fruits or perennial crops like these conditions, blueberries should be grown in containers or in a separate bed designed just for them. The soil for blueberries should contain added peat moss and pine bark fines/compost, and the bushes should be mulched with pine needles or pine bark chips. Annual fertilization should be done with a formulation intended for acid-loving plants. Select at least two blueberry plants, because cross pollination, while not always required, will increase production. Set plants at least two feet apart, four feet apart for the larger cultivars. Blueberries can be incorporated into plantings of ornamentals that like the same conditions. Blueberry bushes will produce a few berries the first season, but their productivity will increase to a peak in their third or fourth year.

Meyer Lemon Curd
and Blueberry Tart

Lemon curd and blueberries seem made for each other, as this luscious summer dessert amply demonstrates. Meyer lemons are actually a type of tangerine, and the juice is not as tart as a regular lemon's. If you use regular lemons, increase the sugar to 1 cup.

YIELD: **4 SERVINGS**

1 9-inch round **pie crust**

2 **eggs**, beaten

¾ cup **sugar**

½ cup freshly squeezed Meyer **lemon juice**

2 teaspoons finely minced Meyer **lemon zest**

3 tablespoons **butter**, cut in small bits and thoroughly chilled

1 pint **blueberries**

1 cup **sugar**

½ teaspoon ground **cinnamon**

¼ teaspoon ground **cloves**

1. Line a 9-inch tart pan with removable bottom with the pie crust. Prick the crust in several places with a fork. Place a circle of parchment on the crust and top this with baking stones or beans. Bake the crust in a preheated 450°F oven until lightly browned, about 9 minutes. Remove and let cool on a rack. Remove the parchment paper and weight.

2. Place the eggs, sugar, juice, and zest in a heavy-bottomed saucepan and cook over medium-low heat, stirring constantly with a wire whisk, until the curd is thickened, about 8 to 10 minutes.

3. Remove the pan from the heat and whisk in the chilled butter, a bit at a time, waiting until each piece is fully incorporated before adding another. Cool the lemon curd to room temperature then cover and refrigerate. It will keep at least a week in the refrigerator.

4. Place the blueberries, sugar, cinnamon, and cloves in a medium saucepan and set the pan over medium heat. Cook, stirring occasionally, until the blueberries release some juice and the sugar is incorporated. Bring the mixture to a boil while stirring, and then remove the pan from the heat. Cool to room temperature.

5. Spread a layer of the lemon curd on the bottom of the prepared crust, top with a layer of the blueberry mixture. Chill until ready to serve. Save any leftover fillings for another use.

Seafood Bisque with Blueberries

We don't often think of blueberries with seafood, but the sweet-tart flavor of blueberries complements perfectly the sweetness of the scallops and crabmeat. This recipe was inspired by a first course we enjoyed at the Victoria Inn in Anniston, Alabama. For a less formal presentation, skip the pastry cups and serve the bisque with oyster crackers.

YIELD: **4 SERVINGS**

1 stick **butter**

¼ cup **shallots**

¼ cup all-purpose **flour**

16 ounces bottled **clam juice**

Sprig of fresh **tarragon**

¼ pound **bay scallops**

1 6-ounce can pasteurized **lump crabmeat**

1 cup **half-and-half**

3 tablespoons **Madeira**

¼ teaspoons **salt**

Freshly ground **white pepper**

Frozen **puff pastry cups**

½ cup fresh **blueberries**, washed and dried

Finely chopped **scallions**

1. In a large saucepan set over medium heat, melt the butter. When the foam subsides, add the shallots and cook, stirring, until they are translucent, about 3 minutes. Add the flour and stir well to combine. Cook, stirring, for a minute, in order to eliminate the raw flour taste. Remove the pan from the heat and set aside.

2. In a second saucepan, combine the bay scallops with the tarragon and the clam juice. Bring to a boil, cook 1 minute, and add the crab meat. Continue to cook another minute. Cover the pan, remove from the heat, and allow the seafood to poach for 10 minutes. Remove the tarragon sprig.

3. Return the first saucepan to medium low heat. Slowly add the seafood mixture, stirring well to incorporate the roux into the liquid. Heat the soup just to the boiling point. Cook gently, stirring constantly, until it is thickened. Add the half-and-half, Madeira, salt, and pepper. Keep the soup hot, but do not allow it to boil after adding the half-and-half. Taste it and adjust the seasoning as needed.

4. While the soup cooks, bake the pastry cups according to the package directions.

5. Set a pastry cup in the center of a warmed soup plate. Ladle the seafood bisque into the cup, allowing some of it to spill over into the plate. Scatter some blueberries on top of the bisque and garnish with the chopped scallions. Serve piping hot.

TREE FRUITS

Tree fruits include apples, cherries, peaches, plums, pears, and citrus. While a few of these categories include varieties small enough to adapt to container cultivation, the majority of cultivars will be represented among dwarf trees suited to a small property or side yard. Citrus, by and large, are not cold hardy, while apples and pears need a period of cold in order to bloom and set fruit. Gardeners are limited by their climate as to which of these tree fruits they can successfully grow. That said, within any category you can find a remarkable abundance of cultivars. Most of them will require a pollinator, that is, a second tree of a similar but often not the exact same variety. Even those varieties that are said to be self-fertile will produce a bigger harvest if cross pollinated. Therefore, be sure you have room for at least two trees before embarking on your backyard orchard project. Citrus, although limited to mild winter areas, do not typically require a pollinator in order to set fruit.

All fruit trees require feeding, pruning, and often spraying. The labor required to bring in a good crop is significant, but the rewards of freshly picked apples or plums make the trouble worth it for dedicated gardeners. It is impossible to give universal recommendations in such a brief discussion. Research online to discover the fruit tree varieties that are best suited to your location, and focus your attention on those. Poorly adapted cultivars will be disappointing, no matter how much work you put into them.

Campfire Apples

I learned how to make this old standby when I was in the Boy Scouts, and it remains one of my favorite ways to prepare apples.

YIELD: **1 SERVINGS**

1 large **apple**

¼ teaspoon ground **cinnamon**

Pinch of ground **nutmeg**

¼ cup **dark brown sugar**

2 tablespoons **raisins**

1 teaspoon **butter**

1. Preheat the oven to 350°F.

2. Cut off the top of the apple in such a way as to leave the stem attached. Make the cut below the level of the stem depression. Using a melon baller, first core the apple, discarding the core, then enlarge the cavity, transferring the apple flesh to a small bowl.

3. Sprinkle the cavity with cinnamon. Chop the apple flesh and mix it with brown sugar then mix in the raisins. Pack this mixture into the cavity and top with the butter. Replace the top of the apple.

4. Wrap the apple in heavy-duty aluminum foil and bake for 30 minutes. Remove and allow to cool. The apple will continue to cook as it cools. Serve warm.

NOTE: For some reason, the apple is even better if cooked in the ashes at the edge of a campfire underneath a canopy of stars.

Grilled Peaches with Blue Cheese

We are not accustomed to thinking of peaches as a first course, but why not? This recipe can be easily multiplied to serve additional diners.

YIELD: **2 SERVINGS**

1 large freestone **peach**

Safflower oil

Freshly ground **black pepper**

2 ounces **blue cheese**, softened

Basil syrup (*page 88*)

1 teaspoon minced fresh **basil** leaves

1. Prepare the grill.

2. Split the peach in half and remove the pit. Brush the inner surfaces of the peach with safflower oil.

3. Place the peaches cut side down on the grill and cook, shifting position once, for 2 minutes, or until they have grill marks. Remove from the grill with tongs and transfer, cut side up, to serving plates.

4. Grind a little pepper over each peach. Fill the cavity with blue cheese, drizzle the syrup over, garnish with the basil leaves, and serve.

Cherry Barbecue Sauce

I would be run out of Memphis, not to mention Knoxville, if I proposed this as barbecue sauce to any of our diehard barbecue experts. Nevertheless, it is pretty darn good on slow-cooked pork or beef. This sauce contains a lot of sugar. If applied during the cooking process it may burn.

YIELD: **ABOUT 1 PINT**

2 cups **cherry preserves** (*page 239*)

1 cup **tomato sauce**

¼ cup prepared **chili sauce**

2 tablespoons **hot sauce**

1 teaspoon **Worcestershire sauce**

1 teaspoon coarse-grained **mustard**

1 teaspoon **soy sauce**

1. Combine all ingredients in a saucepan. Bring to a simmer, stirring constantly. Cook 1 minute, stirring constantly.

2. Remove from the heat and allow to cool. The flavor is better if it sits overnight.

Poached Pears
with Mint Mascarpone

Poached pears seem to have just the right combination of firmness and silkiness, all shrouded in floral and spice flavors. The mint and mascarpone filling creates a creamy counterpoint to the slightly al dente pear.

YIELD: **2 SERVINGS**

1 cup **water**

1 cup **sugar**

¼ cup **Riesling**

1 piece of **stick cinnamon**, about 1 inch long

1 **allspice berry**

1 large **pear**, such as Bosc

¼ cup **mascarpone**, softened

1 tablespoon **mint syrup***
(*page 88*)

1. Place the water, sugar, Riesling, and spices in a large saucepan. Bring to a simmer, stirring constantly, until the sugar dissolves. Raise the heat and bring to a boil. With tongs, slip the pear into the boiling syrup, reduce the heat, and simmer 1 minute. With the tongs, turn the pear over and simmer another 30 seconds. Cover the pan, remove it from the heat, and allow to cool to room temperature. Keep covered and refrigerated until ready to serve.

2. Remove the pear from the syrup and slice it in half lengthwise. Slice a thin slice off the skin side of each half so the fruit will sit on a plate without rolling over. Scoop out the core with a melon baller and discard it.

3. Mix the mascarpone with the mint syrup, and fill the cavity with the mixture. Serve the pears drizzled with a little of the cooking liquid.

NOTE: *To make mint syrup, follow the basic recipe on page 88, but substitute mint for the basil.*

RHUBARB

Rhubarb is a perennial vegetable grown for its thick, succulent stems with a lemon-like acidity and unique flavor. The leaves and rootstock contain so much oxalic acid that they are toxic and should never be consumed. But many people cannot resist the flavor of the stems, especially when paired with sweet tastes, like strawberries.

Gardeners in the warmer parts of the country will not be able to grow rhubarb successfully, as it is a plant of cool, moist regions. Even in the relatively cool East Tennessee Valley, this plant suffers in summertime and may die back. Rhubarb can be grown successfully from seed if the gardener is patient, but most people will purchase root divisions from a garden center. Set these in organically rich, moisture retentive but not soggy soil in fall or winter, while the plants are dormant. In warmer locations, choose a spot that receives some protection from afternoon sun. After the foliage appears, keep the rhubarb patch well watered; plants should receive an inch of water per week. Apply a balanced organic fertilizer as new shoots appear in spring and again after each harvest. It is wise to wait until the second year after transplanting before harvesting. In any case, take no more than one-third of the stalks on any given plant. If you are a big fan and have room, you may want three or four clumps. Rhubarb is generally trouble free once established.

Rhubarb and Strawberry Pie

Rhubarb generates a lot of liquid when it is cooked. Hence, this pie is made with precooked filling and a prebaked shell. Trying to cook the filling in the pie shell may result in the filling boiling over and making a mess in the oven.

YIELD: 1 9-INCH PIE

1 9-inch **pastry crust**

3 cups diced **rhubarb**

1 cup sliced **strawberries**

1½ cups **sugar**

2 tablespoons **cornstarch**

1 tablespoon threads of **orange rind**, removed with a zester

1. Preheat the oven to 450 °F. Line a pie pan with the pastry crust. Trim and flute the edges as you prefer. Cover the bottom of the crust with a circle of parchment paper cut to fit. Place a layer of beans, rice or baking stones on the parchment. Place the pan in the oven and bake until the crust is lightly browned, about 10 to 12 minutes. Remove from the oven, cool, and remove the weights and parchment before continuing with the recipe.

2. While the shell is baking, prepare the filling. Combine the remaining ingredients in a large saucepan and bring to a boil, stirring constantly until the sugar is dissolved. Reduce the heat and cook, stirring occasionally, for 12 minutes. Remove the pan from the heat and allow to cool.

3. Spoon the filling into the prepared pie shell. Refrigerate until ready to serve.

EDIBLE NORTH AMERICAN NATIVE PLANTS

Numerous plants that are native to the North American continent are edible. Indeed, they provided human sustenance for centuries prior to the arrival of European colonists. Undisturbed stands of native plants are becoming increasingly rare outside of parks and preserves, and yet native plants adapt easily to garden cultivation. It is no surprise, therefore, that some gardeners are looking to include native plants in their food-centric landscapes.

It is worth noting that many native species, the pawpaw and persimmon, for example, have not escaped the attention of horticulturists bent upon improving on nature. Cultivated varieties of these and a number of other native plants offer superior flavor, better growth characteristics, and other advantages over their completely wild counterparts. For example, all blueberry varieties are derived from the several species found in eastern North America.

What follows is a brief introduction to the world of native plants and their uses, together with a few recipes. The focus is upon the southeastern United States, but all regions of the country have native food plants. Readers are encouraged to research the indigenous foods of their region for a broader range of possibilities.

Nuts

American walnuts, pecans, and hickory nuts can provide a bounteous harvest to anyone with enough room for a pair of the towering trees. Walnuts can be problematic because not many other plants will survive underneath them. For smaller properties, hazelnuts make more sense, as the trees remain relatively small.

Fruits

Blueberries were discussed earlier, and pawpaw and persimmon have already been mentioned. Both are trees found in the rich hardwood forests of the eastern United States, and both remain small enough to be accommodated on a typical suburban lot. Chokecherries, botanically *Aronia*, are small, shrubby plants that produce a berry high in antioxidants. Elderberries are available as

several selections and hybrids with both European and American parents. Wild plums, such as the Chickasaw plum, *Prunus angustifolius*, and native grapes, such as muscadines, can also be incorporated into the landscape. All these plants favor organically rich, moisture retentive soils, but most are somewhat adaptable.

Miscellaneous Plants

The sassafras tree is the source of filé powder, used in the Deep South for thickening gumbo. Young, tender leaves are collected in spring after they are fully unfurled, then dried and ground to a powder. The small tree is easy to grow and trouble free but not always easy to find in nurseries.

Sumac is a woody plant with bright red seed clusters that can be harvested, dried, and used to add a lemony tang to a variety of dishes. The plants are decorative and easy to grow but can spread aggressively.

Filé Gumbo

Native Americans taught French colonists how to use the leaves of sassafras trees to thicken soup. Gumbo can be thickened in other ways, such as by the addition of okra. However, sassafras, or file powder, also lends a subtle and unique flavor to the gumbo.

YIELD: **8 SERVINGS**

4 ounces **andouille sausage,** *or* other smoked pork sausage

4 **chicken thighs**

Ground **cayenne pepper**

Kosher **salt**

1 tablespoon **bacon drippings** *or* vegetable oil

1 quart **chicken broth**

3 **bay leaves**

3 whole **garlic** cloves

1 cup chopped **onion**

¾ cup chopped **celery**

¾ cup chopped **bell pepper**, any color

1 teaspoon minced **garlic**

2 cups canned **tomatoes**, with their juices

½ teaspoon fresh **thyme** leaves

1 teaspoon **filé powder**

2 tablespoons chopped fresh **parsley**

Steamed **rice**

1. Slice the andouille into ¼-inch thick slices.

2. Sprinkle the chicken with cayenne pepper and salt and set aside in the refrigerator.

3. In a heavy cast-iron skillet over medium heat, cook the sausage in the fat until it is lightly browned. Remove it with a slotted spoon to a bowl and reserve.

4. In the fat remaining in the skillet, cook the chicken, turning it once or twice, until it is lightly browned. As the chicken is cooked, transfer it to a large soup pot. When all the chicken is browned, remove the skillet from the heat, saving the drippings.

5. To the soup pot add the bay leaves, whole garlic cloves, and broth. Bring to a boil and simmer for 20 minutes or until the chicken is done. Skim any scum that rises to the surface. Using tongs, remove the chicken to a plate. Remove and discard the bay leaves and garlic cloves. Keep the broth simmering hot.

6. Pour off all but two tablespoons of the fat accumulated in the skillet. Place the skillet over medium heat, then add the onions and cook, stirring occasionally, until the onions are softened, about 3 minutes. Add the celery and bell peppers and cook, stirring occasionally, until the onions are translucent. Add the minced garlic and cook 30 seconds. Ladle some of the chicken broth from the soup pot into the skillet and deglaze, scraping up any browned bits from the bottom of the skillet.

7. Transfer the contents of the skillet to the stock pot. Add the tomatoes, thyme, and filé powder to the stock pot, adjust the heat, and simmer 20 minutes. Meanwhile, remove and discard the skin and bones from the chicken. Add the chicken meat to the soup. Serve the soup over steamed rice and garnish with the chopped parsley. It will be tastier if prepared the day before it is served.

NOTE: If you prefer a thicker consistency, add more filé powder.

A Soup of Nuts

Native Americans knew how to extract "milk" from nuts gathered from the forest floor. They boiled them in a pot and skimmed the oily "cream" from the surface. This creamy soup was inspired by that dish. For a different take, use sweet potatoes instead of white potatoes.

YIELD: **4 SERVINGS**

2 tablespoons **butter**

½ cup finely minced **shallots**

1 cup diced peeled **white potatoes**

3 cups white **vegetable stock** (*page 230*)

1 cup pecans, **English walnuts,** *or* hazelnuts, *or* ½ cup native black walnuts, toasted (*page 244*)

½ teaspoon **salt**

⅛ teaspoon ground **white pepper**

2 teaspoons **walnut oil** (*optional*)

1. In a saucepan over medium heat melt the butter.

2. Add the shallots and cook, stirring occasionally, until they are softened, about 3 minutes. Add the potatoes and cook until they take on a waxy appearance, another 1 or 2 minutes. Add the stock, bring to a simmer, and cook 20 minutes.

3. Add the nuts, salt, and pepper and cook 2 minutes.

4. Remove the soup from the heat and allow it to cool at least 15 minutes.

5. Transfer the soup to a blender and purée. Return the soup to the saucepan to heat through. Serve the soup in warmed bowls, garnished with ½ teaspoon of the walnut oil, if you wish.

NOTE: If using an immersion blender, it is not necessary to cool the soup before you purée it.

CHAPTER 5

The Pantry

In this chapter you will find recipes for ingredients called for in recipes elsewhere in the book.

Broths and Stocks

Nothing else you can do in the kitchen will improve the flavor of your cooking like making homemade broths and stocks. Although time is needed to extract the flavors, the effort required to prepare the ingredients is minimal and requires no special skills. All these preparations, except where indicated otherwise, can be frozen for several months.

Rich Beef Broth

This recipe was inspired by one from super-chef Emeril Lagasse.

YIELD: **ABOUT 6 CUPS**

3 pounds **beef marrowbones**, cut in 3-inch pieces, about 6 pieces

2 quarts *(or more)* **cold water**

1 tablespoon **kosher salt**

1 tablespoon **canola oil**

3 tablespoons **tomato paste**

1 cup canned **tomatoes**, with their juices

1 **yellow onion**, trimmed, but with peel intact, quartered

1 **carrot**, scraped and broken in 2-inch pieces

1 stalk **celery**, cut in 2-inch pieces

3 cloves **garlic**, unpeeled

2 quarts **water**

3 **bay leaves**

1 teaspoon **dried basil**

1 teaspoon **dried thyme**

½ teaspoon **dried oregano**

½ teaspoon **dried tarragon**

¼ cup chopped fresh **parsley stems**

¾ teaspoon whole **black peppercorns**

1. Place the marrowbones in a large bowl and cover with about 2 quarts of cold water. Add a tablespoon of kosher salt to the bowl. Soak the bones for 1 hour then drain well.

2. Preheat the oven to 425°F. Place the marrowbones in a roasting pan large enough to hold them in one layer and drizzle with the oil. Roast 15 minutes. Turn the bones with tongs and paint their upper surfaces with the tomato paste, using a basting brush. Return the pan to the oven and roast an additional 10 minutes. Add the tomatoes, onions, carrot, celery, and garlic, and roast another 25 minutes.

3. Remove the pan from the oven and allow to cool slightly. With tongs, transfer the solids to a large stock pot. Carefully pour off any excess fat. Pour in a cup of water, place the baking pan over high heat, and deglaze, scraping up any browned bits with a wooden spoon. Pour this liquid into the stockpot and add the rest of the water, herbs, and peppercorns. Bring to a boil, adjust the heat to a slow simmer, and cook for 3½ hours. Remove the bones with tongs and lift out the vegetables with a slotted spoon. Discard the bones and vegetables.

4. Chill the stock, remove the fat from the surface, and strain through a fine sieve before using. The stock may be stored in the refrigerator for up to 3 days. It may also be frozen or canned using a pressure canner. Frozen stock should be used within 6 months.

Chicken Broth Supreme

Use this delicious broth in any recipe calling for chicken broth or stock. It is also excellent for braising or simmering vegetables, where it really kicks up the flavor.

YIELD: **ABOUT 2 QUARTS**

3 to 3½ pounds **chicken** backs, legs, thighs *or* leg-thigh quarters

3 quarts **water**

1 **yellow onion**, about 3 inches in diameter, left unpeeled but trimmed, washed, and quartered

1½ cups chopped **celery** with leaves

2 **carrots**, chopped

2 cloves **garlic**, peeled

3 **bay leaves**

1 teaspoon whole **white peppercorns**

¼ teaspoon each **dried oregano** and **tarragon**

1. Cover the chicken with the cold water in a large pot. Bring to a boil, then regulate the heat and simmer 30 minutes, periodically skimming the scum from the surface.

2. Add the remaining ingredients. Bring to a simmer and cook uncovered 2 hours on low heat. Regulate the heat to maintain a slow simmer. The surface of the liquid should barely tremble. Remove from the heat and remove the largest pieces with a slotted spoon. Set the pot in a sink full of ice water to cool as rapidly as possible.

3. When cool, store covered in the refrigerator overnight.

4. The following day, remove the fat that has accumulated at the surface and strain the stock through a fine sieve.

Keep the stock refrigerated and use within 1 week. Stock may be canned in a pressure canner or frozen for up to 6 months.

Dashi

YIELD: **2 CUPS**

The ingredients are available in Asian markets, which also stock instant dashi.

2 cups **water**

3-inch square of **dried kelp** (*konbu*), wiped with a damp cloth

¼ cup **bonito flakes** (*katsuibushi*)

1. Place the water in a saucepan, set the pan over medium heat, and add the kelp. Watch the pan carefully, and just before the water comes to a boil, remove the kelp with tongs. Allow the water to come to a full boil, add the bonito flakes, and immediately remove the pan from the heat.

2. Allow to sit 5 minutes, then strain the dashi through a fine sieve lined with cheesecloth. Discard the solids. Use the dashi the same day.

Lemongrass Stock

YIELD: **4 CUPS**

This wonderfully light, refreshing stock was adapted from *Fields of Greens* by Annie Somerville. It can be used as a consommé, garnished with blanched dice of colorful vegetables and some chopped scallions/leaves of cilantro. Cooked tiny shrimp or bay scallops could be added for a more complex dish. Including the yellow peel from the onion tints the stock a lovely golden color.

6 stalks **lemongrass**, trimmed and chopped

1 medium **yellow onion**, unpeeled but washed, trimmed, and coarsely chopped

8 slices fresh **ginger**

¾ cup chopped **cilantro** stems and roots

1 teaspoon **coriander seed**

6 cups **cold water**

1. Combine all ingredients in a medium saucepan, bring to a boil, and simmer until reduced to 4 cups, about 1 hour.

2. Strain the stock, discarding the solids.

Vegetable Stock

YIELD: **ABOUT 3 QUARTS**

4 medium **onions**, chopped

3 **carrots**, chopped

3 stalks **celery**, chopped

1 small **turnip**, peeled and chopped

12 large **parsley** sprigs, chopped

6 cloves of **garlic**, peeled and crushed

1 cup well-washed **potato peelings** (optional)

¼ cup dry **green** or **brown lentils**

1 teaspoon whole **black peppercorns**

1 **bay leaf**

¼ teaspoon whole **fennel seeds**

3½ quarts **cold water**

1. Combine all ingredients in a large stock pot. Place the pot over high heat and bring to a boil. Reduce the heat and simmer slowly for 1 hour. If any scum rises to the top, skim it off and discard.

2. Remove the stock from the heat and set the pot in a sink full of cold water to cool. Strain the stock through a fine sieve and store, covered, in the refrigerator. The stock will keep for 3 days in the refrigerator, or it may be frozen for up to 3 months.

Zucchini Broth

This recipe offers a good way to use up overly mature zucchini. Any other summer squash may be substituted.

YIELD: **6 CUPS**

2 cups chopped mature **zucchini**

1 cup chopped **yellow onion**

1 cup chopped **carrots**

1 cup chopped **celery**

4 cloves **garlic**, crushed

5 whole **peppercorns**

1 fresh **bay leaf**

3 quarts **water**

1. Place all the ingredients in a large stock pot. Bring to a boil, reduce heat, and simmer until reduced by half. Strain the stock through a fine sieve into another pot.

2. Place the pot in a sink full of ice water and allow to cool. The stock is best when freshly made. It can be stored, covered, in the refrigerator for up to 3 days, or frozen for 1 month.

White Vegetable Stock

This vegetable stock is a good choice when you want to keep the soup or sauce as pale in color as possible, without sacrificing flavor.

YIELD: **ABOUT 3 CUPS**

4 cups **water**

4 inches of the base portion of four **celery** stalks, chopped

1 **white onion**, chopped

1 **leek**, white part only, chopped

1 **parsnip**, chopped

1 teaspoon whole **white peppercorns**

1. Place all ingredients in a stockpot and bring to a boil. Reduce the heat to a simmer and cook 1 hour. Strain the stock, discarding the solids.

Vegan Tomato Bullion

The hearty vegetarian bullion is a great substitute for beef broth when you want to "veganize" a recipe.

YIELD: **ABOUT 3 CUPS**

1 **leek**, chopped

1 tablespoon **olive oil**

2 cups **vegetable stock**

1 cup canned **tomatoes**, crushed

1 teaspoon **vinegar** *(any type)*

1. Place the leek and olive oil in a saucepan and set over medium heat. Cover, adjust the heat, and cook until the white part of the leek just begins to brown, about 5 minutes.

2. Add the vegetable stock, bring to a boil, and then reduce the heat to a slow simmer.

3. Cover and cook for 10 minutes. Add the tomatoes and the vinegar. Continue to simmer for 10 minutes longer.

PRESERVED FOODS

Oven Dried Tomatoes

The best tomatoes for this recipe are paste varieties, such as Roma. Because the oven-drying process adds and concentrates flavor, you can dry tomatoes from the grocery, but homegrown will, of course, be far better.

YIELD: **40 PIECES**

20 firm, ripe **tomatoes**

2 tablespoons **extra virgin olive oil**

½ teaspoon **salt**

¼ teaspoon freshly ground **black pepper**

1. Preheat the oven to 200°F. Position a rack in the upper half of the oven. Line a rimmed baking sheet with aluminum foil.

2. Wash the tomatoes, dry them well, and slice in half lengthwise. Core them only if the stem scar is large. Arrange the tomato halves cut side up on the baking sheet. Drizzle the tomatoes with the olive oil and sprinkle them with the salt and pepper. Place the baking sheet in the oven.

3. Reduce the heat to its lowest possible setting, and allow the tomatoes to dry undisturbed until they are wrinkled and have a leathery texture. This may take 2 hours or more, depending upon humidity and other factors. Open the oven door to speed the process if you don't mind the extra heat in the house. When the tomatoes are sufficiently dry, remove the baking sheet from the oven and allow the tomatoes to cool to room temperature. They may be stored in a covered container in the refrigerator for a week, or in the freezer for up to 6 months.

Universal Pickling Solution

Use this mixture for refrigerator pickles, or add spices and seasonings to create your own canned pickle recipes.

YIELD: **2 CUPS**

1 cup **water**

1 cup distilled **white vinegar**

1 tablespoon **pickling salt**

1. Combine all ingredients and stir until the salt is dissolved.

Pickling Spice Mixture

Use a teaspoon of this mixture to enliven a pint of any refrigerator pickle, or add to your favorite canned pickle recipe that calls for pickling spice.

YIELD: **ABOUT ¼ CUP**

2 3-inch sticks of **cinnamon**, broken up with a heavy skillet or mallet

1 tablespoon yellow **mustard seeds**

2 teaspoons **black peppercorns**

1 teaspoon whole **cloves**

1 teaspoon whole **allspice berries**

4 dried **bay leaves**, crumbled

1 teaspoon whole **coriander seed**

½ teaspoon dried **ginger root**

¼ teaspoon **hot red pepper flakes**

1. Combine all ingredients and store in an airtight container for up to 6 months.

Pickled Strawberries

The sweet and sour flavor of these pickles goes well with a variety of dishes, both savory and sweet.

YIELD: **VARIABLE**

1 cup halved **strawberries**

½ cup **red wine vinegar**

½ cup **sugar**

2 tablespoons **water**

1. Wash a half-pint jar, rinsing it in hot tap water. Invert on a towel to drain. When the jar is cool, place the strawberries in it and reserve.

2. In a small saucepan, bring the other ingredients to a boil. Remove from heat and carefully pour over strawberries.

3. Cool to room temperature and store in the refrigerator for up to 3 months.

Green Cherry Tomato Preserves

This delicious recipe uses leftover extra syrup from the Ripe Cherry Tomato Preserves recipe which follows.

YIELD: **2 HALF PINTS**

2 cups **green cherry tomatoes**, halved

¾ cup **white vinegar**

1½ cups leftover **syrup from ripe tomato preserves** (next page)

1. Combine all ingredients in a large pot and bring to a simmer. Watch carefully to avoid a full boil, as it will boil over and make a mess. As soon as the boiling point is reached, remove from heat and cover.

2. Allow to stand at room temperature overnight.

3. Using a slotted spoon, transfer the tomatoes to a clean jar, then cover with the syrup and store in the refrigerator.

Ripe Cherry Tomato Preserves

Gardeners often find themselves with an abundance of cherry tomatoes near the end of the season. These preserves are delicious with toast or as a topping for grilled pork or chicken. Use the leftover syrup to make the Green Tomato recipe on the previous page.

YIELD: **ABOUT 6 HALF PINTS**

5 to 6 cups ripe **cherry tomatoes**, peeled

1½ cups plus 2 tablespoons **sugar**

2½ cups **water**

1 sprig **rosemary**

6 sprigs **thyme**

To peel the tomatoes, slash the bottom of each one with a sharp knife, barely cutting through the skin. Drop the tomatoes into a pot of rapidly boiling water, count to 15, and then drain the tomatoes in a colander. Rinse the tomatoes under cold running water. The skins should slip off easily.

1. Combine sugar and water in a saucepan, bring to a boil, reduce the heat, and simmer 1 minute.

2. Remove from heat and cool 10 minutes.

3. Place the herb sprigs in the bottom of a large bowl, add the peeled tomatoes, and pour the warm syrup over all. Cover and let stand at room temperature overnight. You will have some syrup left over.

4. Bring to a simmer, pack into hot jars, and process 15 minutes in boiling water. You will have about a pint of syrup left over.

Pimento Relish

This is a great way to use an end-of-season abundance of ripe peppers. Any color will do, but the peppers should be ripe. This recipe makes eight quarter-pint jars. You can easily decrease the amounts by half or a fourth if you don't want that much relish. Without canning, the relish will keep three months in the refrigerator.

YIELD: **8 QUARTER-PINT JARS**

4 cups finely chopped **sweet red peppers**

1 tablespoon **salt**

1 cup **sugar**

2 cups distilled **white vinegar**

1. In a large saucepan or kettle, combine the peppers and salt. Let stand 4 hours at room temperature, or overnight in the refrigerator.

2. Add the sugar and vinegar to the peppers and place over medium heat. Cook, stirring frequently, 45 minutes.

3. If you do not can the relish, transfer it to a clean jar and cool to room temperature before storing it in the refrigerator. If you are canning the relish, while it cooks prepare jars and lids by washing them in hot soapy water. Rinse well and place the jars in a 200°F oven to keep warm. Place lids and bands on a clean kitchen towel to drain.

   Ready your water bath canner by adding enough water to cover the jars and heating it over medium-high heat. Ladle the hot relish into the prepared jars. Wipe the jar rim with a damp paper towel, apply the lid and band, and place the jar in the canner rack. When all the jars are filled, lower the rack carefully into the canner and bring the water to a full boil. Cover and reduce the heat to maintain a steady, gentle boil. Process 10 minutes. If your elevation is above 1000 feet, process 15 minutes.

Pepper Jam

You can vary the ratios of peppers to create a hotter or milder product. You may also add a few drops of food coloring to the mixture after taking it from the heat. This jam is a great substitute for the duck sauce that often accompanies Chinese appetizers.

YIELD: 6 HALF-PINT JARS

2 ½ cups finely chopped **red bell peppers**

1¼ cups finely chopped **green bell peppers**

¼ cup finely chopped **jalapeno peppers**

1 cup **apple cider vinegar**

1 (1.75 ounce) package **powdered pectin**

5 cups **white sugar**

1. Sterilize 6 half-pint (8 ounce) canning jars according to manufacturer's instructions. Heat water in a hot water canner. Wash lids and bands and spread them out to dry on a clean kitchen towel.

2. Place all the peppers in a large, deep saucepan or stockpot. (Using an extra-large pot helps prevent the vinegar mixture from boiling over.) Mix in the vinegar and fruit pectin.

3. Set the saucepan over high heat. Stirring constantly, bring the mixture to a full rolling boil. Quickly stir in the sugar. Return to full rolling boil and boil exactly 1 minute, stirring constantly. Remove from heat and skim off any foam.

4. Quickly ladle the jam into sterile jars, filling to within ¼ inch of the tops. Cover with flat lids and screw on bands tightly.

5. Place the filled jars in the canner rack, and slowly lower them into the canner. The water should cover the jars completely and should be steaming hot but not boiling. Bring water to a boil, cover the canner, and adjust the heat to maintain a slow boil. Process for 5 minutes.

Universal Recipe for Herb Jelly

Making jelly is a great way to preserve the flavor of summer herbs. Mint jelly is a classic accompaniment to lamb, and other herb jellies can be used to enhance roasted meats of all kinds. Combine herb jelly with cream cheese to make a spread for crackers.

YIELD: **5 QUARTER-PINT JARS**

1½ cups **apple juice**

1 ounce fresh **herb leaves**

3 tablespoons **fruit pectin**

2 cups **sugar**

1. Prepare the jars and lids according to the directions on page 237. Keep the jars warm in a 200°F oven until ready to use.

2. Place the herbs and the apple juice in a large saucepan and heat over medium-high heat until the mixture comes to a boil. Reduce the heat and simmer gently for 5 minutes, stirring occasionally. Make sure all the herb leaves wilt and are submerged in the juice.

3. Remove the pan from the heat, cover, and let stand for 10 minutes. Strain the liquid through a fine sieve into a heatproof container and discard the herb leaves. The infusion may be cooled to room temperature and stored under refrigeration overnight. Bring to room temperature before continuing.

4. Measure the infusion and add enough apple juice to make 1½ cups.

5. Place the liquid in a large saucepan and add the pectin. Place the pan over medium heat and bring to a full rolling boil, stirring constantly. Add the sugar all at once and bring to a full rolling boil again, stirring constantly. Boil for 1 minute, stirring constantly.

6. Remove from heat and quickly skim off any foam that accumulates on the surface. Ladle the jelly into the hot jars, adjust the caps, and process in a boiling water bath for 5 minutes.

Berry or Cherry Preserves

The goal of making preserves is to retain the shape and texture of the fruit.

YIELD: **4 HALF-PINTS**

1 quart freshly picked **berries** *or* cherries

1½ cups **sugar**

1. Pit the cherries. If using berries, wash and pick over the berries, removing any stems.

2. Place the cherries or berries in a large saucepan, add the sugar, and toss gently to combine, bruising as few of the fruits as possible.

3. Set the saucepan over medium-low heat and cook, stirring often, until the juice has dissolved all the sugar. Remove from the heat and allow to cool to room temperature.

4. Cover the pan and refrigerate overnight.

5. The following day, lift out the fruit with a slotted spoon and transfer to clean, hot, half-pint jars. Bring the syrup to a boil and pour over the fruit, leaving ¼-inch head space. Apply lids and bands. Process the preserves for 20 minutes in a boiling water bath.

Compound Butter

YIELD: **1 STICK**

Making compound butter is an easy way to preserve the flavor of any fresh herb. It is particularly useful for herbs that do not dry well, such as parsley, basil, cilantro, chives, and chervil.

1 stick **unsalted butter**

2 tablespoons finely minced **fresh herbs**

Salt or **lemon juice**

1. Soften the butter at room temperature.

2. Using a fork, blend the herbs into the butter until you have a uniform mixture. Season with a pinch of sea salt or a few drops of lemon juice, as you prefer.

3. On a piece of plastic wrap, form the butter into a log. Roll up the plastic to enclose the butter and chill for at least one hour. The compound butter may be frozen for up to 6 months. Wrap heavy duty foil around the plastic wrap, label, and freeze.

Rosemary Oil

YIELD: **ABOUT ½ CUP**

¼ cup **rosemary leaves**, removed from their stems

½ cup **canola** or **sunflower oil**, plus a teaspoon for filtering

1. Place the rosemary in the top of a double boiler or metal bowl. Add the oil.

2. Place the boiler or bowl over simmering water and allow to infuse for 20 minutes. Remove the bowl from the steam and allow to cool.

3. Purée the mixture in a blender and store in the refrigerator overnight.

4. The following day, line a fine sieve with a coffee filter or a clean muslin kitchen towel and "prime" it by brushing with a teaspoon of oil. This will keep the filter from soaking up too much of your rosemary oil. Set the sieve over a bowl. Bring the rosemary oil to room temperature and pour it through the sieve. Allow the clear oil to drip through naturally. It may take several hours for all the oil to drip through the filter.

After filtering, transfer the oil to a sterilized glass bottle and store it in the refrigerator where it will keep for 1 month.

Cilantro Oil

Oil can be used to capture the flavor of fresh herbs to preserve them for winter use. Store all homemade herb oils in the refrigerator.

YIELD: **ABOUT ½ CUP**

1 bunch **cilantro**, rinsed and picked over

½ cup **canola** *or* **sunflower oil**, plus a teaspoon for filtering

1. Spin the cilantro in a salad spinner or use kitchen towels to dry it thoroughly.

2. Chop leaves and stems coarsely and transfer to the top of a double boiler or to a metal bowl.

3. Add the oil.

4. Place the boiler or bowl over simmering water and allow to infuse for 20 minutes.

5. Remove the bowl from the steam and allow to cool.

6. Purée the mixture in a blender and store it in the refrigerator overnight.

7. The following day, line a fine sieve with a coffee filter or a clean muslin kitchen towel and "prime" it by brushing with a teaspoon of oil. This will keep the filter from soaking up too much of your cilantro oil. Set the sieve over a bowl. Bring the cilantro oil to room temperature and pour it through the sieve. Allow the clear oil to drip through naturally. It may take several hours for all the oil to drip through the filter.

After filtering, transfer the oil to a sterilized glass bottle and store it in the refrigerator, where it will keep for 1 month.

Other Herb Oils

You can use the same technique as described above for rosemary and cilantro oils to flavor oil with any herbs you have. Use ¼ cup well-packed, chopped herbs to ½ cup oil. Experiment with different types of oil and combinations of herbs.

Tarragon Vinegar (and Other Herb Vinegars)

Making homemade vinegar is another great way to preserve the flavor of fresh herbs or edible flowers. Experiment with combinations of different herbs and vinegars. Store all homemade flavored vinegars in the refrigerator, where they will keep for a year.

YIELD: **1 PINT**

4 cups moderately packed fresh **herbs, flowers,** *or* a combination, in two batches

2 cups **vinegar,** any type

1. Fill a jar with two cups of the herbs. Pour the vinegar over the herbs.

2. Using a wooden spoon, tamp down the herb leaves, bruising them slightly, to ensure they are covered by the vinegar.

3. Place the jar in the refrigerator for 2 weeks.

4. Strain the vinegar through a fine sieve, pressing down on the herbs with the back of a spoon to extract their flavor before discarding them. Wash and dry the jar, fill it with another 2 cups of herbs, and pour the vinegar back over them. Tamp down as before and return the jar to the refrigerator.

5. After another 2 weeks have passed, strain the vinegar again, once again pressing down on the herbs with the back of a spoon. Store the vinegar in a bottle in the refrigerator.

How to ROAST BEETS

1. Preheat the oven to 375°F.

2. Trim the tops off the beets, leaving about an inch attached to the root.

3. Wash the beets thoroughly, drain well, and place in a baking pan large enough to hold them in a single layer.

4. Drizzle with a tablespoon of oil, shaking the pan and rolling the beets around to coat them.

5. Place the pan in the oven. After 20 minutes check for doneness by piercing the beets with the tip of a paring knife. If the knife meets little resistance, they are done.

6. Remove the pan from the oven and carefully cover it with foil. Allow the beets to steam until the pan is cool. Slip off the skins and the beets are ready to use.

How to ROAST PEPPERS

1. Preheat the oven to 500°F.

2. Place whole, washed, and dried peppers in a baking pan large enough to hold them in one layer. Drizzle with olive oil.

3. Place the pan in the oven and roast 5 minutes. Using tongs, turn the peppers and continue roasting until the tops are blackened and the peppers have begun to collapse, about 5 minutes more.

4. Remove the pan from the oven and cover it with aluminum foil. Allow the peppers to steam in the pan until they are cool enough to handle.

5. Remove the skin and stems from the peppers, slice them open, and scrape out the seeds and membranes with your fingers. Store the peppers covered in the refrigerator until ready to use. You can pour the flavored oil from the pan over them if you wish.

How to ROAST SWEET POTATOES

1. Preheat the oven to 375°F.

2. Scrub the potatoes and trim off the ends.

3. Place the potatoes in a baking pan. Drizzle with a tablespoon of oil, shaking the pan and rolling the potatoes around to coat them well.

4. Place the pan in the oven and cook, shaking the pan now and then, until the point of a paring knife meets no resistance when inserted into the largest potato.

5. Remove the pan from the oven and allow it to sit until the potatoes are cool enough to handle.

6. Slice the potatoes in half lengthwise and scoop the flesh into a bowl.

How to ROAST WINTER SQUASH

1. Preheat the oven to 350°F.

2. Using a large, heavy knife, slice the squash in half lengthwise. Using a melon baller, scrape the seeds and pulp from the seed cavity.

3. Brush the cut side of the squash with vegetable oil. Place the squash cut side down on a foil-lined baking sheet. Place the sheet in the oven and roast until the skin has wrinkled and begun to brown on top.

4. Remove the pan from the oven and allow to cool to room temperature. Scrape the flesh from the skin using a soup spoon. If you wish, place the squash seeds in a colander and rinse them under running water until most of the pulp has been removed. Drain the seeds, dry them in a kitchen towel, and spread them in a single layer on a foil-lined baking sheet. Drizzle the seeds with a little vegetable oil. Place the seeds in the oven while the squash is roasting. Stir them occasionally with a wooden spoon. When most of the seeds have begun to brown, remove them from the oven, transfer to a heatproof bowl, and sprinkle with salt, if desired. Use the seeds as a garnish or snack. They will keep covered in an airtight container for a week.

How to TOAST NUTS or SEEDS

1. Place the nuts or seeds in a small, heavy skillet, preferably cast iron.

2. Set the skillet over medium-high heat and cook, stirring and tossing, until the nuts are lightly toasted and fragrant. If using seeds, cook them until a few seeds pop like popcorn. As soon as they are done, transfer the nuts or seeds to a metal bowl to stop the cooking and prevent overbrowning.

BAKED GOODS AND BATTERS

Pizza Dough

Just about everyone agrees that the crust determines the quality of the pizza. Try this homemade crust and you will never go back to grocery store pizza crust again.

YIELD: **2 10-INCH PIZZAS OR 1 LARGER ONE**

1 teaspoon **dry yeast**

1 teaspoon **sugar**

1 teaspoon **salt**

2 cups all-purpose **flour**

⅔ to ¾ cup **warm water**

Olive oil for the bowl, about ¾ teaspoon

1. Mix the dry ingredients together in a large bowl.

2. Add the water, beginning with the smaller amount. Work with a wooden spoon until the dough comes together, adding the additional 2 tablespoons of water, one at a time, if necessary. Do not allow the dough to become too sticky. If it does, add a little more flour.

3. With your hands, gather the dough into a ball. Knead in the bowl for 1 minute.

4. Drizzle a little oil into the bowl, add the dough, turning it to coat, cover the bowl with a dish towel, and let rise at room temperature for 1 hour. If you wish, you can divide the dough in half and keep one-half in an oiled zipper bag in the refrigerator for up to 3 days. Refrigerated dough is never as crisp as the freshly made dough, however. For the crispiest crust, use a pizza stone, preheating it along with the oven. You will also need a wooden peel to safely transfer the prepared pizza to the hot stone. If you do not have a stone, simply place the dough on a lightly oiled baking sheet.

5. Flatten the dough into a disk with your hands. Top as desired and bake in a preheated 500°F oven until crisp and browned.

Basic Yeast Bread and Variations

Homemade bread is always a welcome accompaniment to a meal featuring vegetables from the garden.

YIELD: **1 LOAF**

1 package **dry yeast**

¼ cup **warm water** (*110°F*)

½ teaspoon **sugar**

1 teaspoon **salt**

1 tablespoon **sugar**

2 tablespoons **vegetable oil**

1 cup **milk**

3 cups **bread flour,** or more if needed

1. In a large bowl, dissolve the yeast in the water and sugar. Wait 5 to 10 minutes, until foamy. (*If no foam forms, discard and start over with fresh yeast.*)
2. Add the salt, additional sugar, oil, and milk, and stir to combine.
3. Add the flour, about a cup at a time, stirring with a wooden spoon and switching to your hand if the dough becomes too stiff. When the dough comes together in a ball, cease adding flour.
4. Knead the dough in the bowl, turning and folding it with your hands for 3 or 4 minutes. Drizzle a little oil into the bowl and add the ball dough, turning it to coat all surfaces. Cover the bowl with a kitchen towel. Set in a warm location, free from drafts, to rise until doubled in bulk, about 1 hour.
5. Punch the dough down, knead 30 seconds, and shape it into a rounded loaf. Place the loaf on a parchment-lined baking sheet. Cover with a dry kitchen towel and let rise another hour.
6. Preheat oven to 375°F after the dough has risen for 30 minutes. Slash the top of the loaf with a razor blade or very sharp knife. Bake 35 to 40 minutes, or until bread sounds hollow when tapped.
7. Remove from the oven and cool on a wire rack.

Variations:

Add ½ cup of nuts or seeds before kneading the dough. Large nuts should be chopped. Seeds can generally be left whole. Don't forget that grains, such as amaranth and millet, are also seeds and can be included in the mix.

Add up to ½ cup minced fresh herbs along with the flour.

Substitute beer, wine, juice, or stock for the milk.

For a glossy finish, brush the top of the loaf with an egg wash. Combine a beaten egg with a tablespoon of water and brush the top of the loaf before baking. You can also use the egg wash to attach a nut and seed mixture to the top surface of the loaf.

Soak a tablespoon of rolled oats in a tablespoon of milk. Sprinkle the soaked oats on top of the loaf before baking.

Cornbread

If you cannot find White Lily Cornbread Mix, you can substitute any self-rising cornbread mix, so long as it does not contain added sugar. Sweet cornbread, while fine by itself, is not recommended for any of the recipes calling for cornbread elsewhere in this book.

YIELD: **1 9-INCH SKILLET**

¼ cup
vegetable oil,
divided

1 cup
White Lily
Cornbread Mix

1 **egg**

½ to ¾ cup
milk, a little
more if needed

1. Preheat oven to 425°F.

2. Place 2 tablespoons of the vegetable oil in a 9-inch cast iron skillet. Set the skillet in the oven to heat while you prepare the batter. The skillet should heat for at least 10 minutes.

3. Meanwhile, place the cornbread mix in a large bowl.

4. In a second bowl, combine the egg, the remaining 2 tablespoons vegetable oil, and ½ cup of the milk. Mix well with a wire whisk.

5. Make a well in the cornmeal and dump in the liquids. Whisk until just combined. You may need to add more milk to make the batter pourable.

6. Carefully remove the skillet from the oven and set it on the stove top. Quickly pour the batter into the hot skillet. It should sizzle at the edges.

7. Carefully place the skillet in the oven. Bake until the cornbread has begun to pull away from the sides of the pan or until a toothpick inserted into center of the pone comes out clean. Remove from the oven and allow to cool for a few minutes, then invert the skillet over a serving plate. The cornbread should drop right out on the plate.

Cornbread with Corn Kernels and Bacon

You can turn cornbread into a serious side dish with this variation. Add ½ cup cooked corn kernels and 2 strips of cooked and crumbled bacon to the batter just before pouring it into the skillet.

Scratch Biscuits

Homemade biscuits can make any meal a special occasion, and making them is easy if you understand a few simple tricks. Keep everything cold when mixing the dough. Handle the dough as gently as possible to avoid building up the gluten, which makes the biscuits tough. When cutting out the biscuits, avoid twisting the cutter, which will seal the edge and impede rising.

YIELD: **6 BISCUITS** (RECIPE CAN EASILY BE DOUBLED)

1 cup soft **wheat flour** (*not bread flour*), plus a little more for kneading the dough

1½ teaspoons **baking powder**

½ teaspoon **salt**

4 tablespoons **unsalted butter**, chilled (*¼ stick*)

½ cup **buttermilk**

Melted butter for brushing finished biscuits

1. Chill a box grater overnight in the refrigerator.

2. In a mixing bowl, combine the flour, baking powder, and salt. Set the bowl in the refrigerator to chill for at least 10 minutes before you continue with the recipe.

3. Using the box grater, grate the butter into small bits directly into the bowl with the dry ingredients. Return the bowl with the butter to the refrigerator for 5 minutes.

4. Preheat the oven to 400°F.

5. Using a rubber spatula, make a well in the center of the dry ingredients. Pour in the buttermilk. With the spatula, combine the ingredients into a soft dough by pulling the flour in from the sides and folding it into the liquid. Work quickly, but gently.

6. Flour a pastry board, using about one tablespoon. Turn the dough out onto the board, apply another tablespoon of flour to the top of the dough ball, and roll the dough out, using a floured rolling pin, into a square about a half inch thick. Fold in thirds like a letter, turn, and fold in half. Roll out again. Repeat this procedure a second time. Using a biscuit cutter, cut six biscuits and transfer them to an ungreased baking sheet. You can combine the scraps and form another biscuit or two, but these will be tougher that the first six.

7. Place the pan in the oven and bake until the biscuits are lightly browned, about 15 minutes. Check about halfway through baking and rotate the baking sheet to ensure even browning. Remove the biscuits from the oven, brush the tops with melted butter, and serve.

CONDIMENTS

Warm Dressing of Two Vinegars with Sorghum

I came up with this dressing for leftovers. It goes great with any combination of roasted or steamed vegetables. It is also excellent with assertive salad greens, such as mizuna, dandelion, tatsoi, radicchio, and arugula.

YIELD: **ABOUT ¾ CUP**

2 tablespoons **red wine vinegar**

2 tablespoons **sherry vinegar**

1 tablespoon **sorghum syrup**

1 tablespoon **water**

1 clove **garlic**, minced

½ cup **extra virgin olive oil**

Steamed **broccoli florets**

Roasted **potatoes**, cut in bite-size pieces

Roasted **zucchini**, cut in bite-size pieces

Roasted **red sweet pepper**, cut in bite-size pieces

Roasted **mushrooms**, cut in bite-size pieces

A few leaves of **Italian parsley**, to serve

1. Arrange the vegetables on a platter or individual plates.

2. In a small saucepan, combine first five ingredients. Place the pan over low heat, bring to a bare simmer, and simmer gently until reduced to ¼ cup. Add the olive oil, stirring to combine.

3. Remove from heat. Pour over the vegetables while still warm. Scatter the parsley over the salad and serve immediately.

Toasted Seed Mixture

This mélange of seeds is not only packed with nutrition, it makes a delicious, crunchy alternative to croutons or other salad toppings. Use it anywhere you want a little healthy crunch.

YIELD: **ABOUT 1/2 CUP**

¼ cup raw **pumpkin seeds**

2 tablespoons **sesame seeds**

1 tablespoon golden **flax seeds**

2 teaspoons **amaranth seeds**

2 teaspoons **soy sauce**

Dash of **hot sauce**

1. Place the seeds in a small, heavy skillet. Set the skillet over medium-high heat and cook, stirring occasionally, until one or two seeds pop.

2. Immediately transfer the seeds to a metal bowl. Working quickly, stir the soy sauce and hot sauce into the hot seeds. The mixture should sizzle. Stir until no more sizzling occurs, cool completely, and store the mixture in an airtight container until you are ready to use it.

Creole Seasoning Mix

Commercial preparations are loaded with salt and preservatives. Make your own seasoning mix using organic spices and flavorings, and you can add as much or as little salt to the dish as you prefer.

YIELD: **ABOUT 3 TABLESPOONS**

1 tablespoon **sweet paprika**

1½ teaspoons **onion powder**

1½ teaspoons **garlic powder**

1 teaspoon ground **black pepper**

1 teaspoon dried **oregano**

1 teaspoon dried **thyme leaves**

½ teaspoon ground **white pepper**

½ teaspoon ground **cayenne pepper**

1. Combine all ingredients in a small bowl.

2. Store in an airtight container at room temperature, where it will keep for 6 months.

Minestra of Summer Vegetables

I devised this recipe fifteen years ago to celebrate a particularly bountiful summer in the garden. A minestra, or serving, consists of a variety of vegetables/meats braised in a small amount of flavorful liquid. You can vary this recipe endlessly by changing the ingredients to reflect what is currently available. As long as you follow the basic technique, the result will be delicious. Another good thing about this dish is that it can cook while you do other projects. It reheats perfectly, so don't worry that the recipe makes a lot. After cooling to room temperature, cover leftovers and store in the refrigerator for up to three days. Reheat over low heat, stirring occasionally.

YIELD: **8 SERVINGS**

½ pound **ground beef**

¼ cup **pesto sauce** (*page 87*)

½ cup fresh **bread crumbs**

2 tablespoons **olive oil**

1 large **onion**, chopped

2 **carrots**, chopped

1 cup minced **par-cel**

3 cups **beef stock**

1 clove **garlic**, minced

3 cups unpeeled **potatoes**, cut into bite-size pieces

1 cup broken pieces of **green beans**

2 small **summer squash**, cut in bite-size pieces

½ cup **shelled peas**, *or* chopped snap peas

1 can (*19 ounces*) **chickpeas**

¼ cup chopped fresh **basil**

¼ cup chopped fresh **parsley**

½ cup chopped **zucchini** blossoms (*optional*)

Salt

Freshly ground **black pepper**

(Continued on page 254)

The "par-cel" called for in the recipe is an herb that looks like parsley and tastes like celery (only more strongly, so a little goes a long way). You can substitute celery tops or ribs of celery for this ingredient. You can also grow par-cel from seeds. It grows like celery.

1. Combine the ground beef, pesto, and crumbs in a bowl. Add salt and pepper, and combine thoroughly.

2. In a large, heavy-bottomed pot, heat the oil until it is fragrant. Wet your hands and form the beef mixture, a teaspoon at a time, into meatballs about ¾ inch in diameter. As you make them, add them to the hot oil. Cook, turning frequently, until nicely browned. Transfer the meatballs as they are cooked to a plate, using a slotted spoon.

3. To the oil remaining in the pot, add the onions and cook until they are translucent. Add the carrots and parsley, and cook until the onions start to turn golden brown. Add the stock, garlic, reserved meatballs, and potatoes, and bring to a boil, stirring well and scraping up any browned bits on the bottom of the pot. Reduce the heat and simmer, uncovered, until the potatoes are tender, about 15 minutes.

4. Add the green beans, peas, and squash, and cook for 10 minutes more.

5. Add the chickpeas and cook until heated through. Add salt and pepper to taste. There should be only about 1 cup of liquid remaining at the end.

6. Ladle the minestra into bowls and top with the fresh herbs and squash blossoms. Pass additional pesto sauce at the table.

NOTE: Because the stock is reduced in cooking, it is important to start with a low-salt or salt-free stock. Otherwise, the end result may be too salty. For a lower fat content, substitute ground turkey for the beef and chicken stock for the beef stock and proceed as directed. For a vegetarian minestra, use vegetable stock. Omit the meatballs and instead add 1 drained can of red kidney beans along with the chickpeas. Add the pesto directly to the minestra with the beans for this variation of the recipe and omit the breadcrumbs.

CHAPTER 6

How to Grow Great Vegetables

This chapter contains all the basic information you need to grow vegetables, regardless of the variety, your skill level, or the amount of space you have available. Armed with the recommendations presented here, the aspiring grower can make appropriate choices to create a garden that is unique, beautiful, and productive.

The Four Essentials

All vegetables, herbs, and fruits need four basic things to thrive: sunshine, water, minerals, and air. Sunshine is by far the most important of these, as it provides all of the energy necessary for utilization of the other three. Solar energy drives the conversion of water and carbon dioxide into sugar during the process of photosynthesis. The minerals are needed for other aspects of the plant's growth and development.

Sunshine

You can do very little to replace sunshine outdoors. If your property is heavily shaded, it will be a challenge to grow the vast majority of vegetables. Indoors, artificial light can take the place of the sun, but providing that light for anything but a tabletop-size space can be costly, both to set up and to maintain. This is the main reason our discussion of windowsill growing was limited to a few varieties that remain small and tolerate low light conditions.

If you garden outdoors, locate your vegetable plants where they will receive at least six, and preferably eight, hours of sunshine every day during the growing season.

Water

Water is vital to the success of any vegetable garden. All vegetables should receive at least an inch of rainfall per week, or the equivalent amount of irrigation. For a twenty-five-square-foot growing bed, one inch of rainfall is about sixteen gallons of water. In all cases, a thorough soaking of the roots every few days is more satisfactory than a light daily watering. Always avoid wetting foliage as a hedge against disease problems, and endeavor to water early in the day so the plants can dry off before nightfall.

Despite some claims to the contrary, plants will do just fine if irrigated with chlorinated water from a municipal supply. Rainwater is preferable only because it is free.

To determine how much water your hose delivers, set a five-gallon bucket near your vegetable bed and time how long it takes to fill the bucket from the hose. Simple math will enable you to determine how long to apply water to a given amount of garden space. For example, suppose it takes three minutes to fill the bucket. Dividing five gallons by three minutes gives a flow rate of 1.67 gallons per minute, or 100 gallons per hour. For the twenty-five-square-foot bed mentioned above, therefore, we would need to run this hose for about 10 minutes to deliver the equivalent of one inch of rain (16 gallons).

Minerals

Plants require several chemical elements, or minerals, in order to carry out their life processes. Chlorophyll, for example, contains the element magnesium. The three major elements plants require are nitrogen, phosphorus, and potassium. These are the components identified by the NPK numbers found on packages of fertilizer. If a bag of fertilizer (organic or otherwise) is labeled 14-12-8, it contains by weight 14 percent nitrogen, 12 percent phosphorus, and 8 percent potassium. A fertilizer that contains roughly or exactly equal amounts of these three minerals, for example 10-10-10 or 6-7-5, is said to be balanced.

Of the three major nutrients, nitrogen is by far the most important one because it is relatively rare in nature. There are plenty of ways to obtain phosphorus and potassium, but fixed nitrogen (nitrogen in a form that can be used by plants) is produced only via the action of certain types of bacteria, or through an industrial process that consumes a lot of energy. Much nitrogen in the environment is recycled through the decomposition of plant debris and other organic matter. Decay releases the nitrogen in a form that plants can use.

Air

Air is all around us, and the small amount of carbon dioxide it contains constitutes the raw material for sugar production via photosynthesis. Air is mostly composed of nitrogen, but in its gaseous form, nitrogen is unavailable to plants. It must be fixed or chemically altered to a form that easily dissolves in water. At night, plants consume oxygen from the atmosphere, just as animals do.

You cannot influence the composition of the air surrounding your plants, but you should remember that free air movement around the leaves is beneficial. Not only does plenty of air movement facilitate the uptake of gases by the plants, it also helps to prevent disease by keeping leaves free of bacteria and fungal spores. A small fan blowing gently away from indoor plants increases the air circulation around them and improves plant health. Air movement also helps tall plants develop sturdy stems by stimulating the plant to produce structural molecules. Outdoors, pay attention to plant spacing recommendations. Planting too close can reduce air movement and increase the chances for disease.

Gardeners need only manage to fulfill these four basic plant essentials, and your vegetables, herbs, and fruits should thrive with few problems.

Containers, Boxes, and Beds

Choosing suitable containers for your food garden depends upon the needs of the plants, your personal aesthetic preferences, and the practicality of the container for

the purpose. While any number of items can be pressed into service as growing containers, certain characteristics are important to success.

Materials

Anything that resists water and will hold soil can theoretically be used as a growing container. For windowsill, balcony, and patio gardens, traditional terra cotta pots, glazed or unglazed, must surely rank as the most popular. Plastic pots come in all shapes and colors. They are also lightweight and nearly unbreakable. Many of them will, however, succumb to the effects of solar radiation after a season or two. Wooden boxes, crates, and even recycled shipping pallets make great growing containers, although unless they are made of naturally rot-resistant wood such as cypress or cedar, they will need a coat of paint or varnish to weatherproof them. Rustproof metals, such as galvanized steel, copper, and aluminum, are almost indestructible but expensive and heavy. Galvanized steel, in particular, can be used to create dramatic, free-form designs for raised beds.

Size

Bigger is better when it comes to containers, regardless of the vegetable under consideration. Try to use the largest container that can otherwise be accommodated in the growing space. Vegetables need sufficient space for their roots to expand. Pots smaller than eight to twelve inches in diameter are suitable only for growing seedlings to transplant or for true miniature cultivars. A deep, narrow container will give better results than a broad, shallow one. If you wish to group multiple containers in a small space, you will find that square or rectangular shapes will make the most efficient use of the area available.

Where room permits, use containers that hold about five gallons of growing medium for all your vegetables. Tomatoes, peppers, brassicas, eggplants, and cucurbits will all do best in containers of at least this capacity.

Design considerations for raised growing beds, the ultimate plant "container," were discussed in Chapter 3.

Self-Watering Containers

Many gardeners have sung the praises of self-watering containers. Vegetables appreciate evenly moist soil, and that is what self-watering containers provide. With minimal attention from you, the plants receive water from a reservoir at the same rate at which water is transpired from their leaves. This keeps growth going fast and constant. Commercially available self-watering containers come in sizes appropriate to everything from indoor applications to an extensive growing space on a patio or deck. Many of them have accessories, such as trellises or wheels, that render them versatile enough for all types of vegetables and situations. Increasingly, new colors and designs have been developed by vendors, resulting in aesthetically pleasing "grow boxes" that blend with any style or décor.

Planning Your Garden

The space available will, of course, determine how many containers or beds you can accommodate and whether you have room for a separate patch of berries or asparagus. Thus, the scale of your garden will be the primary factor in creating a planting plan.

Get the family together and create a list of crops everyone likes to eat. As a first step, separate your list into cool-season versus warm-season crops. Depending upon the length of the growing season and the general climate in your area, you may be able to follow a cool-season crop with a warm-season one and, in turn, plant another cool season crop for fall or winter growth. For this reason, you do not need a separate container or bed for each individual crop in most areas of the temperate zone. One growing space can produce different crops at different times of the year by practicing succession planting.

A simple garden plan could include three containers or beds, each planted with two vegetable crops for a season. In the cool season, for example, you might grow peas and spinach together in one container. You could grow broccoli and carrots in the second space, and potatoes in the third. When the season warms up, replace the peas with cucumbers and the spinach with bush beans. Replace the cabbage and beets with tomatoes and basil. Plant squash where the potatoes grew.

Numerous online resources and apps are available to facilitate the creation of garden plans. Planning software often links to a gardening database that automatically calculates days to maturity and provides recommendations on plant spacing. Of course, the exact format of your garden plan is up to you. A pen and small notebook can be just as effective as a software package.

At minimum, your plan should include a list of what will be planted and when, together with an estimate of the harvest date. Note that the days to maturity listed on seed packets and in vegetable catalogs are counted from the time of germination, not the planting date. Maturity dates also vary depending upon the weather, soil conditions, and other factors, and so are not ironclad. Expect the crop to mature a week to ten days earlier or later. An unexpected cold spell can delay maturity, while an especially favorable stretch of weather can hurry things along.

Your garden plan will be more useful if you keep track of actual events and their outcomes as a reference for the following year. If you had a bumper crop of container-grown cherry tomatoes, it will be helpful to try to duplicate your efforts in subsequent summers.

Using Transplants

Novice gardeners will find good results easier to obtain when beginning with plants that have already been brought through their critical seedling stage. Using transplants not only avoids seedling diseases, it allows you to space plants precisely, an important factor when plants are grown with limited room.

As a general rule, the following are typically grown from transplants: asparagus, broccoli, cabbage, cauliflower, celery, eggplant, herbs (most), kale, leeks, peppers, sweet potatoes, and tomatoes. The following vegetables are direct seeded but can also be grown from transplants: beans, corn, corn salad, cucumber, lettuce, melons, okra, scallions, spinach, and squashes. Special precautions must be taken with some of these. For example, beans and cucurbits should be started in peat pots that can be buried without disturbing the plant's roots. Otherwise, they don't transplant well.

Whether you start plants at home yourself or purchase them at a garden center, in order to keep them healthy and growing, they must be correctly transplanted. Young plants are often tender and easily damaged. Removing the root system from the container without damage is necessary if the plant is to grow properly.

Decide first where each plant will go, using your garden plan. Start the process by watering all the seedlings thoroughly. This will cause the growing medium to cling to the roots, reducing the potential for damage. Remove a seedling from its nursery pot by pushing gently upward on the bottom of the container with one hand, while simultaneously grasping the plant by the uppermost leaves and gently pulling it from the cell. Take care not to pull too hard, lest you tear leaves. If the plant seems stuck in its pot, run a kitchen knife around the perimeter between the pot and the growing medium. This should free up the plant and it should slide easily out of the pot.

In the plant's new location, make a hole a little larger than the root mass, using a hand spade or your hands, and place the seedling's root mass in the hole. If recommended, add fertilizer to the hole before inserting the seedling. Firm the soil around the seedling. Make sure the crown of the seedling is sitting at the same level as it was in the nursery container. Water the transplant thoroughly to settle the soil around the roots.

Sometimes you will find seedlings that have sat a little too long in the nursery container. Their roots may be matted at the bottom of the pot. In this case, after removing the seedling from the pot, pinch or cut off the entangled portion of the root mass, freeing it from the rest of the roots. This will stimulate the plant to produce new roots in its new location, and it will set growth back only slightly.

Tomatoes present a special case. When the plants have grown too large in a nursery container, remove all but the top two or three tiers of leaves before transplanting. Bury the stem up to within an inch or two of the bottom leaf tier. This will cause roots to develop all along the buried portion of the stem, and result in a healthier plant with a bigger harvest later in the season. Also, remove any blooms on the tomato at transplant time. This forces the plant to establish a healthy root system before it expends energy in flower and fruit formation.

Sowing Seed

The majority of root crops do not transplant well, often developing misshapen roots as a result. Besides beets, carrots, radishes, and turnips, the crops most often sown directly in the garden include arugula, Asian mustards, beans, cress, cucumbers, dandelion, field peas, greens, melons, okra, peas, scallion, spinach, and squashes.

Sowing seed can be done in various ways. For greens like arugula, spinach, and the Asian mustards, seeds may be broadcast; that is, scattered over several square feet of growing space. These plants are later thinned out. Tiny seeds, like those of carrots, can be planted this way also. Thinning to the proper spacing, however, is essential.

One way to achieve proper spacing with small seeds is to use seed tapes. This is merely a strip of absorbent paper tape to which seeds have been affixed at their proper spacing. You simply place the tape where you want the plants to go, and cover it to the proper depth with growing medium. Seed tape saves a lot of time that would be spent thinning baby plants. You may have to pull a plant here and there, but the time required will be much less.

Larger seeds that are easy to handle are typically planted in hills. The growing medium is mounded slightly where plants are to grow, and three to five seeds are planted. When germination is complete and plants have grown a bit, all but two or three are removed, leaving the rest to mature. Beans, cucurbits, and peas are frequently planted this way. Hills are placed to provide the proper spacing between plants, so no further thinning is required.

It is important to cover seeds properly. They should be buried no deeper than twice the width of the seed. Light is required for germination of some seeds—notably lettuce—and these should be barely covered. After sowing, many gardeners cover small seeds with a thin layer of vermiculite, which not only holds the seeds in place but maintains high moisture needed for germination. Large seeds, like those of squashes, can be poked into the soil, burying them up to the depth of the first joint of your forefinger. This also works well for beans, corn, and peas.

Always water the growing area thoroughly after planting seeds. This ensures good contact between the seed and the growing medium and provides the water necessary for proper germination. Seedbeds should be watered frequently, more so than a maturing vegetable garden. Wilted seedlings seldom recover.

Trellises

Many vegetables perform better and are easier to pick if the plants are trained upon a support of some kind. Growing on a trellis also helps to prevent diseases, as the plants stay cleaner and air circulation is improved.

What kind of support to use depends upon the materials you have available and what plants you are growing. The trellis must be strong enough to support the weight of plants and their fruits, and it must be securely anchored to prevent wind damage. A trellis covered with vines presents a large surface area to the wind. If possible, orient the length of the trellis parallel to the direction of the prevailing wind.

A sturdy trellis support can be made of wood, but a more long-lasting one can be fashioned from electrical conduit. Using parts available from any DIY store, you can make a U-shaped structure that can be attached with appropriate brackets to a growing bed, a deck post, or some other secure foundation. Once you have this support structure in place, you can use wire, strings, nylon or plastic netting, or any number of other things to allow plants to climb. Garden centers and online vendors also sell a variety of ready-made trellises suitable for all sorts of applications.

Maintenance

The chief maintenance activity you will likely engage in is watering your vegetables and herbs. Other tasks include applying fertilizer, checking for problems and solving them, and pulling weeds. You may also spend a little time tying some plants to their supports, applying mulch, and making notes about the progress of your garden.

Watering

As previously mentioned, vegetables need an inch of water per week, or about sixteen gallons per twenty-five square feet of growing space. For smaller gardens, an old-fashioned watering can may be all you need. If there is a faucet nearby, a hose with a simple watering wand attachment does a great job and is easier than lugging a watering can.

Self-watering containers have already been mentioned and are great time savers. For a raised bed or in-ground garden, a soaker hose allows you to automate irrigation. Soaker hoses release water slowly. Placed near the crown of the plant, the soaker hose saturates the soil without wasting water. Connect it to a water timer and you can water automatically. Soaker hoses work great for raised beds, where a single hose down the middle waters the entire bed.

Fertilizer

Vegetables growing in containers need more fertilization than those grown in raised beds or the ground. This is because frequent watering flushes nutrients from the growing medium. Container plants should receive a weak dose of balanced fertilizer once a week while they are actively growing. Plants grown in beds or in the ground need feeding only about once a month. These recommendations are for fertilizers that contain about 10 percent nitrogen.

The most convenient fertilizers are concentrates designed to be diluted with water before application. These types of fertilizers can be applied with a watering can. Using them gives you complete control over the amount you apply, and very little is wasted. Granular fertilizers are also widely available. They tend to be less costly than liquid concentrates and deliver less nitrogen per pound. Apply granular fertilizer by sprinkling it on the growing medium around the base of the plant. After application, water well.

Composting

Taking the kitchen scraps you generate when cooking from the garden and converting them into compost that is eventually returned to the garden to nourish another crop seems like the ultimate in recycling. Composting merely takes advantage of the natural process of decomposition. Organic wastes become nutrient sources for plants through the activities of beneficial invertebrates, bacteria, and fungi.

Compost contributes to the soil's capacity to hold both air and water. It also contains varying amounts of major, minor, and trace elements that plants require. Compost also introduces bacteria, fungi, and tiny invertebrates to the growing area. These organisms interact with one another and with plants, reducing complex materials into plant-available forms. They also help to keep harmful organisms under control, so plants are less affected by pathogens and pests.

Compost Ingredients

Compost is made from three ingredients: brown organic matter, green organic matter, and water. Brown organic matter consists of dry, woody materials like fallen leaves. Green organic matter includes wet materials like vegetable peelings. You should add equal amounts (by weight) of green and brown matter to your compost pile or bin. Irrigate the compost along with the rest of the garden. Locate the compost pile or bin in the shade to facilitate keeping it moist. Gardeners who grow indoors or on a patio or balcony can still obtain the benefits of compost. Various devices are available for indoor composting of kitchen scraps, or you can purchase ready-made compost in plastic bags.

How to Make a Compost Pile

This is the simplest approach to outdoor composting. Simply pile everything up, hose it down, and cover it with a tarp. Keep adding materials as you have them available, mixing them in well. Keep the pile evenly moist but not wet. Compost will be ready in a couple of months to a year.

Using a Compost Bin

Use a compost bin for tidier, faster composting. You can purchase a plastic or wooden bin, or build an enclosure. A three-sided bin, four feet on each side, accommodates about 500 gallons of material.

To make compost in a bin, start by placing six inches of brown material in the bottom of the enclosure. Add two inches of green material. Keep the volume ratio of brown to green around three to one. Add a commercial compost starter or a shovelful of good garden soil. Mix the materials together with a garden fork. Water the compost thoroughly.

Turn the compost with a garden fork weekly, and add new material on top as you have it available. After a week, the compost should heat up. Keep adding material, mixing, and watering. Once the compost stops generating heat, it is ready for use. This will take one to four months.

Indoor Composting

Indoors, the process is basically the same, although the much smaller volume of material means it will be ready to use more quickly. You can find multiple plans for DIY indoor composters online, or you can purchase a ready-made indoor composter at your local garden center. A properly designed indoor composter will do the job quickly without attracting insects or producing unpleasant odors. Make sure to follow the manufacturer's recommendations for proper use. Indoor gardeners can use their compost as a component of growing mix.

Starting Plants Indoors

Sooner or later, you will want to start your own plants from seeds. You will need a brightly illuminated space indoors. If you have a long growing season, you can start seeds for some vegetable crops outdoors, also. Vegetable seedlings are cared for just like their larger counterparts, but you must pay attention to prevent them from drying out and to keep them warm enough.

Seed-Starting Equipment

For plants that are transplanted after a month of growth, nursery trays that are divided into eighteen or twenty-four compartments, or cells, are the most satisfactory. These trays, together with plastic flats for holding them, and other accessories, are available at most garden centers. You will also need a growing medium for seed starting. Typically, this is merely the same medium used for potting but of a much finer texture. Make your own by combining equal parts of screened peat moss and vermiculite.

A transparent cover that fits over the flat, holding in humidity without excluding light, is a good idea.

Instead of plastic cells with growing medium, you can also purchase peat planting pellets. These serve the purpose of both the container and the growing medium. You simply add water and the pellets expand to a usable size. Like cell trays, peat pellets are usually grouped in a plastic flat for convenience.

For transplants that will remain in their seedling pots for more than a month, select larger containers to permit more root growth. Four-inch plastic pots are a useful choice for tomatoes, peppers, and brassicas. Ten such pots will fit a standard flat. Fill them with growing mix and plant as described for cell trays.

Sowing Seeds

Fill a cell tray or plastic pots with growing medium, or set out as many peat pellets as you intend to use. Water the growing medium or pellets thoroughly, then wait about twenty minutes for them to soak and allow excess water to drain away. Sprinkle a few seeds on the surface of each container. Three to five seeds should be sufficient. All but one will be removed soon after they germinate. Cover the flat with a transparent cover or with plastic wrap. If you use the latter, inspect the flat daily and remove it immediately when you see green shoots. Otherwise, plants may be trapped under the plastic and grow improperly. The transparent cover is high enough to allow the plants to grow an inch before they bump into it.

Caring for Seedlings

When all the seeds have germinated, remove the plastic cover if you have not already done so. From this point on, take care not to allow the growing medium to dry out. Check daily and water the plants when the soil surface is dry. Feed seedlings according to the recommendations given elsewhere in this book. Most vegetables should receive a soluble fertilizer solution every two weeks from germination until transplant time.

When all the seedlings in the flat have a pair of true leaves, thin them, leaving only one plant per cell, pellet, or container. The best way to do this is to cut off the weaker seedlings at the soil line, using a small pair of scissors. Pulling them up by the roots risks damaging the plant you want to keep.

Transplant seedlings as soon as the roots protrude from the drainage holes in the container. If weather conditions do not permit transplanting, it is okay to leave them in the container a little longer. See the recommendations for trimming crowded roots (page 261) before transplanting.

Pest Management

Although integrated pest management, or IPM, was developed for commercial growers, the backyard vegetable gardener can greatly benefit from applying this approach to control plant pests and diseases. When multiple elements of the pest management strategy are used together, the crop is least likely to suffer pest problems.

Healthy, unstressed plants are least prone to developing problems. Plant health begins with proper amounts of the four essentials: sunshine, water, minerals, and fresh air. Planting at the proper season is of obvious importance. Less obvious is the need for proper plant spacing, which allows for better air circulation and keeps plants from competing with one another. One of the simplest things you can do to manage pests is to check the condition of the plants daily. The earlier problems are detected, the easier they are to solve.

Trapping Pests

Simple traps do the least environmental damage of any form of insect control. Aphids and other sucking insects may be trapped with sticky yellow-colored traps, which attract them. Potato beetles will be foiled by a trench around the potato patch, which acts like the trenches around a military encampment. Hapless beetles fall into the trench and cannot escape, and can then be drowned with the hose. Squash bugs may be trapped by placing pieces of wood or cardboard on the growing medium underneath plants. Bugs collect under the wood at night. Check in the morning and sweep the bugs into a bucket of soapy water.

Barriers to Pests

Creating a barrier to pest invasion is a simple, environmentally friendly pest control technique. Covering vulnerable crops with a floating row cover is an example of this. Another good example is the use of copper to thwart slugs and snails. The mollusks will not crawl over a copper barrier. You can purchase inch-wide copper tape. Attaching the copper to the top of your growing bed with small nails will prevent snails and slugs from climbing in. You can also use bare copper wire or copper flashing. Wrap several turns of wire around the base of a pot to protect the plants growing in it. Set a pot on a piece of copper flashing to hold slugs and snails at bay.

Biological Pesticides

Spraying with soap solution can be an effective way to kill many types of insects. The soap breaks down the insects' natural defenses against dehydration, and the bugs die from lack of moisture. Choose a soap made for killing bugs. Household cleaners may contain components that will harm plants.

Diatomaceous earth, an industrial product used for numerous purposes, is an effective control for many types of insect pests. It is composed of extremely fine particles of silica, produced by trillions of marine algae called diatoms. When sprinkled on plants, diatomaceous earth affects insects in two ways. The crystals prevent some insects from chewing leaves, presumably because they damage the insects' mouthparts, and the crystals may also clog the insects' respiratory systems, asphyxiating them. The product is completely harmless and washes right off the plant like sand.

An effective control for caterpillars, Bt is an abbreviation for *Bacillus thuringensis*, a species of soil bacteria that causes fatal disease in insects. Sold under various brand names, Bt is effective against cabbage worms, armyworms, tomato hornworms, and a host of other chewing pests. Repeated application is necessary because rain will wash off the dust, but the product is almost 100 percent effective in controlling some pests.

Extracted from a tropical tree, neem oil has insecticidal, repellant, and fungicidal properties. It is an effective repellant for squash bugs and stink bugs. This product also controls powdery mildew and other fungal foliar diseases. It is sold as a concentrate that is diluted and applied with a sprayer.

Spinosad is an insect toxin derived from a type of bacterium. It targets the insect nervous system but is harmless to birds and mammals. It is effective against many insects, but you should use it with care.

Pyrethrin is extracted from a type of chrysanthemum. This natural insecticide is safe for birds and mammals but toxic to fish. It is an effective control for many agricultural pests.

Ferrous sulfate, a harmless chemical sometimes added to human food, is toxic to snails and slugs. Baits containing it are widely available and effective. The attractiveness of the bait to the target mollusks is enhanced when the bait is mixed with coffee grounds. Place small piles of grounds and bait near your growing beds to tempt snails and slugs as they approach.

Season Extenders

For gaining a few weeks on the normal growing season, either at its beginning or its end, gardeners can use a variety of devices collectively known as season extenders. Anything used for this purpose counts, from a simple cover to a cold frame.

Cloches

Anything used to cover individual plants while admitting sunshine is called a cloche. Among the simplest of cloches is an ordinary plastic milk jug with the bottom cut out. Place the jug over a recent transplant to protect it from late frost. Leave the cap off the jug during the day, and replace it at night to hold in heat. For smaller plants or plants growing in pots, use a 2-liter soda bottle for the same purpose, cutting it to an appropriate height.

Covered Tomato Cage

A tomato cage can act as a support for clear plastic sheeting draped over and held down with weights. This produces a mini-greenhouse for the plants. Take care to remove the plastic on sunny days, or the greenhouse may become a death chamber because of excessive heat.

Row Covers

Sometimes it is desirable to cover an entire bed or row of plants to protect them. A row cover provides frost protection without crushing the tender plants beneath. The cover is supported above the plants by a series of wire or plastic hoops. You can also purchase a floating row cover. This lightweight insulating fabric is placed over plants without crushing them. It is floating because it needs no hoops or other supports.

Cold Frames

A cold frame is actually just an unheated greenhouse. It can be small and simple or elaborately constructed. The basic point of any cold frame design is to shield plants from cold air while admitting sunlight and trapping heat during the day.

One way to make a temporary cold frame is to arrange bales of hay or (better) straw around a raised bed, stacking them two high on the ends and along the north side of the bed. Cover the whole thing with transparent plastic. Make sure the cover is secured against wind. The temperature inside the enclosed space will be much warmer than outside, and you can continue to grow cool-season plants in the bed for at least a month beyond your fall frost date.

If you live in USDA Zone 5 or farther south, you may not need all the insulation a straw-bale cold frame will provide. You can install a plastic grow tunnel over any size bed or a group of containers. Use ½-inch PVC pipe, bent into a semicircle, to span the growing area. How you secure the ends of the pipe depends upon your set-up. If you have a rectangular wooden growing bed, attach the pipe to the sides with conduit clamps. Bend the pipe over to the other side and install a second clamp. Place one of these hoops at each end, and one or two in the middle, spacing them evenly. Using plastic zip ties, attach another piece of PVC horizontally across the top arc of the hoops. This ridge pole greatly enhances the stability of the arrangement. Cover the entire thing with transparent plastic film, and secure the edges with weights, such as stones or concrete blocks.

Gardeners who prefer a more professional, finished look can choose from an array of ready-made cold frames, some offering helpful features like automatic venting when the interior temperature becomes too warm. Depending upon the size of the unit and the quality of construction, a ready-made cold frame can cost several hundred dollars. But for producing fresh greens on your patio in winter, this may be a reasonable investment, given that a good-quality cold frame can be used for many seasons.

Learn As You Grow

Learn from your gardening mistakes and triumphs. The best way to do this is to keep a journal, but simply being a dedicated observer of the life in your garden will lead to insights. You will discover which insects are friends, how growing some vegetables side by side seems to improve both, and possibly that it is pointless to try to grow okra in Bangor or cauliflower in Mobile.

No book on vegetable gardening can cover all the possible scenarios for gardens in a country as large and climactically diverse as the United States. Fortunately, gardeners everywhere can access information that is specific to their region. The US Department of Agriculture has extension offices in every state. Find yours at *http://nifa.usda.gov/partners-and-extension-map*. This web page also has links to university agriculture programs across the country. These programs regularly publish information pertinent to backyard vegetable gardening, food preservation, and related topics. For the most up-to-date information about preserving your harvest, visit the National Center for Home Food Preservation web site, maintained by the University of Georgia at *http://nchfp.uga.edu/*.

Public gardens recognize the ever-increasing popularity of home food gardening and are responding with seminars, workshops, and demonstration vegetable gardens. A visit to a public garden near you will provide inspiration for designing your own garden. For the novice grower, a public garden provides an objective view of what plants will fit into a given amount of space, something that may be difficult to visualize without direct experience. You can find a public garden in your area with the help of the National Gardening Association's locator tool at *http://www.garden.org/public_gardens/*.

Do not overlook opportunities to communicate with other gardeners in your area. Talk to the pros at the farmer's market. They are often willing to share tips if the market is not too busy. If you notice corn tassels peeking above a neighbor's fence, you may have discovered a gardening ally. Most gardeners are eager to talk about their passions, vegetable gardeners no less so than rosarians or orchidists. If there is a Master Gardener program in your area, participating in it will bring you into contact with your most experienced gardening neighbors. The American Horticultural Society has links to Master Gardener program information at *http://www.ahs.org/gardening-resources/master-gardeners*.

Food gardening challenges the intellect, requires healthy physical exertion, and brings the freshest, most nutritious produce to your dinner table. My sincere hope is that this introduction to vegetable gardening and cooking with homegrown produce will lead each reader toward a rewarding lifelong hobby.

ACKNOWLEDGMENTS

Many thanks to my husband and masterful gardener, Jerry Yarnell, for his many contributions to this book.

My agent, Grace Freedson, never gave up on this project. Thank you, Grace.

Thanks to my editor, Allison Janse, for her enthusiastic response to the idea of a different kind of garden-to-table cookbook.

Special thanks to all who tested recipes: Graham Byars, Lori Chavez, Melanie Hall, Connie Killian, Russell Peeler, and J.R. Shute. Your comments and suggestions made the recipes better and easier to follow.

ABOUT THE AUTHOR

John Tullock is a lifelong gardener, self-taught gourmet cook, and trained ecologist whose previous books have covered a range of topics including aquariums, hardy orchids, sustainable living, and starting a small business. His *Natural Reef Aquariums* sold over 75,000 copies and is considered a "classic" in its subject area. *Growing Hardy Orchids* was named by the American Horticulture Society as one of the five best garden books of 2006. *Pay Dirt*, released in 2010, sold over 10,000 copies during its first six months. *The New American Homestead: Sustainable, Self-Sufficient Living in the Country or the City* has inspired people all over the country to grow food at home. His most recent works are *Idiot's Guides: Vegetable Gardening* and *Idiot's Guides: Straw Bale Gardening*, both published by Alpha Books. He writes, cooks, and gardens on his suburban homestead near Knoxville, Tennessee.